The Conversion of
Senator Arthur H. Vandenberg

The Conversion of
Senator Arthur H. Vandenberg

*From Isolation to
International Engagement*

LAWRENCE S. KAPLAN

UNIVERSITY PRESS OF KENTUCKY

Scholarly publisher for the Commonwealth,
serving Bellarmine University, Berea College, Centre College of Kentucky,
Eastern Kentucky University, The Filson Historical Society, Georgetown
College, Kentucky Historical Society, Kentucky State University, Morehead
State University, Murray State University, Northern Kentucky University,
Transylvania University, University of Kentucky, University of Louisville,
and Western Kentucky University.

Editorial and Sales Offices: The University Press of Kentucky
663 South Limestone Street, Lexington, Kentucky 40508-4008
www.kentuckypress.com

Library of Congress Cataloging-in-Publication Data

Kaplan, Lawrence S.
  The conversion of Senator Arthur H. Vandenberg : from isolation to
international engagement / Lawrence S. Kaplan.
      pages cm. — (Studies in conflict, diplomacy and peace)
  Includes bibliographical references and index.
  ISBN 978-0-8131-6055-9 (hardcover : alk. paper) —
  ISBN 978-0-8131-6060-3 (pdf) — ISBN 978-0-8131-6061-0 (epub)
  1. Vandenburg, Arthur H. (Arthur Hendrick), 1884–1951. 2. United States.
Congress. Senate—Biography. 3. Internationalists—United States—Biography.
4. United States—Foreign relations—1945–1953. 5. United States—Foreign
relations—1933–1945. 6. Isolationism—United States—History—20th century.
7. Republican Party (U.S. : 1854–)—Biography. 8. Legislators—United
States—Biography. I. Title.
  E748.V18K37 2015
  328.73'092—dc23
  [B]   2014047972

In memory of Wayne S. Cole, 1922–2013,
historian of isolationism

Contents

Photographs follow page 142

Preface

The inspiration for this book goes back to 1951, when, as a fledgling historian with the Historian's Office, Office of the Secretary of Defense, I was tasked with conducting a study of the impact of the new North Atlantic Treaty Organization on the Defense Department's Military Assistance Program. Having just completed a doctoral dissertation on the origins of isolationism in Jeffersonian America, I was—and still am—intrigued with the recognition that NATO represented the termination of the U.S. tradition of nonentanglement with the Old World. It was symbolized by the absence of an entangling alliance with any nation in Western Europe since the Convention of Mortefontaine in 1800. Almost 150 years had to pass before the United States was prepared to challenge that tradition.

It did not take quite that long before I was able to publish a book-length monograph on NATO's origins. Over the past thirty-five years I have written a few books on NATO's formation as archives opened and new insights became possible. In each of my studies, Arthur Vandenberg has occupied a place of importance but never quite the central role in America's conversion to a new status in the world. Such influential figures as George Kennan, Dean Acheson, and John Foster Dulles have occupied that position.

Vandenberg, as chairman of the Senate Foreign Relations Committee in 1947 and 1948 and the ranking Republican on that committee in 1949, was arguably the key factor in moving the nation from its isolationist past to an internationalist future. The Truman Doctrine, the Marshall Plan, the North Atlantic Treaty, and the Military Assistance Program owe their passage to the passion of this legislator. While disclaiming the position of co–secretary of state, Vandenberg was as important as any member of the Truman administration in convincing his party, the Senate, and the nation at large to share his vision of the nation's future. Scholars have paid attention to his role, and articles have appeared in the sixty-five years since his death. But no comprehensive study has been undertaken. This study attempts to flesh out his conversion from isolationism to internationalism, with appreciation for the limits as well as the extent of his achievements.

The voluminous correspondence in the Vandenberg Papers at the Bentley Historical Library at the University of Michigan offers a picture of a public man, well aware of his importance to community, party, and nation. He was not an introspective person. His letters and diaries, his speeches in the Senate, and his queries in Foreign Relations Committee hearings make up the essence of the public man. Behind the rotund phrases and glib tongue is a political figure who fully reveals himself. There seem to be no inner thoughts that were not brought to the surface.

This study follows the odyssey of a major political figure from archisolationism in the 1930s to ardent internationalism after World War II. He was a major factor in bringing the Republican Party into a bipartisan relationship with the Truman administration At the same time it concentrates on the devotion Vandenberg gave to the United Nations as the template for U.S. foreign policy after 1945. His insistence on the authority of the UN Charter in legitimizing the Atlantic Alliance accounted for the charter's preeminence in the articles of the North Atlantic Treaty. In fact, his Vandenberg Resolution in June 1948 set in motion the negotiations for the treaty. While Vandenberg objected to its military component, and particularly to the implicit powers that military assistance would give to the presidency, he eventually accepted the need for a military assistance program. Did his fear of Soviet intimidation of the West in 1949 overcome the priority he had claimed for the UN Charter? Or was there a nationalist bias that pushed the UN aside and called into question his conversion to internationalism? Such are the issues that will be discussed in the forthcoming chapters.

Two generations have passed since I became acquainted with this subject, and I cannot do justice to the many institutions and individuals who have assisted me along the way.

I begin with the Office of the Historian, and its leaders, Rudolph A. Winnacker, who sponsored my studies from 1951 to 1954, and Alfred Goldberg, his successor in the 1970s as head of the office, who was instrumental in facilitating the completion of my first book on NATO's formative years while I served as a consultant in his office. In the 1980s, as director of the Lyman L. Lemnitzer Center for NATO Studies at Kent State University, I benefited from the work of its staff, particularly Mark Rubin and my successor, S. Victor Papacosma, in organizing conferences on NATO's history. After my retirement from the university in 1993, Georgetown University's History Department offered me an opportunity to continue teaching and to refine my NATO history course. Its chairs have been supportive of my studies over the subsequent twenty years as I pursued further research into NATO's history. This book is a product of my engagement with the subject.

I have received support from multiple sources. For the Vandenberg project I thank the Harry S. Truman Library and its director, Michael Devine, for a second grant to visit the library in 2012. Its resources were especially valuable for understanding the roles of President Truman and Dean Acheson. The primary resource for this volume is the Bentley Historical Library of the University of Michigan that houses the Vandenberg Papers. I appreciate the efforts of Malgosia Myc, assistant reference archivist, in dispatching the disks containing the extensive records of Senator Vandenberg. Similarly, I thank Christine A. Lutz, assistant university archivist at the Seeley G. Mudd Manuscript Library of Princeton University, and Kristen McDonald of Manuscripts and Archives at the Yale University Library for sending, respectively, relevant copies of the John Foster Dulles and George Kennan Papers and the Robert A. Lovett and Walter Lippmann Papers. A visit to the Franklin D. Roosevelt Library Hyde Park, New York, in 2012 gave me access to the Henry Wallace Papers as well as President Roosevelt's. I am grateful for the help of the library's staff and to Vera Ekechukwu, Fulbright research assistant at the University of Arkansas Library, Fayetteville. Ineke Deserno, the NATO archivist in Brussels, made an effort to make available the few documents in Brussels important for this project. It is a pleasure to recognize at this time the special contributions of Marie Gallup, former consultant to NATO, for opening up the archives in Brussels to scholars. Regular visits to Britain's National Archives in Kew once again yielded valuable documents. Closer to home, I want to thank the staff of Georgetown University's Lauinger Library, particularly Shane Hickey, the interlibrary loan officer, for his many services. I am especially appreciative of the encouragement that Steve Wrinn, director of the University Press of Kentucky, and Allison Webster, executive assistant to the director, have given me at every stage of this project.

Once again friends have come my aid. Bob Ferrell gave me tips on the status of Vandenberg scholarship, while Steve Rearden and Stanley Kober vetted the manuscript. Had Wayne Cole been in better health, I know he would have been interested in the evolution of Vandenberg from his affiliation with Senator Nye to a new role in American foreign relations. Wayne's successor as the leading American authority on isolationism, Justus Doenecke, offered knowledgeable advice after reading the prospectus. While I have not followed all of it, I am grateful for his commentaries and those of other readers.

My family has patiently followed my studies for two generations. Cristina deserves special appreciation for her computer expertise, which I have exploited on more than one occasion. My thanks to Deb and Josh for never failing to display my books on their shelves. The most deserving member is my wife, Janice, who has been living with these projects ever since she helped type my dissertation in 1951.

Abbreviations

CEEC	Committee of European Economic Cooperation
CR	*Congressional Record*
ECA	Economic Cooperation Administration
ERP	European Recovery Program
FDIC	Federal Deposit Insurance Corporation
FRUS	*Foreign Relations of the United States*
MAP	Military Assistance Program
MDAP	Mutual Defense Assistance Program
NATO	North Atlantic Treaty Organization
NIRA	National Industrial Recovery Act
NSC	National Security Council
OEEC	Organization for European Economic Cooperation
SACEUR	Supreme Allied Commander, Europe
SC	UN Security Council
UN	United Nations
UNRRA	United Nations Relief and Rehabilitation Administration
WU	Western Union

1

Hamilton's Impact,
1906–1928

Arthur Vandenberg's background does not quite fit the Horatio Alger story. His father was a prosperous harness-maker and the owner of a leather-goods factory in Grand Rapids, Michigan. The family was firmly in the middle class. His Dutch origins in a region filed with immigrants from the Netherlands reinforced this position, which in turn was complemented by his mother's membership in the Park Street Congregational Church. Through his mother's Yankee family, Vandenberg could claim a grandfather who helped to nominate Abraham Lincoln at the 1860 Republican Party convention as well as an ancestor who served in the American Revolution.[1]

Yet the experiences of his youthful years mirrored the rags-to-riches stories turned out by Alger in the late nineteenth century. The panic of 1893 destroyed his father's business, forcing the nine-year-old Arthur to spend much of his youth living by his wits. Adversity promoted the rewards of hard work but also taught him how to make the most out of odd jobs. These included selling vegetables, flowers, lemonade, and newspapers. He showed a spirit of enterprise in his first job, carrying shoes from the company plant to the railroad station for fifteen cents a week. Within a year he had two other boys working for him and was netting twenty dollars a week. Reflecting on his life during the 1890s, he embraced the Republicanism of his father, blaming Grover Cleveland Democrats for the depression in 1893. *New York Times* columnist James Reston in 1948 attributed the "qualities of enterprise" of the self-made man as a reason for Vandenberg's political successes. The young journalist was determined "that when I grow old I would not be in the position my father was."[2]

1

It was the newspaper world that most attracted him; he saw it as the vehicle for financial success that could ultimately propel him into the political arena And it was a newspaper, specifically the *Grand Rapids Herald*, that invokes a Horatio Alger image. To earn money for his freshman year at the University of Michigan he asked for a job at his local newspaper. The editor and publisher did not have an opening at the moment but remembered Vandenberg for his work on his high school yearbook. He put him on the state desk at a salary of six dollars per week. This was a stroke of luck that was replicated six years later when Congressman William Alden Smith, majority owner of the newspaper, was unable to find a replacement after the sudden death of the editor. He offered it to the twenty-two-year-old Vandenberg. Smith surprised the young newspaperman on March 17, 1906, by saying, "Well, I'm going to make you managing editor of this paper and your salary will be $2500 a year."[3]

This was an extraordinary opportunity—a job carrying considerable responsibilities and a princely stipend for a young man of college age. Was this the result of hard work and effort beyond the normal duties of an ambitious youngster who was constantly in the lookout for scoops that would draw attention to his writing as well as to his reportorial skills? Vandenberg was in the right place at the right time, as were the Alger heroes in his many books. When a fire threatened to burn down the office, the hero was on the spot to put the fire out and even rescue the boss's wife, or if the boss's daughter was about to be run over by runaway horses, there was the Alger boy rushing out to rescue her. In both cases the young hero would be rewarded with prospects for a prosperous career if not the daughter's hand in marriage.

The moral of these stories suggests more than luck. One has to be prepared to take advantage of opportunity, and to do this a youth must be clean-living, fit physically and morally to perform tasks that would make his way in the world. In his introduction to Alger's *Struggle Upward; or, Luke Larkin's Luck,* Rychard Fink observed that the "hero is manly, self-reliant, kind and generous. He is modest, even when successful."[4] Vandenberg's modesty may be challenged but not the other characteristics.

Vandenberg did not perform acts of Alger's derring-do. But like an Alger hero he was ready to make the most of an opportunity. His family fortunes required him to look for income wherever he could find it; his personal habits fitted the clean-cut youth Alger portrayed; his talents as a writer and orator were early in evidence. Arguably even more important, he was adept at winning friends wherever he went. In high school he displayed a love for speaking and pleasure in writing. His elocutionary models were the great nineteenth-century orators of the U.S. Senate John C. Calhoun and Daniel Webster, whose voices carried them to national prominence. As representative of his high school in his senior year at the state oratorical contest, he won a silver medal speaking about the peace conference at The Hague. Although he did not win the contest, he believed his interest in world peace had its origins on that occasion. He liked to recall that the political interests aroused in him in high school determined his path to the U.S. Senate.[5]

THE TR PROGRESSIVE

Lack of money had limited Vandenberg's time at the University of Michigan to one year, but as his close ties to Randolph G. Adams, director of the university's William L. Clements Library, attest, he remained a loyal Wolverine, compensating for his incomplete formal education with an amateur's passion for history. As senator he used his considerable influence to supply important documents to the Clements Library's collections.[6]

His tenure at the *Herald*, where he would remain as editor and publisher until his election to the Senate in 1928, was marked by continuous success. His only deviation was to accept an appointment in 1903 in the art department of *Collier's* magazine in New York City. He lasted only a year.

That unhappy experience confirmed Vandenberg's decision to remain a journalist and make his mark in his hometown. He did so with the initial help of William Alden Smith, the owner of the *Grand Rapids Herald* and Vandenberg's patron. After winning election to the Senate in 1906, Smith put his arm around the young man's shoulder and said, "My boy, you are now the editor and publisher of this newspaper." Vandenberg made the *Herald* the leading newspaper in western Michigan and himself a millionaire by the time he took his own Senate seat in 1928. Nearly bankrupt when he took over its management, the paper under his leadership expanded its coverage of national and international affairs as well as offered such features as comic strips and the poetry of Edgar Guest. Vandenberg's biographer C. David Tompkins observed, "The circulation of the paper rose from less than twenty-seven thousand in 1906 to nearly thirty-four thousand in 1928. In 1907 the *Herald*'s net profit had been $6,609; during the 1920s the average net profit was $112,000 per year."[7]

Vandenberg rose to become secretary of the newspaper's board of directors in 1906 and then was elected vice president and treasurer in 1912. In 1919, when he was thirty-five, the board appointed him publisher of the paper and president of the Herald Publishing Company. In the course of this climb he invested in the *Herald* and in the Grand Rapids Savings Bank, where William Alden Smith was chairman of the board of directors. Wealth and status followed from his successful management of the paper.[8]

Vandenberg's political views in these years were fully expressed in the influential editorials he enjoyed writing. Not that he slighted the business or the social sides of his position. While he spent his mornings on the affairs of his newspapers and midday often at cards or billiards with leading lights of the city, his primary attention was on his editorials, to which he devoted his afternoons. He took pride in his ability to articulate quickly and effectively the national issues of the day. He was a compulsive writer in the flamboyant style of the great American orators, not only in daily notes for his diary but in scores of short stories that he sent to prominent journals and that were rarely accepted.[9]

Vandenberg had much to write about on matters of national interest as he took over his duties on the paper. In his first decade as editor they centered on the Progressive movement, which he identified with Theodore Roosevelt. The president, as the Rough Rider of San Juan Hill fame in the Spanish-American War and subsequent tamer of the trusts, appealed to the young editor. When he was honored by the Theodore Roosevelt Memorial Association in 1949, Vandenberg remembered that "as a lad of sixteen I lost my first job because I briefly knocked off, without leave, one afternoon in order to see Theodore Roosevelt" when he was welcomed "to my home town as a candidate for Vice President. I just had to see my hero. Nearly half a century has passed. I haven't changed my mind."[10]

His hero worship of larger-than-life figures persisted throughout his career. Even his ambivalent assessment of Woodrow Wilson reflected this tendency. It did not apply to Franklin Roosevelt but it did to General

Douglas MacArthur. As the election of 1944 loomed, Vandenberg envisioned MacArthur as the Republican answer to a fourth term for Roosevelt. He claimed to be happy to be part of the movement to nominate the general, both out of the party's need for a successful challenger and for his own admiration of MacArthur's virtues. The latter was arguably the more important factor in his identification with the movement. When the MacArthur boom collapsed, Vandenberg told a Battle Creek editor that "I still think MacArthur would have been our best nominee—the easiest one to elect—and that he would have been incomparably our best President."[11]

His adulation of TR was hardly surprising. Vandenberg became editor in the heyday of the Progressive movement and quickly associated himself with its causes. Trust busting was a major issue for the president, and Vandenberg's zeal was reflected in his editorials supporting the principles of competition in place of oligopoly. Applauding the work of the Interstate Commerce Commission, Vandenberg indicated his belief that "these investigations have served to show the innocent purchasers how the market is rigged in support of manipulators and promoters." He named names. "The recent testimony of Mr. Harriman [Edward H. Harriman, president of the Union Pacific Railroad] was especially illuminating, and he is only one of the masters of modern finance who have disclosed how the insiders lift themselves to affluence at the expense of the confiding public."[12] Seeing himself as a small businessman, Vandenberg could empathize with those threatened by the trusts' price-fixing practices.

A lesser but enduring passion of Roosevelt's was Gifford Pinchot's ambitious plans for conservation, particularly of the nation's forests. The founder of Yale University's School of Forestry, Pinchot was an influential adviser to President Roosevelt. Vandenberg agreed with the president's removal of coal lands from private exploitation, writing, "This is an unusual order, and may be frowned upon in 'conservative' circles as showing a tendency to government ownership of the coal mines." But, he editorialized, "the action will serve as a check upon the concentration of the country's coal supply in a few hands. This may be socialistic but it is nevertheless in line with public policy and public safety. Government ownership of large tracts will safeguard the nation against monopoly and greed."[13]

Vandenberg's Progressive credentials were further burnished by his sympathy with unions and opposition to child labor. Perhaps remembering his own childhood hustling for jobs, he could empathize with the women and children being overworked and underpaid in factories. "Lacking organization and too often driven by dire necessity to work for anything they may be offered," he wrote, "they are not in a position to protect themselves against the greed and rapacity of unscrupulous employers."[14] He used his newspaper to plead for humane conditions for women and children in the workplace.

While there was youthful exuberance driving Vandenberg's Progressivism, there was nothing in his daily outpouring of views that was not to be found elsewhere in journals and books that followed Teddy Roosevelt's path. This was true as well in his display of patriotism and nationalism in this period. America's destiny was manifest to him: namely, to accept the white man's burden as in the Spanish-American War. America's expansion into the Pacific and Latin America served to elevate the natives so that they could assimilate the values of the superior Anglo-Saxon peoples. The validity of the Monroe Doctrine was unquestioned, as was its Rooseveltian corollary that would keep foreign powers out of the American-protected Western Hemisphere.[15]

Vandenberg took a special interest in the newly acquired Philippines, working its way to independence under American supervision. This would be a theme that endured long after his strident nationalism had waned. As senator and a member of the Territories and Insular Affairs Committee, he introduced a bill in 1930 to establish the Philippines as a commonwealth, with a plan for progressive autonomy that would result in independence in ten years. Addressing the Senate on January 31, 1931, he asserted that "the American people are under solemn promise as a result of an act of Congress on August 29, 1916, to give the Philippine Islands complete independence when a stable government is established." His bill was a modification of an earlier plan that would have mandated twenty-five years before full independence was granted. Vandenberg felt that "it would be a disservice to all concerned to create a long twilight zone of indefinite sovereignty."[16]

The senator's position reflected his awareness of the nation's economic self-interest, and it assumed that the independent Philippines would not be protected by American tariffs. "Until independence day arrives," he observed to the Philippine governor general, the United States "must maintain unquestionable authority. . . . Our Flag must stay all the way up until it comes all the way down." Vandenberg understood the negative effect that duty-free sugar from the Philippines would have on the Michigan sugar industry. As he told the Senate in January 1930, he wanted his colleagues to understand how important a tariff on beet sugar was to the agricultural vitality of Michigan. He considered his proposal a trial balloon to provoke discussion and followed it up with a visit to Manila in May 1931.[17] After President Hoover vetoed the bill, it took a depression and a world war before full independence was achieved. Vandenberg's intervention was part of his ongoing interest in U.S. foreign relations as well as in the economy of his home state.

Once Roosevelt left office, Vandenberg's Progressive views changed, as his position on the presidential election of 1912 revealed. The increasing prominence of the *Herald* and its editor would have moderated his radical passions even if a new Republican administration had not required him to make choices. Vandenberg developed a cadre of prominent friends within the Republican Party who were more conservative than the young editor had been during the Roosevelt years.

The most influential figure molding Vandenberg's positions on the Progressive movement was his patron, William Alden Smith, the owner of the *Herald,* who served in the Senate from 1907 to 1919 after twelve years in the House of Representatives. When the Progressivism of the Roosevelt years was at its height Smith was one of its champions. After Roosevelt's successor, William Howard Taft, sought reelection, Smith and Vandenberg had to choose between the Republican Party with Taft as its representative and the insurgent Roosevelt challenge in the presidential campaign of 1912. Vandenberg, increasingly visible in the party, was torn between his sentimental attraction to the former president and the more conservative Republicans that rallied behind Taft's reelection. Michigan Republicans were sharply divided, but when a decision had to be made in 1912, Vandenberg's initial neutral stance yielded to political realities. He used his editorials to avoid a decision by pushing the legislature to enact a presidential primary in Michigan. The legislature did respond favorably, but the primary's implementation in 1913 would not relieve Vandenberg in 1912 from having to decide between Roosevelt and Taft.[18]

When Roosevelt walked out of the Republican convention to create his Bull Moose movement, Vandenberg rationalized his decision to remain with Taft by asserting that "the party is bigger and more important than either man, for in the final analysis it is the instrument of reform." And he emphasized in his editorials that the Republican Party remained "intensely progressive." Taft may have made mistakes, he felt, but so had Roosevelt, who could have backed another Progressive, such as Charles Evans Hughes. Because Roosevelt refused to propose a compromise, there remained no alternative to Taft, whose nomination merited support from Progressives.[19]

Vandenberg's youthful enthusiasm for Roosevelt had faded before he reached the age of thirty. He had become a person of consequence—and ambition. If he were to achieve future state or national office, it would have to be in the Republican fold, an increasingly conservative party. He might still talk of Progressivism, but it was a watered-down version as he became more visible in party circles.

AMBIVALENT VIEWS ON WOODROW WILSON

The election of Democrat Woodrow Wilson in 1912 eased Vandenberg's path toward a more Republican orthodoxy. Not that he officially abandoned Progressivism. He initially credited Wilson as a moderate, free from the radicalism of William Jennings Bryan even though he appointed Bryan as secretary of state. But Vandenberg felt, regrettably, that Wilson followed traditional Democratic tariff policies and carried them to an extreme in the Underwood Tariff. Notwithstanding Vandenberg's former support for a federal income tax as a Progressive reform, he now saw the provision in the Underwood Tariff as "grossly un-American, undemocratic, and unfair." He invoked the image of the Cleveland tariff reductions in 1893 to charge that the Underwood Tariff would damage the American economy and cost the nation a depression like the one that so damaged the Vandenberg family fortunes. And in line with traditional Republican views, but contradicting his position in the Roosevelt years, editor Vandenberg denounced the Clayton Act for its denial of a fair profit to businessmen.[20]

Vandenberg also carried his anti-Wilson editorial campaign into the realm of foreign policy. This was more consistent with his Progressive past. Teddy Roosevelt's appeal had always been grounded on his nationalism. And Wilson's appointment of the radical Bryan, the opponent of the Spanish-American War and putative pacifist, as his secretary of state only confirmed Vandenberg's suspicions of the Wilson administration. Yet Vandenberg was also unhappy with Wilson's "missionary diplomacy" in Mexico and Central America, where intervention resulted in "establishing the purchase of Central American Sovereignty. It lays [a] trail of trouble which is bound to damn us now and hereafter."[21] His quarrel with Wilson seemed less over intervention in the foreign affairs of Latin American nations, which Roosevelt had initiated a few years earlier, than in its apparent failure. Or was it simply another opportunity to polish his credentials as a traditional Republican?

Vandenberg's attitude toward Wilson's European policy was more nuanced when war erupted in the summer of 1914. He had no quarrel with Wilson's position of neutrality. Nationalism and isolationism merged in his thinking, as he saw the blessings of an America unburdened by the deplorable history of European nations. He fully agreed with Wilson's neutrality policy as well as his insistence on the rights of neutrals on the high seas. Again, like Wilson, Vandenberg hoped the United States could promote a just peace. As he asserted in August 1914, "This struggle will have a sobering influence upon the whole world."[22]

There were limits to his endorsement of Wilson's foreign policy. Vandenberg regarded Bryan's pacifism as an insult to America's self-respect. There was an element of Roosevelt's bravado in this criticism. He censured Wilson when the president seemingly failed to support preparation for war should it be forced on the nation. He asserted in an editorial that it was "essential that we maintain our army and navy in such a state of preparedness that our national honor will be protected and upheld, come what may." He was critical as well of Wilson's bias against Germany. In his stance on neutral rights, the president overlooked Britain's violations.[23]

That Wilson would lose much of Vandenberg's initial support was hardly surprising. The presidential election of 1916 required a clear reason for Charles Evans Hughes to replace Wilson as president. Hughes, a former governor of New York with strong Progressive credentials, reluctantly left the Supreme Court to accept the Republican nomination for president. No matter the candidate, the Grand Rapids editor, a rising star in Michigan party politics, would have his newspaper clearly on the side of the Republican candidate.

As the nation entered the world war, the strain of romanticism in Vandenberg's character manifested itself. While his Progressivism was in recession, his nationalism was not. Once war seemed imminent, he put all his energies into support of U.S. entry and into support of the reelected President Wilson. Even before the declaration of war Vandenberg reminded his isolationist readers that Germany's resumption of submarine warfare against American merchant ships might make war necessary. He solemnly announced that "the President has had no more persistent critic, almost of constant disagreement with his policies than The Herald." But Wilson would have "no more consistent supporter in whatever he shall deem necessary in this crisis."[24]

Vandenberg followed the logic of his position three weeks before the president asked for a declaration of war in a speech at Grand Rapids' First Methodist Church, approving Wilson's action even if it should lead to war. The Republican editor had become a committed Wilsonian, at least in foreign affairs, by the time the nation was at war. As he later recalled, "I was in Washington . . . and heard President Wilson deliver his war message to Congress. From that date Wilson was my President just as completely as though I had personally named him." Only a month into the war the president told Vandenberg how appreciative he was of "the generous support you have given the administration in these days of critical moment."[25]

Vandenberg did not stop with simple approval of Wilson's conduct of the war. He used his own bully pulpit to rally his readers to campaign against German-language newspapers, to remove the German language from the Michigan high school curriculum, and even to prevent the distinguished violinist Fritz Kreisler from performing in Grand Rapids. He succeeded as well in keeping the Progressive Republican senator Robert M. La Follette of Wisconsin from speaking there because of his opposition to American participation in the war.[26] Ten years earlier La Follette had been one of his heroes, advancing the cause of liberal Republicanism alongside President Roosevelt.

The romance with Wilson did not survive the war. Vandenberg's patriotic fervor eventually competed with his nationalist sentiments and with his party loyalties. Wilson's partisan approach to peacemaking, excluding Republicans from the peace process, offended Vandenberg's sense of fairness, particularly in light of his own abandonment of partisanship in the interest of winning the war. His disillusionment echoed some of the comments he had made in 1914 and 1915: namely, that Wilson's weakness in handling neutral rights before 1917 prefigured his weakness in dealing with the European allies at Versailles. It also prefigured his own arguments as senator: that making the treaty in 1919 was as much the responsibility of the Senate as it was of the president: "The Herald insists that while the Senate owed it to the World to join the League, it owed it to the God-blessed independence of the United States to proclaim 'reservations' . . . which shall make it clear to all the world for all time that we shall never construe the League Covenant as . . . creating any obligation, moral or otherwise, which seeks to abrogate the Constitution of the United States."[27] By 1919 he was upbraiding the president for abandoning constitutional responsibilities—that were not exclusively his.

Vandenberg always claimed that he was not opposed to the League of Nations, with its objective of preserving world peace and making impossible another world war. But an American commitment to collective security was a step he could not accept. While collective action against aggression that threatened American national interest was acceptable, he joined the reservationists who rejected any permanent commitment that the covenant of the league would require the nation to make. Ignoring the fact that the league would exclude such regional arrangements as the Monroe Doctrine, he still wanted a specific statement removing the doctrine from the reach of the covenant: "Accepting the Covenant means that we are transferring sovereign authority over our own immigration laws and our own tariffs and our own Monroe Doctrine to an Old World from which we have been successfully independent for 143 years."[28]

His was not the dogmatic opposition to the league of Idaho's Republican senator William E. Borah, however, or the crippling reservations of Massachusetts's Republican senator Henry Cabot Lodge, chairman of the

Foreign Relations Committee in 1919. Vandenberg's position was closer to that of the moderate reservationists, former secretary of war Elihu Root and former president Taft. It was no coincidence that these prominent political leaders were all Republicans. Moderate though Vandenberg may have considered his views, they betrayed emotions that distorted his judgment, much as they had during the war when he passionately supported the Wilson agenda.

Vandenberg's critical objection to the Covenant of the League of Nations was its Article 10, an objection he shared with Senator Lodge, the primary spokesman for the reservationists. He feared its application. This article was at the heart of the covenant and was seized upon by its American critics as the most subversive of a nation's sovereignty. It read, "The Members of the League undertake to respect and preserve as against external aggression the territorial integrity and existing political independence of all Members of the League. In case of such aggression or in case of any threat of danger of such aggression the council shall advise upon the means by which this obligation shall be fulfilled."

Critics were unwilling to concede that the league, through its council, could only ask, not force, nations to enforce the provisions of Article 10. Recognizing the sensitivities of the United States, the framers specifically exempted the Monroe Doctrine from that article. Moreover, under the principle of unanimity in the council the United States could veto any recommendation for action. Conceivably, as historian Herbert F. Margulies pointed out, had Wilson removed two words, the article might have been acceptable to the Senate. "Undertake" seemed more forceful than the original "guarantee," and "advise" left the meaning of enforcement open to debate. Thomas Bailey thought that if Article 10 not been proposed, the president and Senate might have been able to compromise on other matters.[29] Vandenberg would have agreed with these scholars were he not emotionally vulnerable to the charge that the League's covenant would abridge the constitutional powers of the Congress to declare war.

Vandenberg used his newspaper to expound his nationalist theme as the league became the key issue in the summer of 1919. He did not wish to prevent the United States from joining the league. He knew, as did other reservationists, that U.S. membership was vital to its success. His voice was raised to ensure that the nation would not be forced into military action without the explicit endorsement of the Congress. He echoed the Lodge reservation declaring that the United States assumes no obligation to use the armed forces of the United States to preserve the independence or territorial integrity of any member country unless Congress, with its war-declaring power under the Constitution, votes its approval. Without such a reservation he was convinced that the Senate would not accept the Treaty of Versailles or the league that resulted from it. He disagreed, however, with Senator Borah's assertion that Article 10 involved a moral obligation to carry out its commitments by force. It was an indication of the youthful editor's stature in the party that the Idaho rejectionist took the trouble to write that "I am very sorry to disagree with you and sometime I shall speak upon the matter in detail in the Senate when I will send you a copy of my argument."[30]

The Grand Rapids editor was not only addressing the citizens of western Michigan. He was already a presence in Michigan politics. And his wide correspondence with national leaders gave him credibility as a political force that he certainly recognized. Among such figures was Frank Knox, a Rough Rider with Roosevelt in the Spanish-American War, the editor of the *Manchester (NH) Union,* subsequently publisher of the *Chicago Daily News,* and secretary of the navy in World War II. Not incidentally, he was a former resident of Grand Rapids. Vandenberg could write freely to Knox, pleased to know that they were carrying on the same fight in their states to amend the terms of the covenant. He was glad to note that the nation's sentiment "has unquestionably swung our way—although we were in a hopeless minority when we started."[31]

Vandenberg boasted to Knox that "you may not know it, but the Herald is credited—even by Senator Lodge—with being one of the pioneers among American newspapers in demanding a program of American reservations. The real fact is that our first editorial to this end appeared several weeks before Root made the original proposals to this end." Even more impressive was that "we were the first newspaper to directly challenge Mr. Taft on his western tour and, as a result, we were able to print a letter from Taft in which he committed himself to reservations before the nation was aware of the former president's specific views." Vandenberg took pride in his initiatives—and credit for them as well. His newspaper's headline on July 24, 1919, read, "Taft Opens Fight for Interpretations in

League Pact as Advocated by the Herald." Given his sense of achievement it is understandable that in his letter to Knox he added, "I am almost ashamed to confidentially confess to you that I am giving serious consideration to entering into the 1920 governorship fight."[32]

Vandenberg always nourished political ambitions. His many friends encouraged him to consider political office during his newspaper years, including the lieutenant governorship in 1920. He refused each time, feeling the moment was not right. As he wrote to the editor of the *Kalamazoo Gazette* in 1919,

> I do not now expect to be a candidate either for governor or lieu-tenant-governor. Confidentially, the situation is this. I had almost allowed myself to be argued into standing for the lieutenant-governorship. But no sooner did the papers commence a discussion of this possibility then certain cash-register factions in Michigan gave immediate evidences of intent to try to "discipline" me for my past fidelity to my own ideals. . . . It is no more trouble or work to fight for a big nomination than for a little one. If I must "fight," it is not going to be over a handful of peanut snacks.[33]

Vandenberg backed off from that challenge in 1919, but not from his concern for a middle path to America's membership in the League of Nations, a compromise between the inflexible positions of Wilson and Borah. When the Versailles Treaty was defeated in the Senate, Vandenberg felt that "uncompromising extremists at both ends of the line defeated a sensible middle-of-the-road composition which a majority of the country wanted." He almost proclaimed a pox on both sides but gave a larger portion of blame to Wilson's obstinacy in refusing to accept reasonable reservations, even as he recognized the aims of the rejectionists. The Senate's unreasonable reservation on Irish independence in 1920 particularly annoyed him: "The Reservationists based their whole posture on America's insistence that America must hold itself aloof from foreign embroilment (a posture in which they have the Herald's wholehearted and uncompromising support). In the next breath they challenge their good faith by using their own Reservations to deliberately inject America into a particularly delicate foreign embroilment."[34]

It is unlikely that he ever identified Lodge with the rejectionist camp in 1919. Nor did he recognize that his vigorous opposition to Article 10 may have contributed to the failure of the league. His blistering attacks were undoubtedly sincere, but they conflicted with his instinctive sense of moderation. He understood the importance of collective security even as he worked against its achievement in 1919. He looked forward to the day when there would be an international organization that the United States could join. And when that day came Wilson "will be canonized for his implacable fidelity to the germ of a great idea—the close association of nations in the mutual consideration of international concerns."[35] Vandenberg may have had those words in mind when he helped to fashion an international organization a generation later. Francis B. Sayre, Wilson's son-in-law and the U.S. delegate at the UN General Assembly in 1948, thought along those lines when he told Vandenberg in 1949 that "had you been in office in the Senate during the presidency of Woodrow Wilson, I feel sure that our country and the world would have been spared infinite sufferings and would have had a very different history."[36]

THE HAMILTON FACTOR

Despite his obvious preference for a middle path in foreign relations, Vandenberg's sentiments were subsumed under the political pressures of the 1920s. The Republicans returned to office and the nation returned to "normalcy," in the language of President Warren G. Harding. "With Harding at the helm," Vandenberg wrote, "we can sleep nights."[37] Harding's stance on the league was Delphic enough to allow a Progressive gloss for those who looked for it. It was not that Vandenberg had consciously turned his back on his Progressive past. Rather, Progressivism gradually faded in the judgment of a man who by the middle of the decade had become a millionaire, with three children and a comfortable life to accompany his position of affluence. A year after the death of his wife, the mother of his children, he remarried in 1918. His marriage brought contentment to the still-youthful editor and a happy home for his children. As he and his country looked inward in the 1920s, Vandenberg had become increasingly wealthy from his ownership in the stock of his publishing company and from successful investments in the Grand Rapids

Savings Bank, where he served on the board of directors. He was in every way a leading citizen of his community as well as an increasingly influential political voice in the state.[38]

In postwar America the remnants of Vandenberg's Progressivism were too difficult to find. He appreciated the checks and balances in the Constitution that moderated the vagaries of the people. In particular, he emphasized the vital role of the Supreme Court and deplored any effort to subordinate the court to Congress. He invoked Alexander Hamilton's name to ask "which method best protects the 'will of the people'—the existing Supreme Court authority over Constitutional interpretations, or the proposed Congressional supremacy over the Constitution. And the moment we cut through the sophistry, down to the bed rock of logic, we find the former utterly triumphant."[39] The Supreme Court's rejection of unconstitutional acts of Congress was crucial for the protection of individual liberty. The independence of the court remained a cardinal principle of Vandenberg's political life, although applied to the executive rather than to Congress after he entered the Senate.

Vandenberg accepted tolerance of dissenting views as part of the American way but held that tolerance should not be extended to Communists. The Red Scare affected his editorials after the war. The objective of a world revolution made Communist Russia and its agents in the United States a threat to society, and Vandenberg was as diligent as Attorney General A. Mitchell Palmer in seeking to root them out. He developed a visceral fear of the Bolshevik threat to capitalism and to the values of American society.

This was not simply a reflection of the nation's mood at the time. His dislike of Communism was a running theme throughout his career. He took the occasion in responding to criticism in 1939 from the editor of the *Hackensack (NJ) Record* to protest the charge that his demand to sever diplomatic relations with the Soviet Union in the wake of its invasion of Finland had "no motive except one of domestic politics." He proceeded to demonstrate the consistency of his anti-Communist convictions by noting that he "was against the American recognition of Russia in 1933—just as I had opposed it for the preceding decade. I voted against the confirmation of any Ambassador to Russia. There is nothing new in my present attitude."[40]

If anti-Communism was a hallmark of Vandenberg's increasing conservatism, it did not encompass the whole range of "normalcy" in the Harding years. He continued to defend labor's right to collective bargaining and encouraged state and federal governments to recognize labor unions. This position was in keeping with his dislike of powerful corporations, a carryover from his Progressive days. Furthermore, his newspaper was not hesitant to buck the Republican establishment by backing Gifford Pinchot's nomination for governor of Pennsylvania and Albert Beveridge for senator in Indiana, both in 1922. He retained a mix of Progressivism and conservatism, repudiating both reactionary conservatism and radical liberalism.

Vandenberg discovered in one of the nation's founding fathers, Alexander Hamilton, a figure worthy of his hero worship who embodied the best qualities of conservatism and Progressivism. A love of history was certainly a factor in his devotion to the memory and legacy of Alexander Hamilton that flowered in the 1920s. Vandenberg's enduring interest in the collections of the University of Michigan's William L. Clements Library and his close association with its director over the years attest to the importance he attached to the past. Writing came easily to him, and in the long list of stories, articles, and editorials that he produced before he entered the U.S. Senate were two biographies of his favorite founding father. *The Greatest American, Alexander Hamilton: An Historical Analysis of His Life and Works together with a Symposium of Opinions by Distinguished Americans* and *If Hamilton Were Here Today: American Fundamentals Applied to Modern Problems* were both published with a well-respected New York publishing house, G.P. Putnam's Sons. The books appeared in 1921 and 1923, respectively.

With his customary hyperbole, Vandenberg introduced Hamilton as "the master craftsman of American government. He crowded into one short life more dynamic service to the American foundation than any other patriot who ever lived. He was the inspired oracle of the Constitution. His lucid exposition of its purposes, his matchless interpretation of its spirit, his implacable determination to save it—and through it, to save a stumbling people from the tragedy of disintegration—were the dominant factors in the creation of the Republic. He clearly saw that ordered freedom required protectorate."[41]

Vandenberg also identified Hamilton as a guide to the direction in which the nation should be advancing. The contemporary world was very much on his mind when he observed, "It is inconceivable that a man who could think continentally as did Hamilton . . . would be a narrow-visioned provincial, with blinders at his eyes, in this present period of world-wide international economic involvements." Hamilton would have understood America's role in the world after the world war. But as the "putative" author of the Neutrality Proclamation in 1793 and the statesman who warned America against "entangling alliances" in his contribution to Washington's farewell address in 1796, he would not have sanctioned "any modern partnership between America and Europe." Vandenberg knew that the term "entangling alliance" did not appear in the farewell address but believed that an instruction against "permanent alliances" carried the same message.[42] Hamilton's was a middle path between isolationism and internationalism, much as Vandenberg saw his own.

Fittingly, Hamilton should be credited as a Progressive and as a conservative. In a series of rhetorical questions the Grand Rapids editor asked, "Was it not 'progressive' to achieve the Constitution, the most forward-looking event in history since the birth of Jesus Christ? . . . Was it not 'progressive' to demand the impartial administration of the Law, for rich and poor alike? . . . Was it not 'progressive'—the most progressive single act in American history—to evolve the constitutional doctrine of liberal construction and implied powers, so that the Great Charter, though holding on to fundamentals, did not become a strait-jacket and a garrotte?" Vandenberg was referring to Hamilton's loose construction of the Constitution. No less than twelve examples of his Progressive credentials were cited in these pages. No wonder Vandenberg could proclaim that "Hamilton was, in the true sense of the word, the greatest 'progressive' of his time."[43]

Vandenberg was proud of his literary efforts and made sure that leading opinion makers were aware of his accomplishments. He sent a copy of *If Hamilton Were Here Today* to President Calvin Coolidge, who promised to read it "with pleasure and profit" when he could find the time. His successor, Herbert Hoover, did read it, and according to Frank Knox, agreed with Vandenberg that Hamilton "was a great democrat in the truest meaning of that word." Even more important to Vandenberg was his correspondence with Senator Lodge, who had written his own biography and edited Hamilton's letters. Vandenberg could have not gone to a higher authority. Lodge did find time to read his 1921 biography and regaled the author with stories of his family's friendship with the Hamiltons.[44]

The exchange of letters between Vandenberg and Lodge was not confined to Hamilton's career. A few years later Vandenberg reminded the senator that Hamilton was not excluded from the presidency because of his foreign birth. The Constitution included citizens of the United States at the time of its adoption. Lodge graciously noted that "the point you raise is a very interesting one, and with all my familiarity with Hamilton I never thought of it in connection with him."[45]

Vandenberg's engagement with history did not stop with Hamilton's life. In 1926, just two years before he was appointed to the Senate, he produced a history of the United States entitled *The Trail of a Tradition*, also published by G.P. Putnam's Sons. This was three years after his second tribute to Hamilton appeared. That Hamilton's portrait appeared as the frontispiece suggested that he remained a Hamiltonian, and the dedication of the book to Senator William Alden Smith indicated that his political ambitions also remained active. Two years later Vandenberg was the junior senator from Michigan.

Vandenberg's "trail" was nothing less than "the epic history of the United States leaping down the years from Washington and Hamilton who set us apart from alien contagions to the seasoned American maturities which won a World War and refused to lose the sequent peace." The journey celebrated "our Independence—not our 'isolation' which is a totally different thing—and our continuing privilege and purpose to captain our own souls."[46] As he ploughed through the nation's history, he recognized Jefferson's presence, flawed though his nationalism was. But it was Hamilton whose guiding spirit was bringing the nation successfully into the twentieth century.

Vandenberg overblown praise was acceptable enough in the 1920s, even if academic historians would not take his historical research seriously. Although his judgments hardly indicate a serous scholar at work, they were certainly building blocks for a projected career in public life. A seat in the Senate was an aspiration he had held since his youth. In 1913, when he was chairman of the commission to place the statue of

Zachariah Chandler, an influential Michigan senator during the Civil War, in the National Hall of Fame, he made a speech that won the attention of vice president Thomas R. Marshall. The vice president observed, "I've heard speeches galore on the floor of the Senate, in the Hall of Fame and in many places, but I have never heard anything more eloquent than the address of the young man from Michigan." In response to this praise, the twenty-nine-year-old editor said, "Some day I hope again to make a speech in Washington on the floor of the United States Senate—as a Senator from the State of Michigan."[47] By 1928 he was ready to act on his ambitions when the opportunity arose.

2

The Republican Moderate, 1928–1936

There were good reasons for Vandenberg to tread cautiously in 1928. No matter how ready he felt to serve as senator, he was aware of political obstacles that had deterred him in 1918 from making a run for the Senate. At that time his friend and mentor William Alden Smith retired rather than challenge the seemingly unbeatable Henry Ford for the Republican nomination. Ford ultimately ran under the Democratic banner with President Wilson's blessing, only to lose to Republican Truman H. Newberry. Smith judged that if he would not face the Ford challenge then Vandenberg would have even less chance of defeating the auto magnate. Smith and Frank Sparks, Vandenberg's successor as editor of the *Grand Rapids Herald* and trusted political adviser, agreed that a defeat at the hands of Ford would be a disaster for Vandenberg's political future.[1]

Vandenberg did not retire exclusively into the world of journalism after deciding not to run against Ford. Rather, he used his newspaper skills and connections to become increasingly visible among fellow journalists and among the larger public of Michigan through a continuing stream of writings. In fact, he turned his attention, as did Ford, to the illegal ways by which Newberry won the election of 1918. Although the Supreme Court nullified his conviction for corruption, Newberry's reputation was sufficiently tarnished to force his resignation in 1922. Despite Vandenberg's prominence in the demonization of Newberry, the governor appointed Detroit's mayor, James Couzens, to fill the seat. Further depressing Vandenberg's political ambition was the election of the popular former Democratic governor Woodbridge N. Ferris to the Senate in 1922, partly as a consequence of his Republican opponent's lukewarm approval of Newberry's behavior.[2] So the immediate result of Vandenberg's leap into Michigan's senatorial races was exclusion from both seats.

Arguably, as C. David Tompkins has suggested, Vandenberg's difficulties in achieving his objective was that "he was not a natural politician, and his sober and colorless personality was a distinct political handicap." This description of his personality does not match the reputation he won in Grand Rapids as a social as well as political leader. His correspondence discloses a wide variety of people. He was able to reach out to people in all stations of life with verve and empathy. Tompkins noted the pleasure he took in cards and billiards at the exclusive Peninsular Club. A legion of friends in Grand Rapids helped to propel him into public life. And his frequent self-professed ambitions were kept alive by the confidence friends showed in his future.[3]

Evidence of indecisiveness can be construed as false modesty. What else can be made of Vandenberg's speech before his fellow editors in April 1928, shortly after his appointment to the Senate, when he identified himself as "a senatorial neophyte of three weeks existence. . . . But I am a journalistic veteran of 28 scarred (not scared) years." Basking in the adulation of his audience, he asserted that he would always be an editor first and foremost, which was "extremely fortunate for my own peace of mind because I may be a senator only until next December—if my constituents are blind to their welfare."[4] These were not the words of a shrinking violet who found it difficult to mingle with people.

His difficulties in 1928 seem to have had other origins. Despite his visibility in western Michigan he was not well known among Republicans in Wayne County and Detroit. Because he resented Republican governor Alex Groesbeck's excessive liberalism (he had flirted with La Follette's presidential candidacy in 1924), Vandenberg backed Groesbeck's successful rival, Fred Green, for the governorship. Although Green was in Vandenberg's debt, he had debts to others as well. The sudden death of Democratic senator Ferris provided Governor Green with an opportunity to make an interim appointment.[5]

At this point Vandenberg's luck turned in his favor. Although Green had contemplated appointing a neutral figure to avoid antagonizing expectant claimants, Sparks and his friends pressured the governor to give the appointment to Vandenberg. On April 5, 1928, with Vandenberg's family in the audience and the entire Michigan House delegation present, Senator Couzens ushered him to meet Vice President Charles G. Dawes, who administered the oath of office.[6] At last, at the age of forty-four, Vandenberg was a senator, a position he gloried in and kept until his death twenty-three years later.

He entered the Senate without the customary deference to his seniors expected of a freshman senator, particularly one in an interim capacity. Rather, he burst on the scene full of confidence in his command of the issues before that body and ready to intrude himself into whatever debates interested him. It is hardly surprising that he left the initial impression— never fully erased over the next generation—of being, in the words of Yale professor Fred Rodell, "a strutting, orating Claghornesque caricature" of a southern senator.[7]

THE "YOUNG TURK" YEARS, 1929–1931

Vandenberg's sense of his own importance was reflected in his efforts to dominate a bill on reapportionment of the House of Representatives. Only a month after his appointment he introduced a bill into the Senate calling for such reapportionment following the census of 1920. He recognized that normally the initiative of reapportionment "should be recognized as a primary prerogative of the House itself." But he also noted that the Constitution did not assign this authority to the House alone, and he was "not agreeable to the expedient theory that the Senate can thus entirely sublet its own concurrent responsibility and thus whitewash its own turpitude" by dodging its obligations.[8]

What presumably precipitated his action was the refusal of the House to act: "This completes eight years of constitutional defiance. This is the issue: When the House of Representatives fails to reapportion itself pursuant to constitutional mandate is it not the concurrent duty of the Senate to discharge its own share of this constitutional function by initiating the legislation?" The junior senator from Michigan made a point of asking for fair representation, "particularly to my own State of Michigan which in 1930 will deserve four more Representatives even with a maximum membership held at 435." He admitted that "it is perfectly obvious that this bill can not pass the present session of the Seventieth Congress. But it is equally obvious that the second session of this same Congress next November can not avoid facing the issue thus raised. It is for this purpose that this bill is introduced."[9]

There was something presumptuous about a newly appointed senator who had yet to win an election on his own advising his colleagues how to act in December, when his constituents might not have returned him to Washington. Without justification he adopted a patronizing tone in concluding that "if the Senate values its own constitutional reputation and if it respects its own constitutional oath, it dare not permit another session to pass into history without affirmative action. In fairness to Michigan's members of the House, it should be said that I believe this action will meet with their unanimous approval. Indeed, I seek only to uphold their hands."[10] Such was his leap into the limelight, an action that Vandenberg would repeat in the future by introducing resolutions or amendments.

In the context of a senatorial debut, this particular action more appropriately might have come from Michigan's senior senator, James B. Couzens. The Senate did not immediately respond to Vandenberg's call to arms. Too many other states would be affected negatively by reapportionment to permit easy passage of Vandenberg's bill. A threat of a filibuster forced its withdrawal. Redrafted after consultation with the Senate leadership, his reapportionment bill passed on May 29, 1929, with twenty-six in opposition. The unanimous approval he confidently expected of his first bill did not materialize; instead, painstaking bargaining was required, bringing with a learning experience for the neophyte senator. President Hoover signed the law on June 18, 1929, more than a year after Vandenberg originally made his case.[11] The junior senator from Michigan, in office less than a year, won the admiration of Vice President Dawes, however, who observed that "Senator Vandenberg is beginning to show his teeth in a righteous cause—the passage of the Reapportionment Bill. He is a coming man, in my judgment."[12]

It was the energy that Vandenberg displayed on the Senate floor that earned him the sobriquet of "young Turk."[13] It should have placed him among the sons of the wild jackasses, as Senator George Moses (R-NH) called the western insurgents in his party. But it is hard to fit Vandenberg into that category. He was no bomb-throwing radical intent on upsetting the established order in the Senate. Rather, he regarded himself as a voice of moderation, but a voice that should be and would be heard in the service of Progressive, but not radical, causes—and in support of the president. As such he was not comfortable in the company of William E. Borah, La Follette, and George Norris (R-NE), dissenters in the Hoover years, who looked upon the president as a tool of Wall Street. But he was even more uncomfortable with the Old Guard that was suspicious of Hoover's putative liberalism. Vandenberg sought the middle ground, where he could be a liaison between the president and the Senate, supporting Hoover's program while seeking suitable adjustments, particularly for relief of the unemployed.[14]

Achieving this position was not always possible. Vandenberg voted against the nomination of Judge John J. Parker for the Supreme Court in 1930 in the face of the president's appeal to party loyalty. In this instance Parker's disparaging remarks about "the Negro's" unfitness for participation in government aroused the senator's civil rights sympathies, reinforced by the campaign of the National Association for the Advancement of Colored People. Reluctantly, he resisted Hoover's appeal, hoping it would not affect their friendship. Hoover was disappointed, losing the nomination by one vote, and implicitly blamed Vandenberg for the loss. As the president recorded bitterly in his memoirs, the senator had often spoken about preserving the bench from group pressures. Hoover was convinced that the failure of his Republican friends to vote for Parker stemmed from their fear over their own reelection.[15] This judgment was unfair to Vandenberg, who had four more years left in his term, after being elected with a comfortable margin in 1928. His negative vote was unusual, and he ultimately succeeded in repairing his relations with the president.

Appointed to the Committee on Foreign Relations in 1929, Vandenberg worked with Hoover in reprising many of the positions he had expressed as a newspaper editor. In fact, he gave more slack to Hoover than he had to Wilson, not simply as a fellow Republican but because the former was less ambitious and less dogmatic in his positions on foreign affairs. Vandenberg's views paralleled the president's for the most part, with a mix of nationalism and guarded internationalism. The senator was aligned with Hoover on reducing the war debts of European creditors and on using his influence to support the president's intentions to have the London Naval Treaty ratified as early as possible.[16]

Most notable was his activity with respect to U.S. membership in the World Court. As a Michigan editor he had been as worried about the World Court's intrusion into the nation's independence, as he had been about the potential impact of the Covenant of the League of Nation's Article 10. But unlike the liberal isolationist Albert J. Beveridge, Vandenberg was less disturbed about the World Court than he was about the league.[17] As a senator he was still concerned about U.S. membership in the World Court, even as he worked with the president to win the Senate's approval. But he was upset over Hoover's submitting the protocols of adherence after promising that the matter would be delayed to the next session. He claimed that he "voted to save the World Court from an unnecessary black eye through inevitable failure at that short session."[18]

Neither the protocols nor approval for U.S. membership in the World Court passed the Senate Foreign Relations Committee in the Hoover administration. Vandenberg persisted into the Roosevelt years in his qualified advocacy of the World Court. He saw it as a means of reconciling national quarrels and minimizing the prospect of a new war. But his efforts always included terms that protected American national interests and, as often was the case, were stamped with his own imprimatur.

Vandenberg's intrusion of his amendment to the protocols of adherence to the World Court in 1935 was illustrative of both the limits of his internationalism and of his unlimited compulsion to be at the center of the political stage. His amendment resolved "that adherence to the said protocols . . . should not be construed as to require the United States to depart from its traditional policy of not intruding upon, interfering with, or entangling itself . . . in the internal administration of any foreign state; nor shall adherence to the said protocols and statute be construed to imply relinquishment by the United States of the traditional attitude toward purely American questions." Was this reaffirmation of American policies necessary, when they had never been subject to approval by foreign governments, Senator Joseph T. Robinson (D-AR) asked? Vandenberg piously replied that "it is never an excess of caution for the American people, and the Senate was speaking in their behalf, to reassert the traditional and fundamental policies which we have pursued in all our international relations for years." He went on to say that if "all that can be said against his amendment" was that it is harmless, "then I submit it should be accepted lest those of us who feel its deliberate rejection would be harmful can be satisfied."[19] The protocols still failed passage, due to the prevailing isolationism of the country and lack of presidential support. It was obvious that the World Court was not a major interest of either Vandenberg or Roosevelt.

It was as a member of the Senate Foreign Relations Committee that Vandenberg most displayed his gift for conciliation, for bringing conflicting parties together. While he had criticized Borah for his destructive opposition to the League of Nations in 1919, he found it difficult to fault the ultimate conclusions of the Idaho senator's judgment. Borah, then chairman of the Foreign Relations Committee, had taken Vandenberg under his wing when he entered the Senate in 1928, and the Michigan neophyte tried to bridge the gap between Borah and the president that widened during the Hoover administration.

As the Depression deepened, the senator felt that the president was too rigid about providing economic relief to the suffering unemployed. Nor was he pleased with what he felt was excessive presidential deference to eastern industrial interests. It was this perception that drove him close to the Borah camp of insurgents in the Hoover years, not as a rebellious Young Turk but as a legislator attuned to the distress of farmers, particularly those affected by the devastating drought in the Great Plains. He empathized with western senators increasingly worried about the collapse of the agricultural sector of the economy.

THE VANDENBERG-FDR CONNECTION

The Hoover presidency ended in an election debacle for the Republican Party. The Democrats won not only the White House but also both houses of Congress. The results in Michigan echoed those of the nation. Not only was there a Democrat as governor but there were also more Democrats in Congress than at any time since the birth of the Republican Party in 1854. Vandenberg was a lonely survivor who remained a defender of President Hoover, even as he had chafed over the president's hesitancy in supporting more drastic measures to counter the Depression.

Throughout the Hoover years Vandenberg's Progressive instincts conflicted with his opposition to direct federal relief for the economy's victims. He empathized with the demands of the veterans' Bonus Army in 1931 but felt compelled to vote against the bonus bill because of concern for an increased national debt. He recognized too the need for insurance on bank deposits but feared the impact on the federal treasury if all bank deposits were insured at full face value.[20] It required the collapse of the banking system as Roosevelt took office to change his thinking. Nevertheless, under Hoover he had appreciated the need for liberalizing the banking system in his endorsement of the Reconstruction Finance Corporation that employed the authority of the federal government to extend needed credit to the business community. He felt he had won a personal victory when the Glass-Steagall Act in February 1932 authorized the use of government bonds as collateral for Federal Reserve notes.[21] His Progressive heritage, although diluted over the years, survived, to be reinvigorated for a time under the presidency of Franklin D. Roosevelt.

Vandenberg's relations with President Roosevelt are usually framed by the senator's vocal leadership against the packing of the Supreme Court in 1937 and then by his vociferous and usually colorful denunciations of the president's role in bringing the United States into war between 1939 and 1941. Given his role as the voice of American isolationism at the end of the decade, it is easy to forget how taken Vandenberg was with much of the New Deal in its first two years.

But it was not simply an appreciation for New Deal legislation that modified if not compromised his position as a senator from the opposition party. Partly it was a recognition that although he would object to some aspects of the policies emanating from the Roosevelt White House, he lived in a political system where his party was in the minority. To keep his standing with fellow Republicans he would criticize key Roosevelt aides from time to time in the early years of the New Deal. Yet there was a personality factor that was always present: namely, to socialize or even fraternize with political opponents even when voting against them.

Vandenberg's style was to present as positive a face as possible in his relations with his opponents, and nowhere was this more evident than in his communications with Roosevelt, notably in 1937. But not in public. He was the scourge of the Second New Deal. This was the year that the president proposed to appoint an additional justice to the Supreme Court, up to six if necessary, if a standing judge reached the age of seventy without offering to retire. This "court-packing" plan united conservatives and liberals, Republicans and Democrats to campaign against what its enemies believed was an assault on the Constitution by unprecedented enlargement of presidential authority at the expense of the Supreme Court. This action struck a nerve with Vandenberg, given his long-standing veneration of the Constitution. He was among the leaders in the effort to defeat the president and at the same time build a coalition of like-minded bipartisan conservatives.[22]

Vandenberg's sharp attacks on the Second New Deal and on the president himself increased after 1937. He would issue another one of his many resolutions at the same time that he was working agreeably with Roosevelt on getting rid of riders on appropriation bills. In fact, the senator was even more supportive than before of a constitutional amendment authorizing the president to veto items in appropriations and tax bills. Roosevelt made a point of thanking Vandenberg "for writing me in regard to the proposal to amend the Constitution and appreciate your expression of approval as to my action in calling attention to the unfairness of shackling the Executive in acting on legislation." In response the senator wondered "if he might stir up some general interest in this proposition if our correspondence were to be made public, either at your end of the line or mine. Certainly your agreement on the general principle would lift the proposition out of partisan politics—and that is where it belongs."[23]

The Vandenberg-Roosevelt collaboration over the item veto came to a halt by the end of the year, but not because of party divisions. The influential senator Alben Barkley (D-KY) convinced the president that while he agreed with the principle of his having the right to veto a rider without having to veto the whole bill, he doubted that the amendment would arouse much public interest at this time without more preparation.[24] There is no reason to think that Vandenberg would disagree with Barkley's judgment.

This congenial correspondence took place after the presidential election of 1936 in which Vandenberg ostentatiously displayed his Republican colors. Listening to typical Vandenberg oratory denouncing the New Deal, one would find little trace of New Deal sentiments and no appreciation of Roosevelt's accomplishments. The Roosevelt administration, he proclaimed in October 1936 in Philadelphia, "gives us a federal government of unchecked and unbalanced concentrations of power that makes 'the super-executive' a virtual monarch of all he surveys . . . [and] in which an inconveniently sturdy Supreme Court is the object of ridicule, resentment, reprisal, and revenge."[25] What stands out in these election rallies is a familiar Vandenberg plea of a linkage between his party and the conservative Jeffersonian Democrats that should have brought victory to Alfred Landon and Frank Knox.

Four years later the stakes were even higher, and Vandenberg was even more strident as Roosevelt sought a third term. Speaking in Battle Creek on September 5, 1940, two months before the election, he exclaimed, "This is more than a campaign. It is a crusade. It is more than a Republican cause. It is just as much the cause of Democrats who love the memory of Thomas Jefferson. We present a common front to a common enemy. We dare not fail. And, Michigan must do her full part." The enemy was not in Europe or Asia; it was in Washington.[26]

Two months later Roosevelt won an unprecedented third term, and the republic had survived, despite Vandenberg's alarm that the nation's survival was at stake in 1940. Senator Vandenberg at this juncture seemed to regard the election as a sporting event after which he could congratulate the victor: "I was wrong. It is not 'Good Bye Mr. Chips.' It is still 'Hail to the Chief!' I wish you every good thing for yourself and for the country and I shall hope to be able to cooperate with you whenever possible."[27] This gracious note was more than just a passing gesture in an increasingly contentious political environment. It expressed a facet of the senator's character that coexisted with his conviction that the president was a danger to the nation. But the New Deal of 1933 that had attracted Vandenberg was long gone by the end of the decade, as was his attraction to many but not all of its objectives.

The Conditional New Dealer

That Senator Vandenberg welcomed what he believed was Roosevelt's restoration of confidence in the capitalist system is undeniable. Given his sentiments on the banking crisis, on the plight of the unemployed, and on mortgage relief for distressed homeowners, he supported the Emergency

Banking Act in the first week of the New Deal and went on to endorse the Farm Mortgage Refinancing Act and the Securities Exchange Act. In doing so he integrated his antipathy toward Wall Street with his empathy for the plight of the farmers that he had exhibited in the Hoover years. These were not radical measures. Rather than castigating the president for rash initiatives, he saw him successfully carrying through reforms that Hoover had been unable or unwilling to effect. Roosevelt in his first two years was a defender of a balanced budget and of the gold standard. In these circumstances the Grand Rapids editor who had worried about the radicalism of La Follette and his split from the Republican Party in 1924 grew closer to the dissidents of the 1920s, including his more liberal colleague Senator James Couzens.[28]

Although the New Deal awakened Vandenberg's Progressive memories, he had reservations even in the early years of the Roosevelt administration. The dispute might be minor, as when he objected to Louis Howe being paid $1,000 for two radio speeches in which he joined the controversy between the president and the Senate over the amount of government economies that should be made in reducing allowances to war veterans. The senator criticized Howe for accepting remuneration for his speech when, as the president's secretary, he appeared to be speaking for the White House. No matter how sympathetic Vandenberg was to New Deal programs he was always ready to defend the position of the Senate against executive intrusion—and, not incidentally, to have his name mentioned in prominent newspapers.[29]

The Michigan senator was never fully in step with the New Deal. He felt that the National Industrial Recovery Act (NIRA) gave too many powers to bureaucrats making codes for the many industries involved. He had mixed feelings about the Agricultural Adjustment Act (AAA), approving the farm mortgage refinancing section but objecting to the excessive powers given to the secretary of agriculture to restrict farm production. His objections were largely on constitutional grounds; the executive branch would receive too much authority at the expense of the legislative branch. Beyond his defensiveness about the role of the Senate, he feared that price fixing would lead to a planned economy, damaging the free-enterprise system. He voted against the NIRA and yet did not join his party in condemning its good intentions.[30] In brief, the Michigan senator can properly be identified in Roosevelt's first term with those Republican insurgents who wanted changes that the Hoover administration could never deliver but at the same time were wary of the authority the president would acquire in pursuit of those goals.

Vandenberg's ambivalence toward the New Deal was evident with respect to labor's right to organize unions. He was in sympathy with the labor provisions of the NIRA's application to sweatshops and condemnation of child labor, sentiments he had expressed so many times in his years as a journalist. Yet the weight of the automobile industry's pressure was too heavy for him to identify with labor interests when the Detroit leaders of the industry were antagonistic to labor unions. He participated in the auto industry's effort to amend the bill's guarantee of the right to collective bargaining. And when the explosive sit-down strike against General Motors broke out, he used his oratorical talents to excoriate its leaders for "all the lawlessness, all the hoodlumism, all the syndicalism, and all the communism" it contained.[31]

Vandenberg's future, after all, was tied to the Republican Party, and this identification made itself felt in the election of 1936. There could be no doubts about his allegiance, unlike those his fellow Republicans had about his more liberal colleague James Couzens. Yet it was his New Deal credentials that may have made the difference between survival and defeat in the senatorial election of 1934, when he was the lone Republican from an industrial state to withstand the Democratic onslaught. His vocal campaign to protect investors from bank failures in 1933 was a factor in his success at the polls.

Arguably, the shining example of Vandenberg's embrace of the New Deal was his leadership in the fight against predatory banks through his defense of the Glass-Steagall Act's creation of the Federal Deposit Insurance Corporation (FDIC) in 1933. If ever the senator was the spokesman for Main Street against Wall Street, for the citizens of Grand Rapids against the financiers of the East, it was in the role he played in this legislation. It encapsulated many of the characteristics, including his inconsistencies, that were visible in his public life—criticizing the president even as he embraced his goals; propelling himself to the center of the political stage; following a social program he had long advocated; and expressing pride in being the prime mover in the success of the FDIC.

The Glass-Steagall Banking Reform Act of 1933 was an expansion of the Glass-Steagall Emergency Banking Act of 1932. The new Roosevelt administration was determined to reform the practices of the Wall Street bankers whom it blamed for the miseries of the Depression. Vandenberg's concern was with the small depositor who had lost so much in the banking crisis of that year, and he recognized that smaller banks would be the chief beneficiary of the FDIC. He encountered considerable opposition not only from the larger banks in the East but from the Democratic Party and the Roosevelt administration itself. The president, along with Carter Glass (D-VA) and the New York banking establishment, feared, as Roosevelt told vice president John Garner, "It won't work, Jack. The weak banks will pull down the strong."[32] The president's hesitancy only emboldened Vandenberg to castigate the Wall Street coterie who would destroy the small banks of America. On the floor of the Senate he saw the salvation of community banks through guaranteeing their deposits. Vandenberg had the quiet support of Garner in inserting his amendment into the Glass-Steagall bill. His proposal to have $1,500 per depositor protected by the FDIC was approved.[33]

He was annoyed by the claims that President Roosevelt and Carter Glass made regarding their role in the creation of the FDIC. It was minimal at best and negative at a critical moment. As noted, it was the intervention of the vice president that allowed Vandenberg's initiative to succeed. Yet Roosevelt regularly took credit for the program, identifying it as one of the great achievements of his presidency.

This was too much for Vandenberg to bear. He asserted in 1943 that "the story of bank deposit insurance is a long one. . . . Nobody can claim a monopoly of credit in connection with this achievement. But least of all can the Roosevelt crowd pretend any such monopoly. I believe I offered the first general Bill on this subject on December 23, 1932. Many Republicans and Democrats in the House and Senate collaborated in finally producing the Bank Deposit Insurance Act—but the President is not 'among those present.'" As for the Banking Act of 1933, "the record will show that I offered an amendment [which became known as the Vandenberg amendment] providing for immediate Federal Bank Deposit insurance up to $2500 per account." Although the amendment passed both House and Senate, the president told the congressional conferees, "I must again express to you my definite feeling that the *Vandenberg* amendment must be rejected in toto."[34] It was not.

When Vandenberg felt he needed confirmation of his successful promotion of the FDIC, Leo T. Crowley, the director of the FDIC, provided it. Upon retiring in 1945, Crowley paid tribute to the senator's role, noting that "since the inception of deposit insurance you have been its most consistent friend and supporter. You will remain here. Because deposit insurance has been as close to your heart as to mine, I know that I am leaving behind a friend of the FDIC, a friend who has continuously protected it over the years and who will . . . take the same active interest in its affairs as in the past." This was a handsome and well-deserved testimonial to the Michigan senator, but it might have been more effusive. It is likely that he preferred the sobriquet of "father of the FDIC," as Crowley once had called him.[35]

Vandenberg's sponsorship of banking insurance legislation placed him in the camp of the early New Deal, an easy transition from his advocacy in the last year of the Hoover administration. It also displayed a resentment of Franklin D. Roosevelt that was to manifest itself more clearly in later years, without being accompanied by rejection of all New Deal reforms. In fact, in the case of banking reform Vandenberg was obviously more adventurous than the president. Not incidentally, the FDIC presented opportunities for displays of ego that the Vandenberg amendment underscored. He never forgave Roosevelt for attempting to deprive him of credit for his sponsorship of the FDIC. As he observed years later, "The [Roosevelt] Administration is not in the habit of permitting minority Senators to sponsor major legislation of this character."[36]

THE PRESIDENTIAL ELECTION OF 1936

Vandenberg's attraction to some aspects of the New Deal did not remove him from the Republican ranks. His caveats were articulated at all times. And they increased exponentially as the election of 1936 approached. His disaffection crystallized in his belief that the Second New Deal gave the president too much authority to expand government bureaucracy. He applauded the Supreme Court ruling in 1935 that the NIRA was unconstitutional. It reflected his perception that Roosevelt had gone from combating the Depression with measures he could approve to redistribution of wealth through the Revenue Act of 1935, which would raise income, corporate, and inheritance taxes. He objected to the Agricultural Adjustment Act, even though he had voted for its farm mortgage financing section. He could not reconcile himself to the secretary of agriculture being given authority to restrict farm production. Nor could he accept the National Labor Relations Act, sponsored by Senator Robert Wagner (D-NY), which would compel employers to accept unionization of their plants.[37]

Vandenberg's disillusionment with the Roosevelt administration's Second New Deal was accompanied by increasing prominence in his party. Given his success in bucking the Democratic tide in 1934 it was hardly surprising that he would be considered a candidate to challenge Roosevelt two years later. The senator had the backing of the Michigan delegation in Congress and of his Michigan colleague in the Senate, James Couzens. He not only had survived the Democratic onslaught but also was recognized as an effective speaker and writer who never avoided an opportunity to be visible in the Senate or in national journals.

Although he refused to participate in primaries in 1936 he was willing to accept a genuine draft. This, he knew, was unlikely. He also knew how difficult it would be to defeat Franklin D. Roosevelt at the crest of his popularity. The columnist Drew Pearson reported in his widely read Washington Merry-Go-Round column on April 30, 1936, that the senator was convinced that the Republican Party didn't have a chance that year. He quoted Vandenberg as saying, "I'm not in the race. I've got my eye on 1940." When Governor Alfred M. Landon of Kansas won the nomination, Vandenberg resisted pressure to accept the vice presidential nomination. Only a genuine draft would have been acceptable.[38] Whether he would have been as firm about the presidency was never tested. He then supported his former Grand Rapids colleague Frank Knox, editor of the *Chicago Daily News,* as Landon's running mate.

Although Vandenberg's ambitions might have been great enough to accept a draft, there is no doubt that he dreaded the outcome of the election. This did not stop him from displaying his eloquence on behalf of the Landon-Knox ticket. He was at the top of his form when he addressed his "home-sweet-home" neighbors in Grand Rapids in July of the election year. He informed them that the campaign was "probably the most significant since Lincoln was elected in 1860." He expanded his command of hyperbole when he proclaimed in October in Philadelphia that the Roosevelt administration "gives us a federal government of unchecked and unbalanced concentration of power that makes the 'super-executive' a virtual monarch of all he surveys [and] in which an inconveniently sturdy Supreme Court is the object of ridicule, resentment, reprisal, and revenge."[39]

Vandenberg's hopes for a coalition between Progressive Republicans such as himself and dissident Democrats that would constitute an anti–New Deal force failed to materialize in 1936. But he still had expectations that those he called Jeffersonian Democrats would join with Republicans to repudiate the New Deal reforms that he felt threatened to destroy the Constitution. He had rejoiced when Alfred E. Smith, Hoover's Democratic opponent in 1928, defected from his party in 1936. Vandenberg declared then that "Jeffersonians can find nothing in this present administration even remotely reminiscent of the faith of their fathers."[40] For a journalist who had proclaimed himself a Hamiltonian ten years before, it was an ironic twist for him to appeal to the states'-rights and limited-government views of Hamilton's great adversary. The anomaly was arguably resolved by his call for "a coalition which would again put Alexander Hamilton and Thomas Jefferson in partnership for the common good, precisely as they once cooperated to save America from Aaron Burr." Historian Wayne Cole suggested that Vandenberg identified Roosevelt as the twentieth-century Burr.[41] By 1936 only the Supreme Court, which had rejected the NIRA and Agricultural Adjustment Act and jeopardized all other New Deal reforms, was left to defend the Constitution from a dangerous executive branch and a supine Congress.

FDR and the Supreme Court

The president opened the way for the coalition that Vandenberg wanted with those he called the Jeffersonian Democrats (primarily from the South) and those New Dealers worried that Roosevelt went too far in his zeal to have his major programs accepted.[42] The occasion was the president's devious effort to deter further damage to the legislation passed in

1935 and 1936. Victory in the 1936 election gave him confidence that he had the mandate to change the composition of a conservative Supreme Court. He maintained that the problem lay with aged or infirm justices and federal judges. To solve it he proposed that when a jurist reached the age of seventy after at least ten years in office and chose not to retire within a six-month period, the president could then add a new judge to the bench, up to a total of six additional judges.[43]

Vandenberg had long been in the vanguard of those warning Americans of the importance of the Supreme Court as the defender of the Constitution against usurpation of power by Congress or the president. As a journalist in the 1920s his worries had centered on Congress. In the Second New Deal it was the executive branch that was the major threat. As the Supreme Court invalidated one after another of the New Deal reforms in 1935 and 1936, the White House seemed bent on challenging the court. Vandenberg's response was to deliver stirring speeches describing the court's defense of the Constitution.

In June 1935 and March 1936 the *Washington Star* arranged with the National Broadcasting Company for the senator to address nation-wide audiences. In his first speech he applauded the Supreme Court for its decisions that Congress must quit delegating legislative power to the president and lesser bureaucrats. The president, he claimed, must release the hand of dictatorship from important functions heretofore usurped: "the Constitution is something more than a paper napkin at an economic picnic."

In his second address Vandenberg declared that "deprivation of the Supreme Court's veto power would bring a sad day for popular government and the perpetuation of American liberties." He believed that his worst fears for the future of the nation were being realized in 1937 when he spoke "against the startling proposal to force the immediate appointment of six new members of the Supreme Court of the United States. . . . This, in effect, is equivalent to presidential control of Constitutional interpretations in a Court which must not be subordinated to any other branch of the government if the essential checks and balances of the American System shall persist to guard our freedoms."[44]

This "court packing" raised fears in the country and in both parties that the president was subverting the Constitution to accommodate his agenda. And it appeared that Roosevelt had prevailed over his opponents. Justice Owen Roberts's switch in favor of the Wagner National Labor Relations Act gave Roosevelt a majority of five on the court. The resignation of other justices opposed to the New Deal and the appointment of more-liberal members preserved the reforms of the Second New Deal. Vandenberg's contribution to the controversy, suggesting that the Senate be called into special session to pass upon any nominee for the Supreme Court so that the justice would have a clear title before taking his seat, was ignored.[45]

Yet the court-packing bill failed in the Congress. Less than a year after his spectacular victory at the polls, the president inadvertently had invigorated the Republican opposition, including insurgent friends of the first New Deal. Westerners Gerald Nye (R-ND) and William Borah joined conservative southern Democrat Carter Glass and radical Montana Democrat Burton K. Wheeler in defeating the court-packing bill. Small wonder that Vandenberg assumed that his voice was instrumental in achieving this result.

Vandenberg's credentials as a moderate reformer within the Republican fold were fully credible. They were imperiled but not undermined by the political posturing he displayed in the election of 1936. Equally credible was his shrill reaction to Roosevelt's Second New Deal. His perception of threats to the Constitution was not just a product of his opposition to the Roosevelt presidency. His defense of the Supreme Court long antedated both the New Deal and his membership in the Senate. It found an expression in his Hamiltonian enthusiasm when he was a Grand Rapids editor and was deepened by his convictions about the court-packing controversy in 1937. Despite his admiration for Albert Beveridge's contributions to the nation as legislator and historian, he disputed the former senator's suggestion in 1923 that the Supreme Court on "its own initiative" should "change its rule of procedure in relation to 'five to four' decisions on constitutional questions as related to acts of Congress. . . . If the Supreme Court did any such thing as this it would be construed as a plea of guilty to all the charges that have been hurled against 'five to four' since the days of Van Buren. In my judgment such a step would encourage rather than discourage anti-court propaganda."[46]

By the end of the 1930s it was not just the threat to the Supreme

Court's independence that agitated Senator Vandenberg. The power of the president to engage the nation in war, to abandon its tradition of non-entanglement with the troubles of the Old World, was an even greater challenge to the Constitution and to the future of the nation. It was his leadership in this struggle against the White House that would make him the voice of isolationism in a world at war.

3

Toward Insulation,
1934–1937

Arguably, it was Vandenberg's participation in the Nye investigation of the munitions industry's activities in the world war that ultimately propelled him into the leadership of the movement to keep America out of the impending war in Europe. Unlike Senator Gerald P. Nye (R-ND), a spokesman for western farmers and an investigator of the Teapot Dome oil scandal in the 1920s, the Michigan senator had only a small measure of empathy for the radical Republican dissidents of the 1920s. But the behavior of munitions makers profiting from war was another matter. Vandenberg was as upset about them profiting from war as he was about their actions' impact on the maintenance of peace in the world. In supporting an amendment to a tax bill that would virtually confiscate all war profits in the future, he asserted that its adoption "would be a major frontal attack upon the commercial motive in the war equation," which he felt was "public enemy no. 1 insofar as the promotion of practical peace is concerned."[1]

While there was nothing in his diatribe that the Roosevelt administration would reject in 1934, conflict between Vandenberg and the administration grow exponentially in relation to events in both Asia and Europe—from Mussolini's war on Ethiopia in 1934 to Japan's invasion of China in 1937 and Hitler's assault on Poland in 1939. Discussions about how the United States should react to the dictators presented differing views of neutrality between the Republican isolationists and the Democratic administration. In 1934 Vandenberg was not in the vanguard of opponents of future American involvement in foreign wars. By 1937 he was their most eloquent and most impassioned leader.

THE NYE MUNITIONS INQUIRY

The path to Vandenberg's opposition to American involvement was opened by his role in the Nye investigation. It was not a long step from investigating the war profiteers of World War I to assuming that new wars would bring new opportunities for the munitions makers to sell their wares. To stop this movement in its tracks the chief members of the Nye Committee prepared bills in 1935 to prohibit loans to any belligerent. Senator Tom Connally (D-TX) of the Senate Foreign Relations Committee was convinced that any attempt on the part of the administration to compromise on a neutrality bill would lead to more demands and more intransigence.[2]

Connally was right, as Vandenberg worked with such isolationists as Hiram Johnson (R-CA) and William Borah (R-ID) to build legislative barriers against any administration attempt to help one side or another in Europe's internecine quarrels. The issue of war profiteering was never far removed from isolationism. When Nye and Vandenberg submitted Joint Senate Resolution 206 in 1934 to appoint a committee to investigate war profiteers, Vandenberg railed before the Michigan Press Club in Ann Arbor against American engagement in "the next war." He spoke of his conviction "that America shall avoid any avoidable war. To that aspiration I emphatically and prayerfully subscribe." But as often in his messages, he emphasized "that this does not mean that we shirk our co-operative responsibilities as a unit in foreshortened world society—ready always to encourage the impulses which would substitute justice for force in the settlement of international disputes."[3] These sentiments did not signify a full embrace of isolationism. They evoked his stance on the World Court in the 1920s.

When he joined forces with Senator Nye, he did not equate his antipathy toward war profiteers with the rigid isolationist positions that Borah or La Follette, the radical Republican dissidents of the 1920s, had staked out. Long before he entered the Senate Vandenberg had used his newspaper to lambaste the munitions makers who used war for their own purposes. He had linked them with the financiers of Wall Street as advocates of war in 1917 as well as enemies of Main Street. But his hostility did not extend to complete detachment of the nation from the affairs of the Old World.

Nye's personal history, in fact, seemed much like Vandenberg's in 1934. A Wisconsin native, some eight years younger than Vandenberg, Nye entered the Senate after a career in journalism, three years before the Grand Rapids editor. Nye had many of Vandenberg's oratorical talents. Like Vandenberg, Nye was neither a glad-hander nor a man of much intellectual depth. A powerful speaker in the William Jennings Bryan mold, he was not an original thinker. Historian John Wilz likened Nye to Bryan in that he was "uncomplicated and naïve, symbolized a movement which he did not originate, but was confident he could resolve a difficult problem in his time."[4] And like Vandenberg, he was a man of integrity as well as energy.

Yet the differences between the two senators were equally noteworthy. With little more formal education than Nye, Vandenberg had steeped himself in the study of American history, modeling his appearance and oratorical style on his nineteenth-century heroes. Though lacking the good looks and youthful demeanor of Nye, he had the grand style of the stereotypical senator—an ample belly, the ever-present cigar, and the combed-over hair in place of senatorial locks. But the differences were deeper than appearances. Nye followed the Wisconsin Progressive movement, represented by Senator Robert La Follette. He was a true son of the wild jackasses, from the moment he took his seat as senator from South Dakota. Responding to the jibe, he boasted that that "in a sense we Westerners have been jackasses. Year after year we have gone on paying high tariff rates for the benefit of New England and her industries."[5]

Vandenberg's Progressivism was always limited, if genuine. Like Nye, he was sensitive to his regional economic interests, but as a spokesman for industrial as well as agricultural interests in a populous midwestern state, he was hardly one of the jackasses, no matter how vigorous his denunciation of business monopolists or how sympathetic he was to the concerns of the farmers of the Great Plains. His was always a more measured tone in judging adversaries, aside from his extravagant language in political campaigns. The Michigan senator usually preferred the role of moderator. As noted in chapter 2, he was attracted to La Follette in his journalist days but without the passion Nye displayed. He would never have followed Nye into the La Follette camp in 1924. Nor was it likely that his Senate career would have mirrored Nye's in the 1920s.[6]

Although Nye was only three years ahead of Vandenberg in the Senate, and like him an interim appointee, he launched his career almost immediately with investigations of bankers and oil speculators. His most notable case was the Teapot Dome scandal, involving the leasing of naval oil reserves in Wyoming that had stained the reputation of the Harding administration. Not that the leaders of the Republican Party welcomed Nye or his initiative. As spokesman of the radical farmers' Nonpartisan League, he was understandably suspected by the Republican establishment of being an agitator. Nye saw bankers and eastern industrialists enriching themselves at the expense of workers and farmers. It was the Progressive emphasis on industrialists' manipulation of the economy, not isolationism or the prospect of involvement in European affairs, that animated him in the 1920s.

In the absence of more seasoned candidates, in December 1927 Nye was put in charge of an ongoing probe of the activities of such prominent figures as oil company executive Harry F. Sinclair. It was hardly surprising that senior Republicans had little taste for pursuing the financial activities of such politically influential figures. Nye had no such inhibitions. He displayed both zeal and oratorical skills in sending Sinclair to jail. His condemnation of the capitalists responsible for the scandal went beyond the judgment of Senator Thomas J. Walsh (D-MT), who had directed the investigation from its beginnings. Nye's supplemental report used harsher language, observing that the oil scandals were "conceived in darkness and selfishness and dedicated to the cause of privilege and the privilege must be served."[7]

Nye's appointment in 1934 as chief investigator of the munitions industry's behavior in the First World War was a fitting tribute to his accomplishments in the 1920s. The subject, after all, embraced so much of what Nye had opposed as a Progressive—the dominance of eastern financiers, industrialists' manipulation of government in their own interest, and profiteering at the expense of the public. While their perspectives on the Progressive tradition differed, Nye and Vandenberg both supported Main Street in opposition to Wall Street. Vandenberg admitted that "in many respects the senator from North Dakota and I approach this problem from different viewpoints. Indeed, the interesting thing to me is that men who do have very different viewpoints relatively speaking . . .

in regard to national defense, can find such completely common ground as we find in respect to this particular pending resolution."[8] The differences were manifest in Vandenberg's support for bills strengthening the navy and particularly in his more positive approach to the World Court. As noted in chapter 2, he had been instrumental in securing the Senate Foreign Relations Committee's approval of protocols that would reduce the possibility of war without deviating from traditional America foreign policy.

By contrast, Nye had lined up with the isolationists in opposing American membership in the World Court. Indeed, it was the subject of his first speech in the Senate, warmly endorsed by Borah and Johnson, in which he emphasized that the "World Court is being forced upon our Nation, not by the people who would provide against future wars, but by men who are the makers of war, the international bankers."[9]

Nye's response to the munitions industry's influence centered less on regulation than on government ownership. In this context he was susceptible to arguments of pacifists, who identified munitions makers as the primary instigators of war. Prominent among peace activists was the Women's International League for Peace and Freedom, which had failed to persuade any senator in 1932 and 1933 to initiate an investigation of the international munitions traffic. Now guided by Senator George W. Norris, Dorothy Detzer, the league's executive secretary, found in Senator Nye the person best equipped to lead the movement. Nye introduced Senate Resolution 179 on February 8, 1934, with Detzer watching from the gallery. The reaction in the Senate initially was not encouraging; Senator Key Pittman (D-NV) was not interested in taking responsibility for the investigation and turned the issue over to the Military Affairs Committee.[10]

At this juncture Vandenberg's position on investigation of the munitions makers was critical. He had frequently expressed unhappiness over bankers and arms manufacturers growing rich at the public's expense, just as he had been upset with speculators who had corrupted the political system in the 1920s. But his voice in 1934 did not echo that of the pacifist isolationists; rather, it spoke for the American Legion, the powerful veterans' organization that resented the profiteers of World War I and called for legislation to eliminate excessive profits in the future.

President Hoover had established a War Policies Commission in 1932 for this express purpose. The bipartisan commission included Vandenberg, who quickly exerted leadership by writing a report calling for high taxes on extraordinary war profits. The report and its recommendations died at the end of calendar year 1932. Vandenberg proposed to resubmit it in 1933: "My joint resolution (SJ Res. 42) proposing an amendment to the Constitution of the United States providing for the fixing of prices in wartime and the prevention of profiteering." Despite the American Legion's support, he was no more successful in 1933 than he had been in 1932.[11]

Given the conservative composition of the American Legion and the encouragement its position on the munitions profits received from the influential conservative magazine *Fortune* in 1934, Dorothy Detzer sensed an opportunity to align a munitions investigation with her own objectives in linking munitions makers with the making of wars in general. Merging the Vandenberg resolution (S.J. Res. 42) with Nye's could be the only way to counter the seeming indifference of Senator Pittman, chairman of the Senate Foreign Relations Committee from 1933 until his death in 1940. A prominent but colorless Democrat, Pittman was in the middle of the struggle between isolationists and internationalists, as historian Wayne Cole noted. Pittman's discomfort with the discretionary powers of the president gave comfort to isolationists. More problematic was the potential hostility of the Military Affairs Committee. A majority of its members might be inclined to whitewash the munitions industry, since tarnishing the image of the munitions industry could affect the readiness of the army.[12]

This was not an idle fear. Eastern financiers and industrialists, particularly the DuPonts, were opposed to any investigation that would further open them to aggressive New Deal discriminatory measures. Such formidable figures as Republican Pierre Samuel DuPont and John J. Raskob, secretary of the Democratic National Committee, seemingly stood in the way of a serious challenge to the munitions makers.[13] Detzer's pacifist alliance itself was not without fissures. Many of the pacifists could support the cause of disarmament without accepting the isolationist abstention from any action on foreign issues.

The key issues in 1934 were the sins of the munitions industry. The president was in tune with Nye in 1934, as he saw the political advantage in associating himself with those who opposed the munitions makers. Even Secretary of State Cordell Hull went along with the investigation, despite his worries about isolationists tying the administration's hands in dealing with the increasing tensions in Europe. Yet Detzer was aware of the Roosevelt administration's caution, to the point of hostility to the potential intrusion of Congress into the management of foreign relations.[14] All of these caveats gave urgency to the Vandenberg-Nye coalition, to ensure that conservatives would not block the progress of an investigation.

The results were even more successful than Detzer had anticipated. The merging of Vandenberg's resolution to revive the War Policies Commission with Nye's isolationist-centered Senate Resolution 179 in February took the form of Senate Resolution 206 on March 12. It linked a charge to investigate the munitions industry with a review of the reports of the War Policies Commission—winning "a double–barreled support from two diametrically opposed wings of public opinion—the peace movement and the Legion." The public mood was on the side of the investigators. *Fortune* published an article titled "Arms and Men" in the same month, unintentionally bolstering the implausible alliance. The magazine was Wall Street's voice, speaking at this moment for Main Street as well. It charged British and French munitions makers with selling supplies vital to the German war effort during the world war. Small wonder that an aroused Senate approved the Nye-Vandenberg inquiry without dissent.[15]

By having the investigation conducted by a special committee rather than a standing committee, the opponents of the munitions industry won an agreement from Pat Harrison (D-MS) to have his Senate Finance Committee adopt the Nye-Vandenberg resolution immediately rather than listen to a lengthy Vandenberg oration on its behalf on the Senate floor. This arrangement was also preferable to holding hearings in the hostile environment of the Military Affairs Committee, where Senator Pittman had consigned the resolution. Yet the allotment of $15,000 rather than the $50,000 Nye and Vandenberg requested implied reluctance on the part of the Senate to extend the committee's inquiry too far.[16]

The composition of the Nye committee was important to the success of the process. It consisted of four Democrats and three Republicans. Nye and Vandenberg were logical Republican choices. Of the four Democrats,

Bennett Champ Clark of Missouri was as aggressive an antagonist of the munitions makers as Nye or Vandenberg. These appointments guaranteed a vigorous implementation of the investigation. Given the mood of the time and the prominence of Nye, he was chosen as chairman at the urging of Senator Clark. This was not a happy choice for the State Department; Cordell Hull wrote later that he would not have supported the investigation had he realized the turn it would take.[17]

Nye and Clark, with their pacifist agenda, were the most active members of the committee, but a more reserved Vandenberg was as penetrating in his queries as they were at the hearings of the Nye committee in February 1935. Isolationist sentiment did not appear to be the driving force in the investigations in 1934 and early 1935. Anger at the greed of the financiers and munition makers and their collusion with the government to assure shipbuilders excessive profits was the theme of the first report, on the results of the first six months in 1935. At this point there was consensus among all the parties in government. The president seemed to share these judgments at the time.[18]

This comity did not last long. Much of the subsequent discord turned on the criticism of President Wilson for seemingly allowing the munitions makers' investments in the allies' economic survival to bring the United States into the war. Such was the primary judgment of Senator Nye. But denouncing the Democratic icon was unacceptable to prominent Democrats on the Foreign Relations Committee.

This was not the only division within the committee. A solution to war profiteering recommended by four of the seven members was nationalization of the munitions industry. This was not the approach of the more conservative minority, Democrat Walter George and Republican William W. Barbour, of Georgia and New Jersey, respectively, the former a traditional spokesman for the military, the latter an industrialist viscerally resistant to nationalization.[19]

The third dissident was Vandenberg, who had a different vantage point from that of the Republican radicals of the Great Plains. He did not approve of the majority recommendation of nationalization of the munitions industry. Like Senator Barbour, he preferred regulation to nationalization. And he made it clear in 1934 that he did not share Nye's pacifism: "The senator from North Dakota voted against the Vinson Navy bill. I voted for the Vinson Navy. . . . We did not approve a single dollar for a single additional battleship. We merely declared a policy, and put the world on notice that arms limitations talks must be a matter of mutual participation."[20]

The journalist Raymond Clapper, writing in 1936, when Vandenberg was a possible presidential candidate, lauded him for his independence and moderation: "As a member of the Nye munitions investigating committee, he didn't lose his nerve and run out on the committee when it got into Morgan['s] records. Neither did he join the attempt to make either Morgan or Woodrow Wilson the scapegoat for our getting into the war. He just tried to get what information he could in how we might be saved from being sucked into another foreign war."[21]

The Neutrality Acts, 1935–1937

No legislation resulted from the extensive hearings on the munitions industry. The presidential election of 1936 absorbed increasing attention as the year progressed. But the influence of the hearings on the public was instrumental in reinforcing the nation's movement toward isolationism.

Isolationism's impact on Vandenberg was indisputable. It was not a long step to take from identifying the crimes of the munitions makers to recognizing the appetite for war that motivated munition makers and their Wall Street enablers. War brought profits, and so curbing profit opportunities would keep the nation out of foreign entanglements. The state of the world—from the aggressions of imperial Japan to Nazi Germany's in the midthirties, at the same time that the munitions hearings were conducted—was impossible to ignore. It posed the same temptations that lured America into war in 1917.

Vandenberg's address to the Michigan Press Club in November 1935 underscored his sensitivity to the issue. He called for the nation to refrain from a dangerous involvement with the outside world. After a brief visit to Europe, the senator told the press club that, if there should be an outbreak of war there, "we can and will stay out of it if we have sense and courage enough to maintain a real neutrality and protect it, on the one hand, against international emotionalism, and on the other hand, against the appetites which love commerce in spite of casualties." A new conception of neutrality was inescapable. The old rules did not keep the country out of war. He criticized the *Wall Street Journal* for saying that the nation could not keep the peace without surrendering its independence of action, adding, "That is not my view. We surrender only the dangerous privilege of trafficking in the misfortunes of others—the hazardous benefit that attaches to profits from external wars. That ought to be surrendered." His unmistakable conclusion was that the arms merchants jeopardized the nation's ability to steer clear of any commitments, economic or otherwise, to any nations or combination of nations, including the League of Nations, that could bring the United States into war.[22]

The significance of current wars in Europe and Asia for Vandenberg may best be viewed through the change in emphasis in his addresses between 1934 and 1936. In the early stages of the hearings his emphasis was on levying an 85 percent wartime tax on all profits in excess of the average for the last three prewar years, as first introduced in the recommendations of the War Policies Commission. His focus then was on the misbehavior of munitions makers, whom Vandenberg blamed for conspiring with Germany to evade the provision in the Treaty of Versailles controlling its armaments. The military conflicts of the 1930s were barely in his sights.[23]

Two years later he had turned his attention to new problems. He wanted to stop all loans, credits, and sales of munitions, given the unsettled conditions of the world. Americans should observe a "mind-our-own-business" code. He now believed that "neutrality must have a new and different meaning if we are to insulate America against other peoples' wars. Heretofore neutrality has consisted chiefly of a demand that our rights to a profitable foreign trade abroad should not be impaired by these wars. The old conception subordinated peace to trade. The new conception subordinates trade to peace and proposes as far as possible to keep out of wars' ways. The new conception may be tough on our cash registers. But it will be far easier on our sons." He went on to say that "there is nothing neutral except in legislative theory when we float vast loans or grant vast credits to one of two belligerents in a war. The other belligerent inevitably is hurt and we inevitably acquire an unwitting stake in the outcome."[24]

Vandenberg's conception of neutrality came close to that of William

Jennings Bryan's during World War I. Bryan resigned as secretary of state when he could not convince the Wilson administration that the principle of freedom of the seas had to be amended. Vandenberg asked, "Why should an American citizen travel on a ship of a belligerent nation? . . . An American citizen on the high seas cannot separate himself from the implications of his citizenship. He cannot travel at his own risk. He risks his country every moment of his journey. His 'rights' should be subordinated to the higher 'rights of our whole people.'" The repercussions from the sinking of the *Lusitania* were now uppermost in Vandenberg's mind. The old neutrality led straight to America's entry into war. Yet ending loans, credits, and sales of munitions to belligerents as well as letting individual Americans travel at their own risk would not be sufficient to insulate the United States from a European war. "The new rules must be defined as positive[ly] as possible," he insisted. And to ensure their effectiveness "it will not do to leave neutrality decisions to the discretion of the President," since the president "is not himself a free agent among his own people—as Mr. Wilson discovered to his horror—when once a large and profitable war has started to enrich large numbers of our own people." The only branch of government equipped constitutionally to enforce neutrality was Congress.[25]

In his address to the Michigan Press Club of Ann Arbor the senator linked his assault against war profiteers in the financial and munitions industry to the dangerous enlargement of presidential powers in the Roosevelt administration, and he linked both to the larger cause of peace in a troubled world. The narrow objectives of 1934 had expanded by 1936 to embrace the lessons of World War I.

The threat of arms merchants entangling the nation in European conflicts was highlighted in 1935 by Italy's attack against Ethiopia, with the League of Nations unable to draw on is putative authority to protect the victim of aggression. One U.S. response would be a constitutional amendment requiring a popular referendum before the nation went to war. There was nothing new about this initiative. Thirty-one referendums and resolutions had been introduced in Congress between 1914 and 1935, with thirty-three more added between 1935 and 1941.[26]

This was just the moment for a relatively obscure congressman, Louis L. Ludlow (D-IN), to submit a constitutional amendment to require a popular referendum barring a declaration of war until the people had decided. A Washington-based journalist and a former president of the National Press Club, Ludlow was a product of the Progressive movement and a personal friend of Bryan. He had been a member of Congress since 1929, with long-standing interest in keeping America out of foreign entanglements. As he told former president Benjamin Harrison, "We have no commission from God to police the world."[27] But it was not until he was caught up in the enthusiasm accompanying the Nye-Vandenberg inquiry that Ludlow submitted his first amendment. While Nye himself had endorsed the idea of a war referendum as early as 1925, Ludlow later speculated that attention to the Nye hearings had left the war referendum proposal "a defunct baby," needing "the breath of life."[28]

Ludlow proposed an amendment to the Constitution on January 14, 1935, in the midst of the Nye-Vandenberg munitions hearings. Section 1 provided, "Except in the event of attack or invasion the authority of Congress to declare war shall not become effective until confirmed by a majority of all votes cast thereon in a Nation-wide referendum." Section 2 aimed at excess war profits.[29] Ludlow found a motley legion of supporters eager to endorse his referendum. They ranged from the editor of the *Nation,* Oswald Garrison Villard, to the retired marine Major General Smedley D. Butler, to the energetic Dorothy Detzer. Their testimony failed to win over Congress.[30]

Failure in 1935 did not deter Ludlow from submitting subsequent proposals that met a similar fate. His quixotic quest, however, differed from Nye's and Vandenberg's. The munitions investigation may have produced no specific results, but unlike the Ludlow proposals, its conclusions would not have removed Congress's power to declare war. Vandenberg might have welcomed Ludlow's challenge to the presidency but not one to the constitutional authority of the legislative branch over war and peace. As he pointed out to a Michigan editor in 1940, "I frankly doubt whether it is practical to put a 'war referendum' into the Constitution of the United States. I am afraid that we might create more hazards than we would avoid."[31]

Unlike the Ludlow proposals, the Nye-Vandenberg hearings, coinciding with rising tensions in Europe and Asia, provided the environment for the successful passage of neutrality laws between 1935 and 1937. Italy's invasion of Ethiopia in 1935 and the impotence of the League of Nations in coping with it set the stage for the neutrality acts that followed. Not that there was disagreement over America's abstention from the conflict, no matter how much sympathy there may have been for Ethiopia. The American public was firmly on the side of the isolationists, who saw this crisis as an occasion to avoid a repetition of U.S. behavior in the world war. But if there were to be legislation to reinforce neutrality, it would not be under the auspices of a special committee, as in the Nye-Vandenberg investigations. Key Pittman, chairman of the Senate Foreign Relations Committee, and his formidable counterpart on the Republican side, William E. Borah, agreed that further action on neutrality legislation more appropriately fell under the jurisdiction of the Foreign Relations Committee. Spokesmen for the administration were ably represented by Joseph T. Robinson (D-AR), Tom Connally (D-TX), and Robert Wagner (D-NY). The proponents of strong neutrality in the global crisis not only had Borah and Hiram Johnson (R-CA) on the committee but Vandenberg as well.[32]

Nye was not a member of the committee, but his voice was immediately heard, along with that of Bennett Champ Clark of Missouri. Although Clark was a Democrat, his liberalism on domestic matters did not extend to foreign relations. Following the conclusion of the munitions investigations, Nye and Clark cosponsored a series of resolutions on neutrality. The first, on April 9, would address the problem of Americans traveling on belligerent ships in war zones by withholding their passports. There would be no reprise of the emotions stirred up against Germany over the sinking of the *Lusitania* in 1915 and the *Sussex* in 1916. A month later, on May 7, 1935, Senate Joint Resolution 120 would have denied export of arms and ammunition automatically in the event of war. Both resolutions were by-products of the munitions hearings. No distinction was made between aggressor and victim. Nor was room left for presidential discretion in the application of the resolution. The last resolution, as presented by Senators Homer T. Bone (D-IN) and George as well as Nye and Clark, was more satisfactory to the administration. It established a National Munitions Control Board under the secretary of state to register and license munitions makers and shippers, bringing the armaments industry under government control. The Foreign Relations

Committee promptly reported it favorably on June 10, with the approval of the president and the Departments of State, Army, Navy, Commerce, and Treasury. The Neutrality Act of 1935 was signed on August 31.[33]

The Neutrality Act of 1935 was temporary. More permanent was the Neutrality Act of 1936, which put into effect one of the resolutions—Senate Joint Resolution 100—that was not included in the 1935 act. This was the provision prohibiting Americans from extending loans and credits to belligerent governments or their citizens. Nye and Clark feared that opponents of mandatory neutrality could defeat the more pressing issues if they continued the fight to deny loans and credits to belligerents. But the issue that was at the heart of the Nye inquiry was too important for the isolationists to delay for long. The Neutrality Act of 1936 extended the 1935 law until May 1, 1937, and included the isolationists' demands for an embargo on loans and credits to belligerents.[34]

The presidential election of that year temporarily shelved the neutrality issue and removed the Munitions Committee investigation from the public eye. But the gathering storms in Europe and Asia returned neutrality to the top of the administration's and Congress's agendas immediately afterward. The civil war in Spain that had begun in the summer of 1936 required rethinking of the neutrality laws. It placed more pressure on the administration to take a stand against the continuing assault on presidential discretionary authority.

This was a familiar story. Secretary of State Cordell Hull had taken the lead since the inception of the munitions investigation to mobilize the administration against congressional encroachment upon the executive authority over foreign relations. At the start of those hearings in 1934 Hull had criticized Senator Pittman for turning over the chairmanship of the special Munitions Investigations Committee to Senator Nye. It was not just that Nye was a Republican adversary of the president; he was guilty, in Hull's eyes, of impugning the motives of President Wilson.[35]

When the Nye Committee opened its proceedings the Italian-Ethiopian war had just begun, and the mood of the nation was clearly opposed to intervention. The Roosevelt administration bowed to its perception of public opinion and the power of the isolationists. The president professed agreement with the pacifists and isolationist senators in deploring the power of Wall Street and the munitions makers. There was no special administration objection to the general objective of neutrality in wartime. But Hull and leading Democrats in the Senate, Robinson and Connally, both members of the Foreign Relations Committee, wanted whatever laws were passed to ensure the president's discretion to distinguish between aggressors and victims. Chairman Pittman appeared too often to defer to the demands of the isolationists. Connally put the case baldly in his memoir when he asserted that "in the spring of 1935 I found out that the chief members of the Nye Committee—Senators Nye, Vandenberg, and Clark—were working on a neutrality bill in order to tie the President's hands should the war between Italy and Ethiopia spread. To me this was abominable, for the history of the world showed that parliamentary conduct of international affairs had never been successful."[36]

This was the key matter underlying the administration's response to Italy's invasion of Ethiopia in 1935, as it was subsequently when Japan was the aggressor in China and Spain was convulsed by civil war. The administration wanted flexibility to help victims of Nazi and Japanese aggression but was forced to employ evasive tactics in the face of America's seemingly intransigent isolationism.

The Neutrality Act of 1937 took into account the impact of trade barriers on the American economy through the addition of a "cash-and-carry" provision to the law. This allowed belligerents to buy goods unrelated to war only for cash. They would have to take title to the goods in the United States and ship them on their own vessels. As Senator Connally noted, Vandenberg called this the theory "of transferred risk": the United States would be transferring the risk involved in shipments entirely to the belligerents themselves. Not all isolationists would agree with the wisdom or the morality of the arrangement. Borah disliked the prospect of Americans avoiding "all risks, all danger, but we make certain to get all the profits." The act included an amendment ensuring that there would be no repeal of the arms embargo. It provided that whenever the president issued a proclamation that a state of war existed, it would be unlawful to export arms and ammunition to any belligerent.[37]

This was simply a reiteration by the isolationists of the earlier neutrality acts. But the times had changed. There was a shift in public opinion as fear and anger over Nazi aggressive action were more obvious in 1937. Moreover, the undeclared war by the Japanese against China arguably aroused more angry emotions in the United States than had the Nazi menace in Europe, particularly after the sinking in December 1937 of the *Panay*, a U.S. gunboat, on the Yangtze River. The increased tension over the difference between aggressor and victim had distressed the president earlier, when he had urged a moral embargo against Italy. This only emboldened the Fascists to equate this call with U.S. passivity in the face of their actions. But Borah's response to the *Panay* incident was not an ultimatum to Tokyo but recognition that "the *Panay* was in a war zone and what happened may be expected . . . in a war zone."[38] By 1937, then, the conflict between the isolationists and the administration over how much authority the president had to put neutrality legislation into effect was fully engaged.

The Neutrality Act of 1937 did not embody all the discretionary authority the president wanted over neutrality, but the restraints in the 1936 act were modified by the "cash-and-carry" provision that had been advocated by the president's influential adviser Bernard M. Baruch, head of the War Industries Board in World War I. He assumed that interruption of trade with a belligerent country, even if applied impartially, would be regarded as an unneutral act and a form of U.S. participation in the conflict, and he resolved that problem by recommending protection of business interests in noncontraband trade. The principle rested on U.S. willingness to sell any product except armaments, provided the purchaser paid in cash and carried it at his own risk.[39] American business interests would profit without the danger of being engulfed in a foreign war.

Even pacifists, but not Vandenberg, found the provision acceptable, as long as it applied to nonessential goods. Strategic commodities such as oil, scrap iron, and cotton should still be subject to absolute embargo. Vandenberg, however, by 1937 was wedded to his concept of a new version of neutrality. As he put it in December 1936, "In my view we want a neutrality which quarantines us against the wars of others to the last possible practicable and realistic extent. . . . It cannot be done under the old rules which subordinate peace to commerce."[40] At the hearings of the Senate Foreign Relations Committee on the neutrality laws in 1936 and 1937, Vandenberg was particularly concerned about the president's discretionary powers with respect to an embargo on war materiel. When Assistant Secretary of State W. Walton Moore and Legal Adviser to the State

Department Green H. Hackworth tried to justify presidential flexibility, the senator spoke for mandatory prohibition, beyond the president's discretion. "I am so fearful that the exercise of discretion under section 4 could inherently become unneutral in its net effect, and therefore, the exercise of discretion itself becomes unneutral." Chairman Pittman offered examples of the problem: "For instance, one country has to import oil. If the President places an embargo on oil, . . . it would not injure the belligerent which had oil, but it would injure the other belligerent which had to import oil. Is that in your mind?" Vandenberg agreed: "If the President has the power to make the selection after the controversy arises there is danger of our attitude being interpreted as unneutral."[41]

The controversy over presidential authority resumed in 1937, with the focus centering on the cash-and-carry provision. The Pittman-McReynolds resolution on January 22, 1937, provided that "the President shall promulgate such rules and regulations not inconsistent with the provisions of this act as he shall deem necessary for the administration and enforcement of the provisions of this act." This resolution would apply to the Spanish Civil War, in which Germany and Italy were aiding the Franco rebels against the government, and could be used to help the Republican regime. Pittman was convinced that this joint resolution and Vandenberg's were not very different in substance.[42]

The Michigan senator, referring to his resolution as the "Clark joint" resolution, disagreed with Pittman and with Assistant Secretary of State Moore, who felt that the only difference between the two resolutions was in details. "I think this is the fundamental difference between the two joint resolutions," Vandenberg explained. "The Pittman-McReynolds joint resolution permits the President to decide for himself whether any additional commodity may be restricted, and also permits him to choose which commodity shall be restricted; in other words, he has a double discretion. The Clark joint resolution denies either discretion to him and makes the formula mandatory in respect to all commodities."[43]

Vandenberg and Clark's position would have clarified the U.S. stance on the Spanish Civil War. Pittman's resolution, with the administration's backing, would allow the cash-and-carry provision to aid Franco's Fascists at the same time that the embargo on arms to the Spanish government would damage the Republican cause. The cash-and-carry provision not only promoted the interests of the shipping industry but also could be seen as a symbol of unneutrality. It seemed to counter the results of a Gallup poll in February 1937 that showed 95 percent of the public believing that the United States should not take part in any future wars. But the popularity of cash-and-carry in Congress caught Roosevelt in the midst of the fight over the Supreme Court. He chose to abstain from another conflict with the Senate. Arguably, as historian Robert Divine suggested, the president was looking ahead, realizing that in the event of war in Europe Britain and France, with their control of the seas, would benefit from a cash-and-carry policy.[44]

Vandenberg was pleased with the major aspects of the Pittman-McReynolds bill, with its mandatory ban on travel and loans to belligerents and the prohibition against arming of merchant ships. But his opposition to the "carry" part of cash-and-carry led him to vote against the bill on April 19, 1937. It passed by a vote of forty-one to fifteen. His amendment, cosponsored with Senators Clark Nye and Homer T. Bone (D–WA) on May 10, making cash-and-carry mandatory and thus denying the president the authority to determine which belligerent would benefit, failed.

Vandenberg's suspicions of presidential power, always in the background, intensified in the controversy over Roosevelt's challenge to the Supreme Court. This accompanied his new conception of neutrality. Vandenberg's version no longer included protection of Americans on the high seas or promoted freedom to trade with any nation, belligerent or not. The embargo provisions of the neutrality legislation did meet his criteria for keeping America out of a foreign war. But he was not satisfied with their placement in the hands of the Roosevelt administration. He lamented on April 29 that "as the resolution passed the Senate, it seemed to me it went to the extreme border of Executive discretion which could be tolerated. As it came back from the conference it has crossed the limits of toleration. . . . It seems to me that the Neutrality resolution—in the form in which we now confront it—transfers a substantial portion of the war-making power from the Congress to the Chief Executive."[45]

In Vandenberg's evolution from qualified fellow traveler to leader of the isolationists in the Senate there was a genuine, if not clearly expressed, contest with Gerald Nye. They were not equal partners in 1934. Nye's reputation as a forceful inquisitor in the Teapot Dome investigations placed him, not Vandenberg, in charge of the munitions inquiry a decade later. While both men were eloquent orators, the younger Nye displayed a passion for exposing the sins of the munitions makers and their Wall Street enablers that Vandenberg did not show in 1934. When they joined forces to push the Senate into action, it is understandable that the public perceived it as the Nye investigation more often than the Nye-Vandenberg investigation. Nye had the additional advantage of a closer association with the radicals Borah, Norris, and La Follette than Vandenberg enjoyed.

Despite Nye's initial edge over his Michigan colleague, Vandenberg had overtaken Nye to become the voice of isolationism between the beginning of the neutrality debates in 1935 and the conclusion of the third Neutrality Act in 1937. Personality, the presidential election of 1936, the increasing likelihood of war in Europe, and the expansion of the war in China all played a part in elevating Vandenberg's status in his party and in the country. For all his talents and accomplishments, Nye was still a loner from the Great Plains, outside the circle of power in the Republican Party and sidelined with fellow western radicals who had backed the early New Deal.[46] He did not become a member of the Foreign Relations Committee until Borah died in 1940.

Vandenberg, by contrast, was a midwesterner from a swing state whose style in politics was that of a conciliator. The election of 1936 gave him an opportunity to show off his skills in self-promotion through correspondence and articles that made him a potential contender for the presidential nomination in 1936. While he delighted in the acclaim he received, even the proposal of a vice presidency, he astutely recognized the odds against victory and the limitations of the office of vice president. These considerations did not prevent him from vigorously participating in the Landon campaign (as noted in chapter 2), even hoping for a "Jeffersonian" alliance with disaffected Democrats.

Although the election ended with a resounding victory for Roosevelt, it only hardened Vandenberg's resolve to oppose the administration's policies. The president's attempt to thwart the Supreme Court's assault on New Deal laws generated the bipartisan opposition that had failed in the election campaign, aimed as it was against the enlargement of the president's discretionary powers. This issue was particularly vivid for Vandenberg in the debates over neutrality. As the most articulate member of the

Foreign Relations Committee, he was recognized by 1937 as the senator most capable of preventing the Roosevelt administration from entangling the United States in European or Asian wars.

Nye would share Vandenberg's sentiments, but he was no longer the symbol of protest. The Michigan senator earned his position by the vigor with which he contended with the administration over neutrality, and even with his isolationist-minded colleagues over cash-and-carry. Borah and Johnson, for example, would not abandon America's rights as a neutral to defend itself on the high seas. Vandenberg's insistence on his new conception of neutrality would do just that. If rising sentiment against Nazi and Japanese aggressors defeated his efforts to deny executive discretion in the application of the cash-and-carry provision, he was comforted by the Neutrality Act of 1937's provision of a mandatory ban on travel, on loans to belligerents, and on the arming of merchant ships. His long-standing antagonism to executive overreach dovetailed with his conversion to absolute neutrality—complete insulation from the wars of the Old World.

Evidence of Senator Vandenberg's ascent to primacy as an isolationist leader may be seen in the treatment the *New York Times* gave to his pronouncements between 1935 and 1937. When Nye and Vandenberg both opposed aiding the League of Nations' sanctions against Mussolini's Italy in 1935, it was Nye who saw "peril in sanction," while Vandenberg took a "like stand."[47] By the end of 1936, after Vandenberg had delivered his speech on his "new conception" of neutrality, he received special attention with a full text of his statement.[48] In August 1937 the senator's speech before the Veterans of Foreign Wars urging firmer neutrality to "insulate" America from any war was on the front page of the newspaper. The National Broadcast Association carried the address. Rebutting the argument that application of the neutrality laws tended to help one belligerent and hurt another, he claimed that "if one belligerent has some natural advantage over another, it would be unneutral of us to seek to off-set this advantage by our treatment of belligerents. It is not our duty to equalize the effect of our neutrality program as between two belligerents. That would be equivalent to direct participation in the belligerent equation."[49] The reference was to China, the victim of Japan's aggression in 1937 and the object of considerable popular sympathy. Isolationism could not be more rigid, and Vandenberg was now its most aggressive champion.

4

Isolationism Challenged, 1938–1941

Vandenberg's primacy as the spokesman for the foreign policies of the Republican Party, if not for the party itself, was widely understood after the debacle of the 1936 presidential election. *Newsweek* implicitly recognized his position as a leader of the party when it observed that the Republican National Committee selected him to frame a set of party principles that would revive its fortunes. As the magazine noted, "With the same sense of astute timing that has helped to make him the most talked-of prospect for his party's presidential nomination," the Michigan senator managed to broadcast his own ten-point program over a national radio network.[1]

Abrogating the 1911 Treaty with Japan

Vandenberg may not have won all his battles for neutrality over the previous two years, but among his ten points was the adoption of a firm "policy of insulating neutrality," as contrasted with the president's failure to invoke the Neutrality Act in the Sino-Japanese War. The war in Asia was a problem for Vandenberg that separated him from fellow isolationists such as Senator George W. Norris (R-NE). Like them he was appalled over Japan's brutal behavior toward China. He recognized too that the cash-and-carry provision in the Neutrality Act of 1937 benefited maritime powers such as Britain and Japan. He also recognized that Japan had legitimate interests in China. He feared that the naval expansion bill in 1938 implied a naval race with Japan that could lead to war.

In this context he had opposed Roosevelt's quarantine speech in October 1937, aimed as it was at Japan's behavior in China. And while he understood the emotions that impelled isolationists as well as the administration to impose an embargo against Japan, he opposed it, fearing it would lead to war as well as violate his conception of neutrality. Norris, however, felt so strongly about Japanese aggression against China in 1937 that he wanted a neutrality law that would include a boycott of all Japanese goods.[2]

Vandenberg did not dominate the hearings on new neutrality legislation in 1939. In fact, Senator Nye, who was not a member of the Foreign Relations Committee, was present and vocal, along with the isolationist Democrat Senator Bone of Washington, at the hearings in the spring of 1939. But Vandenberg's incisive queries about the compatibility of the cash-and-carry program with neutrality marked his participation at the hearings, which he enlarged on in an exchange with the Columbia University professor and leading peace advocate James T. Shotwell at the Senate Foreign Relations Committee hearing in May 1939. His concern was always with the excessive powers of the presidency in foreign affairs, but at this point of time it was linked to the integrity of neutrality in a world at war or on the verge of war.[3]

As of September 3, 1939, it was war between the Western Allies and Nazi Germany. In the wake of the German attack on Poland, Vandenberg responded to a query about the cash-and-carry program substituting for the arms embargo. He worried about any change in the neutrality laws becoming "*a SYMBOL of UNNEUTRALITY.*" No matter how much the United States would favor the cause of Britain and France, he argued, "it is *UNNEUTRAL* to favor *ANY* belligerent, and any *UNNEUTRAL* act is a step away, in *some* form, from a purpose to stay out of this war." His emotions were engaged enough for him to employ capitalization as well as underlining to emphasize his points. He resolutely opposed the repeal of the arms embargo by the Senate Foreign Relations Committee on September 28, 1939, and was among the seven members voting against sending the Pittman resolution to the Senate floor. Sixteen voted in favor of the bill. Undermining his position on ending the arms ban was the signing of a German-Soviet pact dividing Poland on the day after the Senate Foreign Relations Committee voted to repeal the arms embargo.[4]

Although he recognized that the European war posed a greater threat to America's neutrality, much of his attention in 1939 was directed toward the Japanese war against China. There was no question about where his sympathies lay in that contest, but he was alarmed by the administration's efforts to evade the neutrality laws by invoking Japan's violation of the Nine-Power Treaty of 1922 to place an embargo specifically against that country in light of Japanese aggression. The plight of China, more than that of Western Europe, induced some isolationists, including Senator Nye, as well as the administration to abandon neutrality at that time. And sympathy for Republican Spain inspired Senator Nye to call for a repeal of the embargo against that country in 1938.[5]

The wave of support for the Chinese victims of the war that affected isolationists seemed to open a way for the president to implement the quarantine speech, at least by indirection. Senator Pittman, chairman of the Foreign Relations Committee, provided that opportunity on April 29, 1939, with a resolution intended to give the president authority until May 1, 1940, to embargo both imports from and exports to Japan for its violation of the Nine-Power Treaty of 1922. Presidential action would be based not on the charge of aggression but on charges that Japan's behavior endangered American citizens or deprived them of their legal rights and privileges. This 1922 treaty had been the product of the Washington Naval Conference and was signed by Belgium, Britain, France, and Italy as well as by China and Japan. Questions about the need to consult other signatories of a multilateral obligation were brushed aside on the assumption that Japan's violations of bilateral commitments, particularly the Open Door policy in China, justified the resolution. Although claiming to introduce his resolution without having consulted the White House or State Department, Pittman would enlarge presidential powers not least by precluding any congressional veto of a presidential initiative. The chairman asserted that he had "no uneasiness in granting this power to the President because of his conduct over many months."[6]

Senator Vandenberg, not surprisingly, was as uneasy about this proposed extension of presidential authority as he was alarmed at an embargo that could be considered a declaration of war. After the Senate defeated the administration's effort to repeal the arms embargo in July 1939, he had to contend with Pittman's intention to submit a resolution targeting Japan alone. To derail momentum for an embargo and divert its direction, Vandenberg submitted his own resolution on July 18, 1939. It would allow six months' notice, in accordance with the 1911 treaty with Japan, before abrogating the treaty. It would be followed by negotiations for a new commercial treaty that would recognize the realities of the balance of power in the Pacific and still protect American interests. The almost forty-year-old Open Door arrangements were no longer applicable. No matter how many emotions it aroused, the quarrel with Japan was not worth a war. As for helping China under the Nine-Power pact, he urged reconvening the Brussels Conference of 1937 to determine what course the signatories should take, given Japan's continued violations of the pact.[7]

The Foreign Relations Committee deferred action on Vandenberg's resolution, although Secretary of State Hull seemed to look favorably upon it. Historians William L. Langer and S. Everett Gleason suggested that "there was some indication that the Democratic majority disliked supporting a measure introduced by a Republican." But this was not at the heart of the administration's rejection of the Vandenberg resolution. Rather, the administration wanted to signal to the Japanese and to the world at large that more than an economic issue was involved. The president formally announced on July 26 his intention to abrogate the 1911 agreement by letting the commercial treaty expire on January 26, 1940, and then placing trade with Japan on a day-to-day basis. This implicit warning to Japan found a positive reception among some isolationists, including Senator Borah. Assistant Secretary of State Adolph A. Berle observed, "It is a serious fact that the United States, which bolts like a frightened rabbit from even remote contact with Europe, will enthusiastically take a step which might very well be a material day's march on the road to a Far Eastern War."[8]

The Michigan senator did not share these sentiments. The president's action upstaged his intentions. He had coupled his recommendation to abrogate the treaty with plans for a new treaty. The president's action also revived his suspicion of the administration's use of the treaty's revision to move its own agenda without the Senate's sanction, but now with more public support. When Vandenberg pressed for implementation of his resolution, the State Department avoided a response by suggesting that his ideas were parallel to those of the administration. He was not satisfied with this attempt to preempt his vision. It was more than a difference in phraseology. He tried to impress upon Acting Secretary of State Sumner Welles that it was vital for Japan to understand specifically "that our desire for 'the formulation of a new treaty' is at the base of our recent abrogation notice." The administration remained cautious, content for the time being to avoid a showdown with Japan over China. Its eye was on the greater threat from Nazi Germany.[9]

Six months later, after Europe was at war, Vandenberg was distressed by Walter Lippmann's assertion that his resolution of July 18, 1939, had precipitated the crisis with Japan by inducing the State Department to accept the judgment of the Foreign Relations Committee. "This is historically inaccurate," the senator remarked, reminding Lippmann that the committee had rejected his resolution. He was particularly disturbed by Lippmann's judgment that "the Vandenberg Resolution was the longest step on the road to war since 1915." Vandenberg insisted, "It was nothing of the sort—unless the incident of abrogation be needlessly used to precipitate a breach and a crisis which the Resolution itself explicitly sought to avoid through its demand for *a new Treaty*." His resolution was "an alternative to a one-sided embargo that *WOULD* have been 'the longest step to war since 1915.'"[10]

The senator 's irritation with the influential columnist only increased two weeks later when Lippmann noted in his column on February 13, 1940, a contradiction in the behavior of this "pacifist and isolationist" who wanted to condemn Japan under the Nine-Power Treaty and then frame a new treaty. "It is this propensity of his to adopt such strange contradictory and extreme views which divided him from the main mass of Republicans," the column stated. Lippmann compounded his sins, according to Vandenberg, by suggesting that "I only asked for a new treaty with Japan after somebody [presumably himself] had called my attention to the consequences of the Nine Power Treaty signatories. This would be funny if it were not so dumb."[11]

The senator also resented Lippmann's gratuitous remark that in favoring the arms embargo, Vandenberg was telling his countrymen that there was no difference to them if the Allies were defeated in Europe. "I have never said the outcome of the war 'makes no difference to us,'" Vandenberg argued. "It *does* make a tremendous difference. My feelings are well known and unequivocal. But it makes a still greater difference, in my humble opinion, if we are drawn into war—and I propose to continue to combat that hazard to the last honorable limit."[12]

There was an implicit paradox in Vandenberg's position, which he did not confront. He had frequently recognized that self-defense must be a priority, and his votes in favor of arms appropriations undergirded a nationalism that went back to his enthusiasm for Theodore Roosevelt's foreign policies. America's entanglement in a European war could not be excluded from the Senate's or the administration's consideration. But he never advocated U.S. entry into World War II. In fact, U.S. involvement could hurt the British war effort. He made a point of observing in a letter in September 1941 to a Michigan supporter of Britain that if "we *are* drawn into this all-out shooting war, it will result in far *less* aid to our allies than they will receive if we maintain our present position because if and when we face the hazards of a two-ocean war in direct contact with it, the American people will insistently demand that a far greater proportion of our resources shall be *retained* for our own physical defense which continues to be in serious jeopardy." Yet he understood that he could not close his eyes "to the fact that there *might* come a time when our participation in a foreign war would be unavoidable. . . . Under *such* circumstances we surely do not want to jeopardize our own chances of victory and we certainly do not want to increase the martial difficulties we must overcome." While he accepted the possibility of U.S. engagement as potentially vital to the Allies' survival, he contended that a partnership in the conflict would diminish the aid they needed as America tended to its own defenses. The only way out for the nation in 1940, then, was to maintain as much neutrality as possible for as long as possible.[13]

Vandenberg remained convinced in May 1940, even after the Nazi blitzkrieg was rampaging across Europe, that the time for participation had not yet come. In answering a Michigan correspondent in May 1940 he admitted that "*isolation* is impossible in this foreshortened world. But *insulation* continues to be entirely practical. This would not mean we would not confront a serious situation in the event of a completed Hitler victory. It simply means we must 'insulate' ourselves as best we may against the possibility of such a victory."[14] How to do this was a dilemma that Pearl Harbor resolved for him on December 7, 1941.

THE ELECTION OF 1940

Such was the cloud of war that hung over the Republican campaign to wrest the presidency from Franklin D. Roosevelt in 1940. By that year

Vandenberg was the unchallenged spokesman for the Republican Party in foreign affairs. He was also the most articulate and most respected isolationist in the field of aspirants for the Republican presidential nomination. The most distinguished of the isolationists, Senator Borah, was well past his prime by the end of the thirties and died in 1940. Senator Nye, the dynamic young spark of the munitions investigation and fiery advocate of strict neutrality, did not lose his voice at the end of the thirties but had to cede authority to Vandenberg. Nye, the agrarian Progressive of the Great Plains, was out of place in "the increasingly urbanized, industrialized, capital-surplus, pluralistic, bureaucratic America of the twentieth century," in Wayne Cole's description.[15] Vandenberg's location in a populous midwestern state thrust the Michigan senator into the political limelight in the election of 1940, where there was no room for Nye. Not that Vandenberg was without competition in that election year. The newly elected Robert A. Taft, an able scion of an Ohio dynasty, was an ambitious contender for the nomination, as was the young New York district attorney Thomas E. Dewey, who had won fame for his conviction of Murder, Inc. But of the three, Vandenberg had the most impressive credentials for a presidential run if he chose to use them.

He was far less reluctant to throw his hat into the ring in 1940 than he had been in 1936. His long-standing worries about the encroachment of the executive branch on the constitutional authority of the Senate had increased exponentially during the court-packing contest and over the administration's deviousness regarding the neutrality laws. While he shared the nation's anger over the behavior of the Axis powers and empathy with the cause of the beleaguered Western democracies, he believed that those situations did not justify abandoning the American tradition of nonentanglement. He did not seek to isolate the United States from the outside world but instead—to use his locution—to insulate the nation from involvement in any foreign war. This was the motivating force behind his increasingly vehement charges against what he felt to be the Roosevelt administration's devious tactics to bolster Britain and France's defense against Nazi aggression and China's defense against Japan's.

Without shifting from his oral support for Britain and France, he could take comfort, as he told a Michigan constituent in May 1940, in the knowledge that the Allies were getting everything they needed. He did not feel they would require additional credits for at least a year. But how credible was this assertion in light of the fall of France a few weeks later? His answer apparently turned on the buildup of America's own defenses. Two months later he told the military analyst for the *Detroit News*, S. L. A. Marshall, that he believed in *"total preparedness,"* noting that he had voted for every emergency defense appropriation and for mobilization of the National Guard, as well as for the acceleration of military production and the acquisition of bases in the Western Hemisphere.[16]

Vandenberg was doing his best to cope with the impact of Nazi victories that made "neutrality" and "insulation" increasingly problematic. The issue had been irrelevant when he debated entering the race in 1938. Other matters more favorable to the Republicans then occupied center stage. In April 1938 he challenged the president to announce unequivocally that he would renounce any ambition for a third term. When there was no response to this proposal, the senator informed Michigan Republicans that he would be willing to "assume whatever responsibilities that lie ahead" and at the same time signaled that he would favor only one term for the next president. At no time did he explicitly say that he sought the nomination, but he did nothing to discourage his Michigan friends from promoting his candidacy in the "Vandenberg movement." His position was that he would accept the nomination if the party named him. He claimed with either modesty or fear of rejection that "it seems like rank presumption to discuss the acceptance of an honor which is not offered and undoubtedly will never be." Vandenberg's interest in the nomination was certainly expressed in his complaint against the gossip columnist Walter Winchell, who asserted, "without warrant and totally false[ly]," that Vandenberg had told Republican senator Arthur Capper of Kansas he would not accept the 1940 nomination. He told reporters that he had made no such statement to Senator Capper.[17]

Although Alfred Landon dismissed him as a remnant of the Old Guard, the program that Vandenberg outlined for the country domestically was hardly reactionary. His essay in the January 1940 issue of the *American Mercury* contained measures to retain the best features of the New Deal. "New problems demanded new answers," he wrote. "The hands of history cannot be turned back, no matter how much we may itch for the so-called good old days. . . . Eight years of the New Deal have launched certain social concepts which, in their objectives, cannot and should not be reversed." Much of his appreciation for New Deal reforms was grudging and backhanded, but still genuine. "If Republicans win in 1940 there will still be a Social Security Law. That is an axiom. It will probably evolve into a far more practical Social Security Law because Republicans notoriously are more practical and more efficient administrators." And when praising the FDIC, he could not refrain from criticizing Roosevelt for trying to eliminate the "so-called Vandenberg Amendment." In brief, what the Republicans in power would do, he asserted, is to retain the framework of the New Deal but to infuse it with fiscal stability and—not least—limit the powers of the executive branch. The Michigan senator was claiming the right to be the candidate who would both reform the New Deal and maintain American insulation from the wars of Europe and Asia.[18]

Vandenberg was not the party's choice in 1940. Nor were the rising new political leaders Taft and Dewey. Instead, an outlier and political novice, Wendell L. Willkie, president of a prominent utility company and acknowledged spokesman in the utility industry's fight against the New Deal's Tennessee Valley Authority, was to be the nominee. Although a Democrat, he was identified by 1939 as an effective and articulate champion of industry against the New Deal. His appeal to Democrats and independents inspired a grassroots effort to make him the Republican candidate in place of the inexperienced Dewey or the overexposed Vandenberg. Like the Michigan senator, he accepted much of the New Deal, but unlike Vandenberg he was not identified as a confirmed isolationist. Willkie appeared more open than Roosevelt to supporting Britain's lonely struggle against the German-dominated European continent. To enthusiastic acclaim, he won the nomination at the Philadelphia convention in June 1940, only to lose the election to Roosevelt in November.

Vandenberg never quite understood how the newcomer from industry took the party by storm. Shortly after the convention in Philadelphia adjourned, the deflated Vandenberg spoke with the wife of the Argentinian ambassador, Courtney Letts de Espil:

> "Courtney," he said with a little smile, "tell me, what has Willkie got that I haven't got?"

"Well, Arthur," I replied, too facetiously. "He has a mop of unruly, curly, black hair that to most women is almost irresistible."

"I hadn't thought of that."

In a speech a few days later Vandenberg referred to Willkie's shock of hair that was irresistible to women.[19]

There was no single factor to explain Vandenberg's failure to win the nomination in 1940. That his political organization was not equal to Dewey's may have been one reason, even if Willkie had not suddenly come on the scene. More likely was his own reluctance to push himself forward sufficiently. When pressed to make more appearances as a candidate, this most visible author of "Vandenberg resolutions" and "Vandenberg amendments" in the Senate, who appeared in magazine articles and press interviews on all current issues, postponed campaigning on the grounds that his obligations in the Senate precluded an early departure from Washington. "I cannot leave here until Congress adjourns," he told a close friend shortly after the war began in Europe, "because I cannot desert the grave issues now pending."[20] A case may be made that his ambition was always directed more toward maintaining his primacy in the Senate rather than toward the competitive atmosphere of a presidential campaign. Still another explanation rests on a fear of rejection that was a familiar factor in his dealings with elections in the past. It is worth noting that he easily won his third election to the Senate in 1940, ensuring that he would be the first third-term senator in Michigan's history.

To Pearl Harbor, 1940–1941

Arguably, it was the international scene and Vandenberg's dogged isolationism that doomed his candidacy and would have defeated him had he won the nomination. The approaching presidential election coincided with the darkest days of the British struggle to survive the Nazi onslaught. But dark days had loomed ahead for isolationists as well when in September 1939 the Nazis invaded Poland, Britain and France went to war immediately afterward, and the Soviet Union, after partitioning Poland with the Germans that month, invaded Finland in December. America's sympathies were with the democracies, seemingly to the extent of encouraging Congress to revise the neutrality laws by lifting the arms embargo and empowering the cash-and-carry provision of the 1937 Neutrality Act.

Actually, the outbreak of war initially reinforced isolationist sentiment in the nation, despite revulsion over Nazi and Communist behavior. Consequently Vandenberg's prospects for the Republican nomination benefited from the war in Europe, according to a *Newsweek* poll in December 1939. Before the outbreak of war both Dewey and Taft ranked ahead of him in the presidential race. But fears of America's entanglement made him the most eligible candidate for the isolationist opposition. Most isolationists could deplore the Nazi invasion of Poland but rationalized it by damning Britain's and France's history of imperial conquests. The absence of a moral difference between the Axis powers and the Allies made it all the more imperative to keep the arms embargo intact and refrain from any preference for one belligerent over the other. Traditional liberals such as Senator La Follette could join Vandenberg in criticizing actions that would favor the Allies.[21]

Over the next two years the isolationist tone became more strident under the aegis of the America First Committee, founded in September 1940 and dominated by conservatives who were not always able to shield the organization from pro-Nazis. Isolationists for the most part concentrated on their conviction that entry into the war would jeopardize America's domestic liberties at the hands of a dictatorial president. Moreover, they claimed that the fate of the Allies would not affect the United States; the Atlantic and Pacific Oceans themselves were barriers to any danger that victorious aggressors in Europe or Asia could impose on the nation. Even if executive power could be restrained, increased military aid to the Allies would come at the expense of America's own defenses. These arguments were often contradictory, but they were deeply felt and expressed fears most Americans felt about being drawn into a foreign war.[22]

In the series of crises that were enveloping Europe, Vandenberg saw himself—and was seen by his supporters—as the most consistent advocate of America's abstention from the conflict. He carried the banner of opposition to the repeal of the arms embargo provision in the Neutrality Act of 1937 in a failed effort to stop what he felt was a stampede promoted by the president and backed by a Democratic majority in Congress to bring the nation closer to war. Vandenberg was among the seven members of the

Foreign Relations Committee to vote against the revised neutrality laws on September 28, 1939. His voice was raised in the Senate on October 4 in a notable dissent arguing that the repeal of the arms embargo deprived the nation of its "indispensable, insulating defense against our involvement in this war. In the long run I do not believe that we can become an arsenal for one belligerent without becoming target for another." The only caveat—but an important one—was his recognition that if America's fate was tied to the survival of one side in a European war, "let us go all the way with everything we have got."[23] This was not his recommendation in 1939, but it undercut the vigor of his rejection of the revised law.

A similar ambivalence had crept into his diary in September. He envisioned and deplored a repetition of the pressures and propaganda that drove the United States into the First World War: "The same emotions which demand the repeal of the embargo will subsequently demand still more effective aid for Britain, France, and Poland. . . . It is a tribute to the American *heart* but not to the American *head*." He went on to accuse Roosevelt of exploiting the "treacherous idea" of believing that we can help the democracies "short of war." In this same entry he recorded that he hated the Nazis and Communists "as completely as any person living" but that it was cowardly as well as deceptive for the president to say that the United States could stop the dictators without going to war. This admission was hardly an endorsement of the repeal, but it opened a gap in his policy of nonintervention in Europe.[24]

When the act passed the Senate by a strong majority of sixty-three to thirty on October 27, 1939, he noted that at least the revised law eliminated presidential discretion in the arming of merchant ships and it barred American citizens from ships entering war zones. In his diary he recorded that "we won a great moral victory . . . it is going to be much more difficult for F.D.R. to lead the country into war. We have forced him and his Senate group to become vehement in their peace devotions—and we have aroused the country to a peace vigilance which is powerful." At the same time he observed that "we have definitely taken sides with England and France. There is no longer any camouflage about it. Repealist Senators speak frankly about it. In the name of 'democracy' we have taken the first step, once more, into Europe's 'power politics.' . . . What suckers our emotions make of us!"[25]

His rueful reflections on the American character were reasonable enough. Less understandable was his flat declaration that the nation now had taken sides with Britain and France. The repeal of the embargo then was hardly a "first step." The Roosevelt administration may have been duplicitous in its tactics, but its identification of America's fate with Britain's in particular was always visible, as Vandenberg had frequently complained in the past. But if he recognized this reality, then his claim of a moral victory in the legislation in making it more difficult for the president to bring the nation into the war is not only dubious but is also at odds with his concerns about the act serving as the first step toward war.

His rationalizations for a moral victory could not pass the test of time, not even for a very short time. The public mood was moving inexorably toward aid to Britain, faster than the senator anticipated. In mid-September, two weeks after war was declared, a Gallup poll showed 57 percent approval of a repeal of the embargo. After the president addressed Congress on the issue on September 21, support rose to 63 percent. Vandenberg was bombarded with reproaches from Michigan constituents, most painfully from Grand Rapids, for not recognizing the importance of keeping Britain afloat. The final vote on the bill was no surprise.[26]

Newbold Noyes, editor of the *Washington Evening Star*, a loyal Republican friend, empathized with Vandenberg's position even as he warned him against his opposition to the repeal of the embargo. Noyes asserted that "Roosevelt has already won this fight I think and I believe you agree with me." He felt that "to prolong and debate further now, or to adopt any tactics which the country will construe as obstructive to a prompt vote on the bill will only serve to further enhance the presidential prestige."[27]

Without retreating from his opposition to the president's initiative, Vandenberg replied that "regardless of the merits of the present controversy I agree with you that there should be no obstructive delays whatsoever, in connection with a decision. From the very start I have opposed any semblance of a 'filibuster.' . . . My great hope is that our battle (though a losing one) has made it impossible for the President to misunderstand the national attitude toward war itself." He did not want England or France to be misled into a belief that the United States would take up arms on their behalf in the way those allies had misled Poland.[28]

Noyes was right. Public opinion continued to move toward increasing entanglement with the Allied cause. As the British situation deteriorated in the spring of 1940, ultimately leaving it essentially the only survivor of the Nazi blitzkrieg in Europe, the nation followed Roosevelt, not the isolationists, on what Vandenberg felt was the unfounded assumption that all the president's steps in aid of Britain would stop short of war. William Allen White, the well-known editor and publisher of the *Emporia (KS) Gazette,* headed the Committee to Defend America by Aiding the Allies, formed in May 1940, to become the major vehicle for the eastern establishment's support of Britain. The committee represented the major economic interests with ties to Britain, cultural as well as economic.[29] In the midst of the election year the administration made such dramatic moves as appointing two prominent Republicans to key Cabinet positions—Henry L Stimson, Taft's secretary of war and Hoover's secretary of state, and Frank Knox, Vandenberg's old journalist friend and Landon's running mate in 1936, as secretary of war and navy, respectively. Roosevelt further won Congress over to bold initiatives by successfully imposing conscription, an unprecedented peacetime draft of young men, in passage of the bipartisan Burke-Wadsworth Act in June, just as France was surrendering to the Germans. The concept of national service even attracted the isolationist Charles A. Lindbergh.[30]

In a more provocative gesture, in September 1940, as Britain was fighting for its life against the Luftwaffe, the president engineered the destroyer-base deal with Britain. It was in response to Prime Minister Winston Churchill's request for a loan of forty to fifty destroyers to serve as antisubmarine escorts on the Atlantic. In exchange for the destroyers Britain would give a ninety-nine-year lease for military bases on British territories from Newfoundland to British Guiana. Roosevelt may have hesitated, fearing Britain, in defeat, might turn the ships over to the Nazis, but he was buoyed by positive reactions from those isolationists who appreciated that America had taken good advantage of British weakness. Historian Warren F. Kimball observed that "shrewdly, Roosevelt appealed to the Yankee businessman and the desire to best the English, which lay just beneath the surface of every American."[31]

Vandenberg admitted being critical at first but came around to recognizing that "we have been fairly treated." Still, he felt that "we should have been given a title in fee simple to these bases rather than just a lease. I think a far better 'bargain' *could* have been made, but I want to repeat that the existing arrangements are not as bad as they have sometimes been painted."[32] This grudging acknowledgement was about as far as he would go in endorsing the deal. In fact, his acceptance in light of his principled stand on neutrality was a measure of his continued conflicting emotions about the Roosevelt administration's policies and the fate of Britain. On the one hand, he had made it clear that the president's tactics, which he condemned, had already moved the nation into the role of cobelligerent in the war against Nazi Germany. The neutrality laws were in tatters. On the other hand, his nationalist instincts, along with an indisputable bias in favor of Britain, compromised his long-standing principle of abstention from war, even over a worthy cause.

Obviously Vandenberg was uncomfortable with all the foregoing actions, including the defection of Republican stalwarts Stimson and Knox. This was just another step toward America's involvement in the war. The selective service act too was predicated on the early onset of war. But this was not the reason he gave for his opposition to the act. He called it unnecessary: "The August quota for volunteers was already filled. It was absurd to say that the system had broken down. There is no breakdown in the volunteer system, but there is a breakdown in the willingness to acknowledge its success." He professed to being opposed "to the peacetime conscription of American youth unless it is reasonably established that a positive national emergency can be served and saved in no other way. I am opposed to tearing up 150 years of American history and tradition in which none but volunteers have entered the peacetime Armies and Navies . . . unless there is a valid reason." He claimed that his "position has always been that I would swiftly support conscription on the first moment that the army shows any signs of failing to obtain *all* the men it wants from the volunteer method."[33]

His primary reasons for opposing the bill were its contribution to war hysteria and the new powers it gave to the president, a familiar refrain in his evaluation of any bill. Besides, as he asked a Michigan editor, "Is there something about a 'conscript' which makes him a better soldier than a 'volunteer'? As a matter of fact, it seems to me that Mr. Hitler would be far more impressed with our demonstration of national purpose if it was based on a *voluntary, spontaneous,* enlistment of Army personnel than on the necessity of resorting to a draft." He pointed out that the administration itself was dubious about the conscription bill: "Under the irresistible pressure of logical criticism, the Bill has been rewritten by its own sponsors to a degree which confesses that the original measure (which it sought to rush through in a hurry) would have been a gross imposition on American democracy. I think it *continues* to be such an imposition unless and until there is some real proof of its necessity."[34]

The senator was especially annoyed by the charge of the *Detroit News* military expert, S. L. A. Marshall, that was he was lax in his support of national defense, on the basis of his skepticism about conscription. Vandenberg contended that he believed "in *total preparedness* and swiftest possible results and every vote I have cast has harmonized with this objective. I have voted for *every* emergency defense appropriation." He went on to list examples from mobilization of the National Guard to the acquisition of bases in the Western Hemisphere in the destroyer-base deal. Vandenberg could not accept Marshall's comment that he was in "complete disagreement" with Marshall's position "since I have been almost a fanatic on the subject of preparedness for the last twenty years. You will understand why I would think that you and I should find ourselves in substantial harmony." The senator's voting record did not fully substantiate his claim. In 1939, for example, he voted against the passage of a national defense act authorizing six thousand planes for the Army Air Corps and against a bill to acquire strategic war materials. Neither vote, however, diminished his nationalist credentials.[35]

But of all the critical issues before the Senate in the wake of war in Europe, it was the Lend-Lease Act of March 8, 1941, that most agitated Vandenberg. Deliberately labeled H.R. 1776, it was introduced on January 10, 1941, in the House by Representative John W. McCormack (D-MA), whose Irish Catholic constituents in South Boston would have been upset with a "McCormack bill" serving Britain. "1776" had a patriotic sound that would maximize its chances in Congress. Its origins may be traced to the inadequacy of the destroyer-base arrangements in September. Britain was running out of money to pay for U.S. goods at the same time that Nazi U-boats were inflicting enormous damage on shipping in the Atlantic. Prime Minister Winston Churchill made his case at the end of the year, stressing the vulnerability of Britain's lifeline across the Atlantic and emphasizing the financial plight that only the United States could resolve: "You may be certain that we will prove ourselves ready to suffer and sacrifice to the utmost for the Cause. . . . The rest we leave with confidence to you and your people."[36]

Roosevelt responded with plans to increase U.S. production and then lend or lease to Britain the supplies needed. The key elements in the bill allowed the president to, "from time to time, when he deems it in the interest of national defense, authorize the secretary of war, the secretary of the navy, or the head of any other department or agency of the Government to sell, transfer title, to exchange, lease, or otherwise dispose of, to any such government any defense article." At the end of the war Britain would return or replace what had been leased. Congress had received the news in the president's State of the Union message on January 6, 1941. Four days later the bill was presented to Congress.[37]

Vandenberg quickly found it to be the culmination of all his old fears—the granting of extraordinary powers to the president, increasing the risks of war at Roosevelt's discretion. The hearings on H.R. 1776 gave the senator an opportunity to vent his feelings in hyperbolic terms: "We have torn up 150 years of traditional American foreign policy. We have tossed Washington's Farewell into the discard. We have thrown ourselves squarely into the power politics and the power wars of Europe, Asia, and Africa."[38]

Vandenberg stirred controversy immediately following the president's State of the Union speech by calling his proposal *"Peace through War by Proxy."* He resented Eleanor Roosevelt's singling him out for criticism for such language. A dozen Democratic senators agreed that "I had been exactly accurate in describing the President's policy—and *that very fact* was probably my chief crime because the Roosevelts did not relish facing the reality of what they are trying to do." But the senator hedged his accusations in his public reaction to the president's message: "It was a strong plea for peace through war-by-proxy. For the sake of America I hope his program will never have to go farther. It is impossible to pass specifically upon his latest plan because it is still too nebulous."[39]

This cautious reaction did not prevent him from blasting the bill for giving the president the authority to lease away America's resources to whomever he pleased. Vandenberg's amendments to the bill were all rejected. As he complained on the Senate floor on March 7, 1941, "It is a matter of desperately important judgment, from day to day, as the bill is administered, what portion of our defense facilities we can safely permit the President to lend, lease, or give in whose defense we have a common interest. I submit, it is not fair to leave that desperately important question solely to the President of the United States."[40]

He felt that turning down the lend-lease bill was the last chance for the administration to change its policy, and he said so on the Senate floor. When it was clear that he had lost his fight, he predicted that "if America 'cracks up,' you can put your finger on this precise moment as the time when the crime was committed. It was at this moment that the Senate passed the so-called Loan-Lease Bill. It was passed because it wore the popular label of an aid-to-England bill and because the Roosevelt administration left no stone unturned to drive its votes in the Senate into a goose-step—backed by a nation-wide emotion and a nation-wide propaganda of amazing proportions." Little wonder that he felt, "as the result of the ballot, . . . that I was witnessing the suicide of the Republic."[41]

The most that opponents of lend-lease could win were amendments in the Senate requiring consultation with the army chief of staff or the chief of naval operations, but these concessions were hardly enough to change the direction of the administration. The isolationist minority was not able even to cut the $7 billion that the administration sought to administer the program. At this point Vandenberg differed with his colleagues: "When H.R. 1776 became law of the land, this issue of foreign policy was settled; . . . certainly, it was settled so far as the $7 billion appropriations was concerned." He went on to say, "With the greatest respect for and understanding . . . of my colleagues who may conclude otherwise, I shall vote for the impending bill." This was not a confession of surrender, he asserted, since he intended to hold the Administration to "strictest accountability for stopping short of actual war and stopping short of any program which would needlessly drag us into war." The senator ended his peroration with a bit of bluster. If the administration failed to keep its commitments, "I shall join in renewed contest with them, and we shall battle to the finish."[42]

It was Congress's surrender of its powers to the president, more than Roosevelt's steps toward war, that inspired Vandenberg to confide in his diary that he was witnessing the suicide of the republic. He told a constituent that repayment under terms of the act was "entirely in the hands of the President. He can make any arrangement he pleases. He can *give* away our equipment and supplies as he pleases without any contract whatever for repayment. . . . This is one of the reasons why I opposed the Lend-Lease Bill. I do not think that any one man—not even the President of the United States—should have such plenary power over the resources of 130,000,000 people."[43]

Shortly before the lend-lease confrontation, Vandenberg unwittingly emitted confusing signals. He opened himself to the criticism of the prominent syndicated columnist Joseph Alsop. At the end of 1940, after Britain had survived the Nazi air blitz in September, the senator seemingly associated himself with the idea of a "negotiated peace." In response to Alsop he pleaded a misunderstanding; he did not "clamor" for a negotiated peace. Rather, "I thought a restatement of belligerent war aims at this time might be useful." This could "(1) either make possible a reasonable termination of the horrible destruction now instead of later, or (2) to make it clear, particularly to millions of Americans who want to know, that no peace *is* possible—which event would do more to unify American thought than anything else."[44] According to a weekly British journal, *Foreign Correspondent,* he believed that the American public "will not support President Roosevelt's program for 'all-out' aid to Great Britain until it is convinced that all avenues to peace have been explored." The senator emphasized that "then—but not until then—I should agree with President Roosevelt's policy, even though I know it is bound to lead to war." But the next day he added that he had not changed his opposition to acts that could lead the nation into war.[45] It was obvious that no matter how he rationalized his positions on the subject, it was an embarrassment that he wanted to put behind him.

Less visible, certainly, in his correspondence or diary was the effect of his enjoyment of the company of British visitors to Washington, official and unofficial, who were later charged with influencing a susceptible senator to blandishments, even sexual favors, on behalf of British intelligence agencies. There is no question of his affection for Mitzi Sims, the wife of a prominent Canadian businessman and onetime attaché at the British embassy in Washington. Rumors of Vandenberg's affairs with Mrs. Sims and

well-connected British women held the women responsible for the senator's conversion to the British cause before the Japanese attack on Pearl
Harbor. Lord Halifax, Britain's ambassador to the United States, observed
to Lord Beaverbrook, the minister of supply in Churchill's cabinet, on
December 3, 1941, "He is apparently wobbling towards us and is worth
hooking."[46] This may have been wishful thinking on the part of British
officials. And while there was no doubt of Vandenberg's pleasure in the
company of attractive women, determining whether they were responsible for the senator's putative Anglophilia needs more than innuendo to
make the charge credible.

More persuasive in situating Vandenberg's positions in 1941 was the
resolution of his debate with himself over how to cope with his distrust
of the president's intentions. Ultimately he decided that no matter how
dangerous the president's behavior was, national suicide was not likely.
He reconciled himself to having fought the good fight and lost. The republic would survive. "I think it [the Lend-Lease Act] will *not* stop short
of war. But it is now the law of the land. It is now our fixed foreign policy
whether we like it or not. We have no alternative except to go along unless
H.R. 1776 is used by the President in a fashion which is *not* short of war."[47]

Despite his acceptance of the law of the land he inserted a caveat with
an implied threat of opposition if the president did initiate war. He affirmed his skepticism about the act's claim to help Britain "short of war,"
concluding that "the White committee [William Allen White's Committee to Defend America by Aiding the Allies] slogan 'Deliver the goods
to England now' . . . strips the mask from the committee's face. War will
result when American bottoms with American convoys are challenged by
submarines." He saw this scenario as an invitation to war "even though
the bill specifically did not justify convoys." It justified his conviction
that "we have a right to constantly remind the Administration that it had
promised to keep us out of active participation in this war through the
medium of this new policy. I think it our duty to hold the Administration
to strict accountability for its actions under H.R. 1776."[48] His was not the
language of compliance with the law of the land.

Although this reaction does not suggest rebellion either, its cynicism
was obvious: "When 1600 Pennsylvania Avenue becomes the G.H.Q. for
all the wars of the world—and when the President has promised to es-

tablish his 'four freedoms' *everywhere in the world,* it takes a very light-hearted moron to be complacent in the presence of such a prospectus." He raised the additional worry of how all the aid the United States was giving abroad would affect its defense needs at home. Yet notwithstanding all his reservations and gloomy prognostications, the senator admitted that the bill was passed by a congressional majority "acting strictly within the constitutional process. . . . When the President *and* majority of Congress—both acting strictly within the Constitution of the United States—have settled any phase of our foreign policy, I consider that I am bound to act accordingly, no matter how much I may disapprove."[49]

Historians Langer and Gleason reasoned that Senator Vandenberg spoke for most of the isolationist minority in pledging their cooperation, since his "isolationist tendencies had already moderated." These scholars may have read more into Vandenberg's position that he would have accepted.[50]

They did have a point. Vandenberg had voted against H.R. 1776, one of thirty-one senators against the sixty-eight in the majority. It was an impressive victory for the president. But the senator not only accepted it, as noted, he also voted in favor of the $7 billion to carry out the program. His isolationist colleagues—Nye, Clark, Wheeler, and La Follette—were among the small band of nine that voted against the appropriation. Vandenberg rationalized his vote: "I opposed it [H.R. 1776] from start to finish. But when it was passed, by Congressional majority—acting strictly within the constitutional process—I considered that we were committed (whether we liked it or not) and, of course, we were committed. So far as the 'lend-lease' program was concerned the die was cast."[51]

Vandenberg never gave his approval to any of the administration's actions that followed in 1941. Even so, the path to war that he had accurately predicted did not weaken his loyalty to the constitutional system that had sanctioned these actions. While he was proud to have "fought the original 'lend-lease' bill from beginning to the end," he recognized that a majority of Congress approved it, it was signed by the president, and it became the law of the land: "I do not consider that I have any more right to depart from *that* law than any other." He explained that his devotion to the constitutional process explains why he voted for the two subsequent lend-lease appropriations.[52]

There is little doubt that Vandenberg was right about the Lend-Lease Act accelerating America's movement toward full participation in the war. When the U.S. steamship *Robin Moor* was sunk in international waters of the South Atlantic in June 1941, he charged the administration with using the event as a propaganda ploy, ignoring the fact that 70 percent of the cargo was contraband. He opposed Secretary Knox's stand on arming merchant ships carrying supplies to Britain and noted that "practically every merchantman that has been armed and then transferred to Panamanian flag has been attacked or sunk. The trouble about arming our merchant ships is that we sacrifice all of our unarmed immunities but we do not give them adequate protection against the hazards which we invite them to face." In the Senate on October 27 he asserted that "under present existing circumstances, I am opposed to arming American merchant ships. Most emphatically I am opposed to arming them as a provocative prelude to sending them into combat zones and into belligerent ports where they inevitably invite the shooting that means war."[53]

Despite all the odds against him he kept seeking ways of avoiding war, down to the Japanese attack against Pearl Harbor. He used every argument he could summon to deter the administration from continuing to bait the Axis powers. Even when he supported Secretary Stimson's intention to replace the British garrison in Iceland with an American equivalent, he felt that the United States should not take such responsibility "because we lack the essential resources. I have the 'heavy responsibility' of asking myself whether we are ready to precipitate a war on two oceans, when we are not qualified to take over in little Iceland." As late as October 27 he pleaded with his colleagues for one more attempt at another recourse before Congress adopted its repeal of all the substantial restrictions of the Neutrality Act of 1939 and thus "needlessly and unwisely asks for war. Before we take the final step into war itself, rather than edge our way into it, as the pending resolution would invite, I should prefer that we present to all the Axis the choice of reasonable negotiations now as an alternative to our frank, all-out entry into war, if reasonable negotiations fail."[54] The Japanese navy and air force settled that question for him less than seven weeks later.

After Pearl Harbor Vandenberg voted with every other member of the Senate to declare war against Japan "in answer to what was probably the most treacherous attack in all history." It was just as well that he qualified his remarks. He could not forget that the administration left the Republican opposition out of its planning, even as its policies bore some responsibility for the attack. He was skeptical about the administration's claim that the war was *thrust* upon the United States. Excluded from the secret diplomatic negotiations with Japan, he had questions about the origins of the Japanese attack on Pearl Harbor and speculated that a wiser foreign policy might have separated Japan from Germany, implying that more flexibility on the part of the United States might have averted the catastrophe. He ridiculed the notion that war had been thrust on the United States. "The thrusting," he asserted, "started two years ago when we repealed the Arms Embargo."[55]

These musings were not reflected in Vandenberg's public role as the Republican spokesman on foreign affairs. He telephoned the White House on December 8 to let the president know that "despite all differences on other things, I would support him without reservation in his answer to Japan."[56] Without apologizing for his past positions, the Michigan senator demonstrated that national unity trumped all political considerations in a time of crisis.

The senator confided to his diary that at four o'clock on December 7, when he learned of the Japanese attack, "in my own mind, my convictions regarding international cooperation and collective security for peace took firm form on the afternoon of the Pearl Harbor attack. That day ended isolationism for any realist." He wrote these words later. Even his son and closest collaborator considered them as the knowledge of hindsight. If Pearl Harbor did not convert Vandenberg into an instant internationalist, Arthur Jr. at least detected seeds of bipartisanship in his approach to foreign policy. The senator, he knew, felt that "unity at home was essential in the face of the world crisis."[57]

Just how meaningful was Vandenberg's professed conversion on December 7 to international cooperation, and how deep were the seeds of bipartisanship implanted on that day? Internationalism, or awareness of the need for cooperation if not collective security, was imbedded in his personal history, separating him from so many fellow isolationists. Representing a state with residents from multiple ethnic backgrounds made him sensitive toward victims of Nazism. While Michigan was home to a large population of German and Irish descent that was indifferent or hostile to the British cause, there were equally important segments of Poles, Finns, Jews, and Dutch who may not have been Anglophiles but who empathized with the plight of their ancestral homelands. Vandenberg responded to the concerns of these constituents with comforting comments. As a former journalist, he was able to develop close ties with editors of influential ethnic newspapers, such as Detroit's *Polish Daily News* and *Jewish News*.[58] He was also able to tout his long record of opposition to Communism, with particular emphasis on his vote against recognition of the Soviet Union in 1933. The Soviet division of Poland with Germany and its invasion of Finland in 1939 were occasions to reemphasize his personal history. If those events did not open the way to America's defense of European territorial integrity, it weakened Vandenberg's isolationism to a degree that was not shared by isolationists in the Senate. These events, more than his past passive support of the World Court, might be cited as forerunners of his subsequent conversion to collective security.[59]

If so, countervailing evidence respecting his deep concerns about the president's executive power at the expense of the Senate, exacerbated in the court-packing issue in 1937, did not disappear as war threatened. In fact, Vandenberg felt that the prospect of a closer connection with Roosevelt was more distant in 1941 than it had been during Roosevelt's first two administrations. No trace of camaraderie, as in his congratulations on reelection in 1936 or his sharing the president's interest in establishing an item veto, could be found in his diary on June 8, 1939. He recorded how Roosevelt introduced him to the British king on the famous royal visit "in an amazingly ungracious way. With a grim growl (and not a bit of facetiousness)—he didn't even give the King my name. He simply said: 'Here's the chap who thinks he is going to succeed me in the White House, but he isn't.'" Vandenberg's ego was understandably bruised, although he professed to have been "greatly amused."[60]

The personal antagonism between the two leaders blended into Vandenberg's resentment over the exclusion of Republicans from the decision-making process that had brought on war and that continued to guide its conduct. Recognizing that the direction of the war was essentially an executive prerogative, he sought unity in his suggestion to the president for "a more intimate connecting link between the Executive and the Legislature," at least for the duration of the war. He invited Roosevelt to consider creating a Joint Congressional Committee on War Cooperation. He felt that such an arrangement might "curb whatever suspicions or irritations may arise if [Congress] were to know that its own elected representatives are in full and first hand contact with all essential facts."[61]

Collaboration of the kind the senator hoped for was slow in coming and never met his standards or wholly silenced his doubts about the president's sincerity. Until he was able to sense the administration's willingness to create a genuine national unity, in which he could play a prominent part, his potential internationalism was in abeyance.

5

The Impact of World War, 1941–1945

In the long run Senator Vandenberg was justified in his belief that the attack on Pearl Harbor "ended isolationism for any realist."[1] In his case, as a realist he recognized that there was no alternative to future international cooperation and collective security. But he was looking back to 1941 when he recorded those words. They did not reflect his judgments at the time. His immediate reactions had little to do with collective security and even less with an international organization and much more to do with lack of unity between the executive and legislative branches of the U.S. government.

It was a unity that seemed elusive to him because of the behavior of the president. When he asked for a more "intimate connecting link" between the executive and the legislature in this critical time, the president responded courteously but with no intention of bringing Vandenberg or other senators into wartime policy making.[2] Bipartisanship in wartime did not signify meaningful power sharing between the president and the Senate. Senator Connally, chairman of the Foreign Relations Committee, however, made good-faith efforts to establish a liaison with the State Department. Secretary of State Hull designated Assistant Secretary Breckenridge Long to give the committee "inside dope."[3]

This informal briefing was frustrating for Vandenberg. He still saw the nation being ruled by executive decree, with the Senate shut out from vital information about the progress of the war. Instinctively, he blamed "a substantial New Deal sector in high places which will constantly think of the war in terms of new opportunities for further New Deal experiments."[4] When he proposed linking defense appropriation bills to a Joint

Congressional Committee on War Cooperation, composed of six senators and six representatives, "I was promptly 'ploughed under.'" He felt
that his proposal "would have made for essential flexibility in executive
power without surrendering Congressional control of the purse strings."
Nor was he satisfied with the Republican National Committee's endorsing
in the vaguest terms not only of victory over the Axis powers but also of
a new world of international cooperation that Wendell Willkie hailed as
a new path for the party. Vandenberg dismissed the former Republican
presidential candidate as a hopelessly naïve internationalist.[5]

The administration's rebuff of the Senate's request for collaboration
appeared all the more dangerous in 1942 when Vandenberg dwelled on
the unlikelihood of the Soviets collaborating with the United States to
construct a better postwar world. That the Soviets—and the British too—
would take advantage of Roosevelt to advance their special interests in
the absence of a congressional check was obvious to Vandenberg.[6] Given
his long-standing opposition to the Roosevelt administration's policies
toward the Soviet Union—establishing diplomatic relations in 1933 and
refusing to sever relations after its occupation of Poland and war with Finland in 1939—it is not surprising that the senator would perceive threats
to American interests in the president's secret dealings with that country.[7]

Part of his frustration with the Allies stemmed from a sense of America's impotence in dealing with them. As he wrote to a Michigan constituent in January 1942, "I have been anti-communist all my life and I
shall continue to be anti-communist all the balance of my life." Yet with
the outcome of World War II uncertain, he saw no alternative to closing
ranks and helping the Soviet armies repel the Nazi invaders. They were
"making a magnificent demonstration of military strength and tenacity
which we must admit (whether we like communism or not) is a source of
vital advantage to us." Similarly, he balanced his support for "true autonomy for India" and sympathy for the imprisoned Indian leader Mohandas
Gandhi against the priority of winning the war against Japan. He doubted
that "a sharp allied breach over the Indian question would be offset by the
greater compensation which would flow from the international effect of
an American proclamation in behalf of India's liberty." The war had to be
won before the United States could take on the British empire.[8]

Given the obstacles the administration placed in the way of collaboration with the Senate on major issues, Vandenberg turned to sniping at such administration failures as the aborted effort to fortify the Pacific island of Guam against a Japanese attack. As he told a Chicago friend in February 1942, "The primary reason why the Guam item was defeated was unquestionably the belief that it would needlessly aggravate Pacific peace at a time when it was endangered even in prospect. I think it would be well worthwhile to have the Republican Research Bureau go through the whole Guam record and develop *all* the facts." He recalled the administration rejecting his own sound advice about dealing with the outdated 1911 treaty with Japan in favor of appeasing Japan for years in a fashion that outdid the Munich pact.[9]

Vandenberg exposed chinks in the administration's armor whenever he could find them. He believed he found one in March 1942 when he learned from the *Detroit Free Press* that two million acres of Kansas wheat were being destroyed at a time when farmers were being urged to increase war production. He fired off a letter to Vice President Henry A. Wallace, former secretary of agriculture, demanding an explanation. When Wallace provided a satisfactory response to this inquiry, it did not stop the senator from asking why some $200 million was on its way to India to equip factories under the lend-lease formula. Vandenberg understood that military necessities required financial aid but was skeptical of any program to build up India after the war. Wallace denied having any postwar plans for India and added that any projects under consideration were intended solely to strengthen the war economy of India. Wallace also questioned Vandenberg's source, a representative of the Board of Economic Warfare in Detroit, since the bureau had no agent in Detroit.[10]

Wallace's response did not soften Vandenberg's annoyance with the vice president's "international milk route," a reference to Wallace's supposed postwar goal of making "sure that everybody in the world has the privilege of drinking a quart of milk a day." He was equally impatient with "kindred Pollyanna crystal gazing," referring to Wendell Willkie's evangelical calls for America to lead a new world of freedom after the war. Instead, he cast the average American in his own image, one that was "neither an isolationist nor an internationalist. He is a middle-of-the-roader who wants to win this war as swiftly and as cheaply as possible, who then wants a realistic peace which puts an end to military aggression, who wants justice rather than force to rule, who is willing to take his full share of responsibility in all of these directions." This was as far as Vandenberg would go in the spring of 1943 in pursuit of a postwar cooperation that would end military aggression permanently. And he carefully hedged this aspiration by asserting that the United States must speak up for its own primary interests—"an 'enlightened selfishness' mixed with 'generous idealism.'"[11]

UNRRA as a Test Case

Before the senator could concentrate on the role of the United States in a postwar world, he would have to sort out both the thorny relationship between the Senate and the presidency and his place as a Republican leader in fashioning a position on the nation's foreign relations. There is no question about his wanting to be a player, and a positive one, in shaping American policy during the war and in its aftermath. For example, he defended on the Senate floor army chief of staff General George C. Marshall's decision to accept French admiral Jean Darlan as high commissioner for French Africa in 1942 despite Darlan's history as a German collaborator in France's Vichy government. The reason for Vandenberg's intervention was clear. Unlike most spokesmen in the Roosevelt administration, Marshall took the initiative in explaining his decision to Vandenberg and his colleagues. This approach to legislators helps to explain why, despite his strong reservations about the lend-lease program in the past, the senator voted in 1943 and 1944 to extend the program for its service to the war effort. In fact, he was present at the signing of the lend-lease extension bill on March 11, 1943.[12]

A more critical test of Vandenberg's willingness to endorse the president's programs was his stance on the United Nations Relief and Rehabilitation Administration (UNRRA) in 1943. The organization was to deal with the plight of people freed from Nazi control. Under the leadership of Governor Herbert H. Lehman (D-NY), whose appointment was signaled as early as November 20, 1942, UNRRA would have considerable power as well as funds to carry out its mission. Vandenberg's initial reaction was negative. When the president announced to Congressional leaders on June 9, 1943, that American participation in UNRRA would be authorized by executive agreement, Vandenberg interpreted it as another step in Roosevelt's accumulation of power at the expense of the Senate. The president's action aroused fear that UNRRA would set a precedent for all future postwar commitments. Vandenberg's response was a resolution on July 6 calling for an investigation of the draft agreement to determine whether U.S. participation in UNRRA constituted a treaty requiring Senate approval.[13]

He was not alone in his concern. Tom Connally, ordinarily a reliable defender of the administration's foreign policies, joined the Michigan senator in the defense of the Senate's prerogatives. As chairman of the Foreign Relations Committee, Connally had the committee approve Vandenberg's resolution unanimously the next day and blamed Secretary of State Hull for setting a dangerous precedent by ignoring the Senate's constitutional role in the treaty-making process. Moreover, he and Vandenberg were annoyed with the president for briefing the minority leaders of the House and Senate without consulting the Senate Foreign Relations Committee. Vandenberg claimed that the issue was not a matter of the administration snubbing the committee but the larger question of determining where the executive's authority should defer to the Senate. Vandenberg was cited in the *Detroit Free Press* as saying that Connally was more heated than he was in denouncing the administration's behavior.[14]

By subsequently toning down his indignation over the Roosevelt administration's unilateral decision to treat UNRRA as an executive agreement excluding congressional involvement, Vandenberg felt that he succeeded in forcing "a highly reluctant Administration to submit the UNRRA agreement to Congress for approval of an Enabling Act." He congratulated himself for compelling the administration to "substantially rewrite the text. . . . It is now practically nothing but an authorization for appropriations . . . with specific statement in the text . . . that we are bound to nothing unless and until Congress makes the specific appropriations. . . . Thus, in my opinion, it has ceased to be a treaty in any ordinary acceptance of that word."[15]

What is noteworthy in this controversy is not the senator's familiar worries about the president bending the Constitution but the reasonable way he presented his case. In retreating from his demand that the administration's participation in UNRRA be considered a treaty requiring a two-thirds vote of approval in the Senate, he found a readiness on the part of Assistant Secretary of State Dean Acheson to seek a middle ground. Stroking Vandenberg's ego paid dividends almost immediately for the State Department. It led to a seemingly happy compromise even as the senator continued to crow about his triumph. The issue of executive agreement was dropped, as was the treaty with all its implications. Instead, a majority of both houses of Congress would be sufficient to approve UNRRA's status.[16]

A pattern of cooperation opened at this time. It required special patience to win over the senator, according to Acheson's recollections. As noted earlier, Acheson came to respect and appreciate Vandenberg's considerable talents but initially saw him as a destructive hurricane, "producing heavy word fall. Senator Vandenberg . . . had the rare capacity for instant indignation, often before he understood an issue, or even before there was one." This metaphor was not quite fair, but it did capture what Acheson saw in 1943, when Vandenberg was "just emerging from his isolationist chrysalis and had not yet learned to manage his new wings."[17] Acheson was certainly right about Vandenberg stirring up initial opposition in both houses of Congress, although his claim that the administration had no intention of bypassing Congress is open to dispute.

Vandenberg's movement to the middle inevitably was difficult. He had to contend with a constituency that recalled his noninterventionist as well as his partisan past and that now charged him with apostasy for collaborating with the administration. Wrangling with a constituent on July 8, 1943, he displayed exasperation when he complained, "I do not know the basis of your comments. If I have become an 'internationalist' then black is white." Still, "it is perfectly clear—it seems to me—that when this war is over we cannot escape certain inevitable international cooperation."[18] Just what this would entail was not a matter he would take up in 1943, at least not before he could fashion an equitable relationship between the Senate and the presidency in conducting the war effort.

In his halting movement toward collaboration with the executive branch he had a partner and rival in Senator Connally, who shared his resentment at the administration's secret diplomacy that ignored the role of the Senate, especially its Foreign Relations Committee. There were limits to the partnership. Connally was a loyal Democrat, appreciative of the

administration's leadership and reluctant to criticize Roosevelt's steward-
ship of the party. For his part, Vandenberg's approach to collaboration
was constrained by Republican mistrust of the president, which he shared
in abundance, and by the part he hoped to play in his party's retaking
of the White House in 1944. The Republicans needed a winning foreign
policy platform and Vandenberg felt he was the person to produce it. Additionally, there was a rivalry based on the two senators' common interest
in being in the limelight and the pleasure each took in hearing the sound
of his own voice. Both senators dressed for their position: Vandenberg
with his white suits, bow ties, and ever-present cigar; Connally with his
flowing mane, string ties, and black-ribboned pince-nez. They sought to
look the part of nineteenth-century orators and succeeded for the most
part.

In 1943 they worked well together. Connally assigned Vandenberg
to key subcommittees: first a three-man subcommittee under the chairmanship of Senator Walter George (D-GA) to study the many postwar
resolutions and then a larger subcommittee chaired by Connally himself
to meet with State Department officials over the UNRRA controversy. It
was in these arenas that Vandenberg honed his budding skills in foreign
relations. It was an intense learning experience, as the Foreign Relations
Committee had to deal not only with the State Department but with res-
tive congressmen from both parties anxious to have their voices heard as
America looked ahead to a postwar world.

The B^2H^2 Problem

J. William Fulbright, a young Democratic congressman from Arkansas
with impressive credentials as a former Rhodes scholar and college president, presented a brief resolution in the House asking for congressional
sentiment in favor of postwar cooperation with the United Nations. His
resolution captured the spirit of other internationalists in Congress, many
of them newly converted. The most successful intervention was the product of a bipartisan group of four in the Senate—Republican Joseph H.
Ball of Minnesota, Republican Harold H. Burton of Ohio, Democrat Carl
H. Hatch of New Mexico, and Democrat Lister Hill of Alabama—known
as B^2H^2. At Ball's initiative they brought specificity to their resolution.

They asked the United Nations, then little more than a year-old declaration signed by twenty-six countries, to form a permanent organization that would prosecute the war and provide machinery for peaceful settlement of future disputes. In addition, their resolution advocated a UN police force to suppress any aggression by any nation.[19] This team of four aroused enthusiasm in Congress and put pressure on the administration to act on their resolution.

Vandenberg had reservations about the resolution, similar to those of Connally and Hull. He was flattered by his inclusion in the Connally circle, which worked harmoniously for the most part with Secretary of State Hull. Indirectly, it included British foreign secretary Anthony Eden, then in Washington, who responded affirmatively to Vandenberg's question about the danger of disrupting the war effort by trying prematurely for allied unity on a future peace settlement. Then Vandenberg, with a bipartisan group of senators known as the Committee of Eight, found Hull almost in a state of panic about B^2H^2 interfering with the delicate negotiations with the British and Russians: "He frankly said he would have given *anything* to have avoided a precipitation of this issue on the floor of the Senate at the present time."[20]

When the secretary of state admitted how important it was to tamp down congressional emotions, the senator was ready with a resolution, drafted with the collaboration of Wallace H. White (R-ME). Vandenberg had demonstrated many times in his senatorial career how facile he was in coming up with appropriate amendments, but now he was turning to international issues, a relatively new experience for him. His resolution began with a recognition that the United States must be involved in "international cooperation" after the war. This was couched in general, not specific terms, to concentrate attention on winning the war. The resolution included in vague terms the hopes of the United Nations for a world where military aggression would be "permanently curbed" and—equally important—where "self-governing people shall be free to work out their own destinies in the closest practical co-operation with each other." This was a reference to Vandenberg's continuing concern for the restoration of Poland, which avoided criticizing the behavior of the Soviet Union. He concluded with another familiar refrain: American cooperation would respect "due Constitutional process."[21]

When Hull responded with what Vandenberg considered "a rather noncommittal reply," the senator offered a revised draft to Senator George. He was convinced that an alternative to the Ball resolution should be introduced to let the public see specifically what the precise issue was. The revision contained only minor changes to simplify the language. Vandenberg intruded his own voice into the effort to sidetrack B^2H^2 by articulating what was to be a Republican version not quite in synch with Connally's or Hull's efforts. He clearly expressed it in a letter to the military analyst Major George Fielding Eliot, in which he described himself as "the average American" in favor of "America's reasonable participation" in a postwar security system. Even though he was a "so-called 'isolationist'" before Pearl Harbor, he emphasized that "this 'average American'—at least west of the Allegheny Mountains—wants, at the same time, to be sure that [an] American spokesman at the peace table is at least as loyal to America's own primary interests as Mr. Stalin is certain to be loyal in respect to Russia and as Mr. Churchill is certain to be in respect to the British Empire." The senator went on to express his willingness to have the Senate "*generalize*" on postwar issues but not to "*particularize*" prematurely. To do so would jeopardize the unity the allies need to win the war and stimulate new decisions in the Senate.[22]

Vandenberg felt he was being realistic rather than cynical in believing that nations follow their own interests. He even suggested to Eliot that when Eden warned the Senate Foreign Relations Committee against trying to particularize peace plans at this juncture, he had to "confess—just to you—that I sometimes wonder whether they [the British] would not like to encourage this non-cooperation idea (on our part) as a justification for their own freedom in their own post-war planning." He was not condemning Eden if this scenario was accurate. Rather, his complaint was directed against naïve Americans who failed to understand America's national interests, such as Henry Wallace and his own party's Wendell Willkie. He had "no sympathy whatever with our Republican Pollyannas who want to compete with Henry Wallace."[23]

In February 1943 Vandenberg had complained about the "complete and total lack of authentic liaison between the White House and Congress in respect to war responsibilities." He rejected Eliot's recommendation for a War Cabinet, presumably in the British model, as a possible solution to the problem. It would not work. The president would have to change "his *own* executive methods and his *own* executive disposition, before your 'War Cabinet' would be anything more than another debating society. . . . There would still be *final* decisions which he alone could make." The senator wrote these words while appreciating that "the President carries a superhuman burden—and it would still be superhuman, if it were streamlined to the utmost extent. I speak of him with the profoundest respect and a very real affection in spite of our historic differences."[24] Probably without fully realizing its extent, Vandenberg was developing a foreign policy for himself—and his party—that would differ from that of the Democrats while sharing a general recognition that there was no alternative to an internationalist future. He was seeking his middle ground. By noting "our historic differences" he was also equating his role with that of the president, perhaps also without fully realizing it.

Vandenberg and Connally disposed of the Ball challenge in the Connally resolution in October 1943. The resolution was only a little more specific than the Fulbright resolution, calling for an "international authority" but not a formal organization, "with power to prevent aggression and to preserve the peace of the world," without any mention of the military force that B^2H^2 had made their centerpiece. On November 5, 1843, the Senate voted in favor of the Connally resolution by a vote of eighty-five to five. Essentially it was a collaborative action by Vandenberg and Connally that incorporated the Vandenberg-White resolution of July 2, 1943, with a final paragraph referring explicitly to Senate ratification of whatever the diplomats signed. Not surprisingly, Vandenberg was happy to join in the subcommittee's unanimous approval as well as in the vote on the Senate floor.[25]

THE MACKINAC DECLARATION, SEPTEMBER 1943

The disposition of the B^2H^2 problem confirmed Vandenberg's conviction that the future of the Republican Party lay in choosing a middle path between the extremes of the old isolationists and the idealism of the increasingly vocal internationalists. Governor Thomas E. Dewey of New York, once again a leading candidate for the presidential nomination, illustrated the problem Vandenberg was so anxious to avoid. On the eve of a Republican conference on the party's direction after the war, Dewey preemptively proposed to continue the Anglo-American alliance that had blossomed in the war. He did qualify this proposal by hoping that Russia and China might be brought into the arrangement. However, the governor did not demand that his suggestion for an alliance be incorporated into the Republican Postwar Advisory Council's resolutions that would come out of the Mackinac conference in September 1943.[26]

Dewey's intervention antagonized Senator Taft, a formidable defender of a modest change in Republican foreign policies, and complicated Vandenberg's efforts to frame a middle-of-the-road approach. Given his experience on the Foreign Relations Committee, Vandenberg saw himself as the person who could formulate a policy that would accept the realities of international cooperation without aping the Democratic Party line. He positioned himself to exert authority by having announced as early as December 1942 that he would not be a candidate for the party nomination in 1944: "As a non-candidate myself I hope to have far greater influence in choosing the right candidate. That is all that matters."[27]

His hope was fulfilled. Harrison Spangler, the national chairman of the Republican Party, found in Vandenberg just the right figure to negotiate among the differing factions in the Postwar Advisory Council. The senator enjoyed this role at a meeting at a resort hotel on Lake Michigan's Mackinac Island. As he told Thomas Lamont, "I am hunting for the middle ground between those extremists at one end of the line who would cheerfully give America away and those extremists at the other end of the line who would attempt a total isolation which has come to be an impossibility." He resented the recurrence of the charge of "isolationist," which should have disappeared with Pearl Harbor, and blamed "anti-isolationists" in the Republican party as much as Democrats in keeping the libel live. The dominant tone, though, in his comments to Lamont was similar to that he had expressed in July. He took pride in knowing that the Mackinac Declaration was his product.[28]

The key elements in the declaration that united most strands of the party was the emphasis on America's national interests in the face of Soviet and British pursuit of their own individual objectives. Additionally, but not secondarily, was the underscoring of the Senate's constitutional authority in the shaping of American foreign policy. Vandenberg had found his middle ground. As he noted in a radio address on September 22, 1943, "There are those who are striving to prove that somebody got plowed under at Mackinac—either the so-called interventionists or the so-called noninterventionists of yesterday. The answer is that nobody got plowed under. There was a rational, tolerant meeting of patriotic minds upon wholly compatible philosophies of action which complement each other." Clare Hoffman, a Michigan congressman, admitted, "As an American Firster, I am satisfied with it." And presidential aspirant Governor Dewey congratulated Vandenberg: "The party indeed should be grateful to you for a major contribution to its welfare as well as that of the country."[29]

Vandenberg was able to tie his resolution of July 2 to the Mackinac Declaration and felt he succeeded in meeting all objections. Granting that some element of total sovereignty is always sacrificed in any cooperative treaty, he stated, "I thought I was doing a good constitutional job when I succeeded." He dismissed interventionists' claim that his very mention of sovereignty was proof that he never intended to cooperate with the Democrats.[30] Vandenberg not only put his personal stamp on whatever foreign policy initiatives the Republicans would support after the Mackinac Declaration, but he also solidified his position as spokesman for foreign affairs. He did this through an informal partnership with Senator Taft, who would be the arbiter of domestic policy.

Yet the Republicans entered the presidential campaign of 1944 under the handicap of conducting a campaign in a nation at war. Challenging Roosevelt's campaign for a fourth term was a formidable task, and the Republicans' stance on war and peace turned out to be an additional handicap. Despite the satisfaction he took in modifying the Connally resolution and the administration's foreign policies in general, Vandenberg was unable to outline a Republican foreign policy program in 1944 that offered a comprehensive alternative to Hull's program. He hoped for a bipartisan policy that would remove differences in foreign affairs from the agenda of both parties. The president, however, had no intention of allowing the Republicans to become equal partners.

The Republicans, for their part, feared that whatever concessions the president might grant could make the party a scapegoat for the administration's mistakes. Senator Taft warned Vandenberg that "the press will play up the Committee in such a way as to try to make you responsible for everything the President does or does not do. You certainly will have to protect yourself at every point against the assumption of such responsibility for I have no idea that the President will really cooperate."[31]

Vandenberg did not need Taft's warning. He demonstrated his understanding of the problem when he expressed his frustration over Roosevelt's freedom to negotiate with the European allies without senatorial restraints. He was dubious about the ability of the administration to cope with the ambitions of the Allies and was even more dubious about the president's secret diplomacy and the potential damage it could cause. He wrote to a Michigan friend in March 1944, "I am totally unwilling to trust these [postwar] negotiations to President Roosevelt's highly internationalistic point of view. I want America to play her full postwar part . . . but I . . . do not believe that Mr. Roosevelt's idea of 'protecting American interests' would square with mine for an instant." He went on to lament that "none of us know what President Roosevelt's commitments on our behalf have been at Quebec and Moscow and Teheran. We can *guess* but do not *know*. My *guess* is that they lean toward Stahlin [*sic*] in a degree with I would *never* approve. Under such circumstances, you will understand why I should consider it a fatal error for the Republican Party to promise to put Mr. Roosevelt at the head of the ultimate peace-making machinery."[32]

The Vandenberg hyperbole was once again in evidence, but his frustration was understandable. There was no way to prevent the president from being "head of the ultimate peace-making machinery." This would account for Vandenberg's gloomy prognosis about the outcome of the election in November with Roosevelt running for a fourth term. It would also account for a desperate attempt to make General Douglas MacArthur the Republican candidate. The general, a hero of World War I and commander of U.S. forces in the Pacific, may have had no political experience, but he had the visibility to match FDR's. Vandenberg's enlistment in the MacArthur boom for the Republican presidential nomination was genuine enough, given a hero worship traceable to his youthful enthusiasm for Theodore Roosevelt, but he maintained reservations that undercut his enthusiasm. Not least among them were reports of MacArthur's unpopularity among soldiers under his command. Vandenberg wanted to be assured that the campaign would be divorced from ordinary political routines that might embarrass the general or compromise his military mission. His premonition was justified when Congressman A. L. Miller (R-NE) published his private correspondence with the general in which Miller attacked the New Deal. MacArthur's response endorsed the sentiments. As Vandenberg noted in his diary, "Miller, in one inane moment, crucified the whole MacArthur movement (and MacArthur with it)."[33]

Vandenberg's ultimate backing of the Dewey nomination was to be expected. Willkie's "one world" idealism removed him from competition, and the Ohio challenge from Governor John W. Bricker, Taft's choice, was a minor hurdle. The Michigan senator had the satisfaction of finding his Mackinac Declaration the basis of the Republican platform on foreign relations. He won over all segments of the party and earned congratulations from John Foster Dulles, Dewey's closest foreign policy adviser and secretary of state–designate after victory in November 1944. Vandenberg found a kindred spirit in Dewey when the governor accepted his redraft of the proposed foreign policy plank of the platform. The senator added, "I should say that my Republican Mid-West is perfectly willing to sanction 'international cooperation' just as long as it knows that we aren't going to 'haul down the flag' and that we aren't going to be international 'saps' in 'giving America away.'" He ignored the earlier Dewey outburst about a permanent Anglo-American alliance. In his statement to the party's Resolution Committee, Vandenberg concluded that the "foreign policy creed" of the Mackinac Charter was where divergent minds found a common meeting place.[34] Whatever optimism the charter generated dissipated in the face of Roosevelt's victory, narrow though it was, in November 1944.

THE DUMBARTON OAKS CONFERENCE, AUGUST–SEPTEMBER 1944

Important though the presidential campaign was, it took place at a time when the senator was more engaged in the effort of Secretary of State Hull to promote a bipartisan image at the Dumbarton Oaks Conference of September 1944. There the Republican leaders presumably would have a voice, or at least a hearing. Vandenberg, now as the spokesman of his party, was a major actor in these proceedings. Given Vandenberg's long-standing suspicions of the president, Secretary Hull had his work cut out for himself. He had to convince Vandenberg that the administration wanted as well as needed bipartisan support for organizing the United Nations without ceding too much authority to the Senate.

Hull set the tone by appealing to Connally as chairman of the Foreign Relations Committee to appoint a small group that would be privy to the details of the State Department's negotiations. He was successful. Connally appointed a genuinely bipartisan group of senators: three Republicans—Warren Austin of Vermont and Wallace White of Maine, along with Vandenberg, each sympathetic in varying degrees with postwar commitments; four Democrats, committed internationalists—George, Alben Barkley of Kentucky, and himself as chair, with Democratic maverick Guy Gillette of Iowa as the fourth; and one Progressive, Robert M. La Follette Jr. of Wisconsin, an unreconstructed isolationist. This was dubbed the Committee of Eight, and its mission provided Vandenberg with the opportunity to expand his increasing sensitivity to the problems of a postwar world. As the most influential as well as the most voluble Republican, he would be a key figure in the success of the Committee of Eight.[35]

Vandenberg's membership in this exclusive group did not preclude his wariness about being co-opted in administration plans that he and his party would find objectionable. "I have taken the position that, no matter how acceptable the program for a new League might be, everything depends upon the kind of peace—whether it is *just*—which this new organization will implement. . . . The *peace* will create a new status quo in the world. The new 'League' will defend this new status quo. It is my position that the United States cannot subscribe to this defense, no matter how hedged about, unless and until we know more about what this new status quo will be."[36] His guarded response was less a reflection of election tensions than a memory of the administration's history of excluding the Senate from its relations with the Allies.

What Hull wanted from the senators was an endorsement of the tentative outline of an organization for the United Nations that had been presented to the committee on April 25, 1944. The secretary informed the committee that there were "three vital pivotal questions: The first was to keep Russia solidly in the international movement. The second was to develop an alert and informed public opinion in support of the program proposed. And the third was to keep the entire undertaking out of domestic politics." For all three he needed the cover of a supportive Senate, especially from the committee's Republican members.[37]

The major elements in his program seemed to meet most of Vandenberg's expectations. These proposals, though conducted in secrecy, relieved the Michigan senator of many of his concerns: "The striking thing about it is that it is so *conservative* from a nationalist point of view. It is based virtually on a four-power alliance. While there is an Assembly in which all nations will be represented with one vote each, the real authority is in a Council of Eight upon which America, England, Russia, and China shall *always* be represented, and no action can be taken if any one of the Big Four dissents. Hull's whole theory is that there must be continued agreement between the Big Four or the post-war world will smash anyway." With appreciation, the senator recorded that he was "deeply impressed (and surprised) to find Hull so carefully guarding our American interest in his scheme of things."[38]

But Hull could not win the senators, particularly Vandenberg, over to his primary goal: namely, unconditional congressional commitment to whatever terms the United States would make with the Allies in forming a new league. Vandenberg insisted on seeing the "actual physical and specific terms of the peace itself" before such commitment could be made, adding, "otherwise we would be signing the most colossal 'blank check' in history." He felt "that our advance action in seeking tentative agreement upon a new 'League' should be *contingent* upon whether the ultimate peace merits our support." What motivated Vandenberg's reservations was his persistent concern that Britain and Russia would manipulate the organization to the detriment of America's national interest and America's conception of a just peace. Without specifying Roosevelt's responsibilities, he implied doubts about the ability or willingness of the president to stand up to the Allies. The senator concluded his response with support for continuing "present efforts to agree upon a tentative international organization formula. I wish to go ahead. But it *does* bear upon the time and circumstance under which we shall be prepared to implement our unofficial prospectus."[39]

Given this carefully calibrated reaction to Hull's plans, the committee refused Hull's intention to approach Churchill and Stalin immediately with a statement of the Senate committee's approval. Differences among the members quickly surfaced. Republican Warren Austin as well as Chairman Connally were willing to go farther than Vandenberg in oral backing of the secretary. The Committee of Eight resolved the problem by agreeing four days later, on May 23, to favor Hull "entering upon immediate negotiations with other United Nations, and stop there." Vandenberg had La Follette on his side in recognizing that "this is no time for Senators (particularly Republican Senators) to 'sign up' *in the dark.*" Underlying his dissent was fear that the president had made secret agreements at the Tehran meeting in 1943 that the Senate could not accept. Vandenberg wondered if Hull himself "*knows* the whole story. I can simply state for myself that I do not feel I have sufficient information to back any specific 'League' plan (although I heartily favor the principle and the idea)." Assistant Secretary of State Breckinridge Long was convinced that Vandenberg "hates Roosevelt. . . . He thinks Roosevelt stands for everything bad and for nothing good. . . . He is the only one of the group that has antipathy to Roosevelt and suspicion of every move he makes." Yet Vandenberg appreciated Hull's efforts to work on plans of the kind that would avoid the Senate's rejection of Wilson's league in 1919.[40]

Hull may not have won over the Committee of Eight to blanket approval of the administration's negotiations with the Allies for a postwar organization, but Vandenberg and his colleagues were agreeable to encouraging the negotiations that would take place in August at Dumbarton Oaks in Washington, D.C., between the United States and its wartime partners—Britain, France, and the Soviet Union. The site was the former home of Robert Woods Bliss, one of Hull's special assistants and a former ambassador to Argentina, who had turned it over to Harvard University as a research center for Byzantine studies.

Hull seemed to have devoted almost as much effort to keeping the Committee of Eight informed as he did to the substance of the nego tiations. The secretary recognized that if the proceedings, which opened on August 1, fell prey to partisan attack, it could destroy the confidence of the Allies in America's credibility as a peacemaking partner. This scenario loomed over the conference a week before it was to begin when Governor Dewey, the Republican candidate in the presidential election, professed to be disturbed by reports that the four major powers intended to subject the lesser nations to their control. Dewey's pronouncement, drawn up with the help of his chief foreign policy adviser, John Foster Dulles, deplored the political ploys that would undermine democracy. "As Americans," he asserted, "we believe with all our hearts in the equality and rights of small nations and minorities. In the kind of permanent world organization we seek, all nations, great and small, must be assured of their full rights. . . . We are fighting this war to a victorious conclusion and for these very principles."[41]

The potential quarrel was settled after Dulles worked with Hull on a mutual agreement to set aside partisanship—but not before they squabbled over the difference between the terms *bipartisan* and *nonpartisan*. Understandably, the State Department suspected that use of *bipartisan* might be seen as making the Republican Party an equal partner in policy making. Dulles, speaking for Dewey, accepted Hull's language on the understanding that it was not possible to have a nonpartisan approach on all other issues in foreign relations. With respect to a new league, they concluded that the Big Four would have to dominate it but would keep lines open for all members to have their voices heard.[42]

Vandenberg was discomfited by some of the information he gathered about the secret conversations among the four participants at Dumbarton Oaks. Particularly sensitive was the question of who would make a decision on the use of American troops to enforce a collective security action. He wrote a formal letter to Hull on August 29, 1944, asking for clarification of this important issue. Invoking military sanctions, he claimed, "is a clear commitment on the part of the United States to promptly engage in the joint military action. Therefore it is tantamount to a Declaration of War. I believe our Constitution clearly lodges the exclusive power to declare war in the Congress. Frankly, I do not believe the American people will ever agree to lodge this power anywhere else."[43]

Despite these strong and very familiar words from the Michigan senator, he conceded that the president's traditional powers gave him the authority to act within the blessing of the Constitution as commander in chief without a congressional declaration of war. The presidential role in the defense of the Monroe Doctrine was a case in point. It would appropriately apply if a member of the new world organization breached the peace in a way "so clearly criminal and so clearly outlawed that our Congress would not for an instant hesitate to join in his military subjugation."[44]

There was no question that the senator was anxious for the new order to succeed, but he still worried that President Roosevelt would consent to the creation of a new organization without recognizing its limitations. He was hopeful, though not convinced, that "no President would dare ultimately to take us into one of these subsequent major wars (if one were to occur) without the clear and obvious support of the American people." The nub of his problem remained mistrust of the president. He feared that by stubbornly pursuing presidential prerogative the Roosevelt administration was jeopardizing the success of the enterprise. Roosevelt could be inviting the kind of congressional resistance that defeated Wilson in 1919.[45]

When the Dumbarton Oaks Conference adjourned at the end of September, there was 90 percent agreement on most of the issues. Dulles, Dewey's surrogate as adviser to the U.S. delegation, observed on September 28, 1944, that "the work of the British, Russian, Chinese and American experts makes a fine beginning in a momentous task. All peace-loving people must rejoice that they have found so large an area of agreement about world organization for peace." Dulles felt that their progress opened the way for deciding which permanent members of the Security Council (SC) would have a veto power when one of them was caught up in controversy. Vandenberg chimed in two days later, questioning whether any of the Four Powers with permanent seats on the Security Council should have the right to veto a charge of aggression against itself: "I am opposed to any such immunity. In my view it would represent a new imperialism. America and Britain are opposed. Apparently Russia favors it." This was a reference to the 10 percent of issues in dispute, which involved "the dreadfully significant question whether we are building a new Peace League in which the four major powers shall be totally immune to discipline." The new league required as well "a World Court to which we shall all agree to submit all justiciable questions. I heartily favor it. (I voted for the old World Court.)"[46]

On balance, Vandenberg shared with his colleagues a hope that the concerns of the smaller nations would be covered under membership of at least two of them on the "new League Council." The Dumbarton Oaks proposals called for a United Nations organization composed of an assembly of all member nations; a Security Council of eleven nations with five permanent members (including France); an Economic and Social Council; and an International Court of Justice. Less specific but most critical was the Military Staff Committee, chosen from the permanent members of the Security Council, which would administer military forces when an emergency occurred. Addressing the Senate on August 22, 1944, a week before the conclusion of the conference, Vandenberg added his endorsement, stating that there was no alternative to a sound international organization "in this foreshortened world."[47] At the same time he was conscious that there was no resolution on the issue of the veto power, over which the Soviets refused to yield. And unspoken but always in the senator's mind was the fear that a duplicitous president would either make secret arrangements that were unacceptable to the Senate or would yield to the unilateral interests of the other Allies.

The Dumbarton Oaks Conference left the administration uncertain as to just where the Republicans stood on the United Nations organization and on postwar foreign policy in general. Hull left office on November 27, 1944, succeeded by his undersecretary the former U.S. Steel executive Edward R. Stettinius Jr., who had led the U.S. delegation at the conference. Stettinius had no more assurance than his predecessor had about the direction the Republicans would take with respect to the future of the United Nations. Still, the administration had been able to come through the election successfully without partisan conflict over foreign relations. But if the new secretary of state was uncertain of the American position, the Republican leadership was even more uncertain.

A few years later Dulles implied that Roosevelt had taken advantage of his party in convening the Dumbarton Oaks Conference. While Dewey tried to warn against creating an organization that would perpetuate the dominance of the Big Three powers (Britain, the United States, and the Soviet Union), Hull had managed to disarm Republicans by asserting that conflict between the parties at that time might jeopardize the development of the world organization after the war. When Dewey went along with Hull's intention to take the UN issue out of the presidential campaign, Dulles reflected that "there was grave doubt as to whether or not this was good Republican politics. It deprived Governor Dewey of one of the few major issues available to him during wartime, and it enabled the Democrats to put him in the position of me-too-ing Roosevelt's foreign policy."[48] After the Republicans failed to dislodge Roosevelt from the White House, this was a retrospective view that Vandenberg shared with Dulles. But this was not their view—or Dewey's—in the summer of 1944.

In the course of the election campaign, Vandenberg had come to appreciate Dulles's expertise in foreign affairs, and particularly their harmonious views on foreign policy. While both were active in the Dewey camp in 1944, the Michigan senator had been a rival of the New York governor four years before, with none of the links Dewey had with Dulles, his presumptive secretary of state. As they collaborated in the summer of 1944, Vandenberg felt they had become "old friends." The senator would agree with Dulles that "the language of the Dumbarton Oaks Proposals may, in spots seem to exaggerate what is now accomplished. . . . The Proposals embody no universally accepted law and make no provision for any law-making body. The use of force is so hedged about by requirements of political unity between the nations that there can be no assurance that the force machinery will work with promptness or certainty." Dulles expressed these views on the day that Vandenberg made his celebrated speech to the Senate.[49]

Vandenberg was locked in the same box with Dewey and Dulles. Like other Republicans working with the administration, he had to fend off critics who felt that he had abandoned his long-standing defense of the authority of the Senate and the limitations of presidential powers. John T. Flynn, a fellow traveler in Vandenberg's isolationist years, feared that the Michigan senator was surrendering to the "professional State Department New Dealers" in recommending that international agreements be accepted by a majority of both houses rather than by two-thirds of the Senate, as prescribed for treaties.[50]

This was a misreading of Vandenberg's position. Flynn was extrapolating from the UNRRA vote. The senator, in fact, was not unsympathetic to Flynn's charge that the administration had been striving for a decade to "rid itself of the restraint of the Senate in international relationships." Vandenberg never retreated from his belief that "the final Constitutional authority to declare war rests with the Congress of the United States. . . .

But the fact remains that we confront a difficult problem in 'definitions.' Since the early days of the nation the President always had the right—and used it—to use the military for national defense on his own responsibility. But this did not include the power to declare war." Vandenberg went on to identify a "twilight zone" between the powers of the executive and Congress: "There has never been a definitive rule to draw the line between them." The Dumbarton Oaks Conference was the occasion to "*now* find this line and definitely draw it and then say to the President: This far and no farther."[51]

Notwithstanding the energy he put into these words, he still did not define the line. Like Dulles, he was not prepared to challenge the White House directly if the consequence was the failure of a postwar organization. He felt that the Dumbarton Oaks Conference moved the Allies in the right direction: "I feel that we *must* have thorough international cooperation to *prevent* future wars because . . . the science of mass destruction is reaching a point which robs us of any *physical* immunities and makes the 'next war' too horrible to contemplate."[52] In this context the need for unity between the executive and legislative branches of government in pursuit of an international organization trumped Vandenberg's doubts about the good faith of the president and the ambitions of the Allies as the Allies looked beyond the Dumbarton Oaks proceedings. But his doubts did not disappear.

"THE SPEECH," JANUARY 10, 1945

On January 10, 1945, as the Allies looked ahead to the end of World War II, Senator Vandenberg delivered a speech in the Senate that was hailed as a turning point in American foreign relations. While the senator was never the orator he would have liked to have been, an equal of Webster or Clay, he was an effective speechwriter with a gift for the telling phrase, no matter how extravagantly expressed. On that day he offered his own prospectus of America's foreign policy in a postwar world. The speech could have been the opportunity to break the bonds that had frustrated his efforts to define his party's position on the nation's appropriate role in a new league of nations.[53]

He hoped it could be significant and labored over his battered portable typewriter to ensure that his words would matter. As he recalled some years later, he felt that "the speech *had* to be made in order to clarify and strongly assert the position of America from the standpoint of those of us who had been so-called 'isolationists' prior to Pearl Harbor." Moreover, he felt it was a "personal challenge" to take on this assignment. He wrote the speech, he claimed, a dozen times before he was satisfied with the results and then checked it with trusted journalist friends.[54] His flair for the dramatic gesture and his timing in making it struck a chord with the Senate and nation at this moment.

If the senator was surprised at the attention his address received, so was the president. The White House initially gave a polite response but offered no word of appreciation from Roosevelt himself. Tom Connally, chairman of the Senate Foreign Relations Committee, hoped its repercussions would not disturb the forthcoming Yalta Conference. He wondered about Vandenberg's sincerity: "To me it seemed rather late in the day to be professing anti-isolationism. But from then on I tried to deal with him as if he had at last learned [the] necessity for international cooperation." But the caution was short-lived, perhaps because the public and the president himself recognized that the speech was intended to strengthen the U.S. position at the forthcoming conference at Yalta. Upon leaving for that conference the president asked Vandenberg's office for fifty reprints to take with him, encouraging the senator to believe "that I had struck a helpful note."[55]

No such reservations accompanied the accolades that the speech quickly inspired. Most were lavish in their praise. Senator H. Alexander Smith (R-NJ) exclaimed that Vandenberg was "two blocks ahead of President Roosevelt in starting a definite foreign policy." And Vandenberg himself displayed a letter from a president of a major eastern university who was about to leave the Republican Party until he read the speech. The leading national pundits joined in the applause, including those who had differed with the senator in the past, with the influential Walter Lippmann writing, "It cannot be said of many speakers that they affect the course of events; but this may well be said of Senator Vandenberg's speech." The *Cleveland Plain Dealer* and the *Omaha World Herald* used the same terms to describe its impact: "a shot heard around the world." The liberal *New Republic* gushed, "Quite possibly historians a quarter century from now may say that the speech of Senator Vandenberg marked a turning point in world affairs."[56]

Probably the most moving commentary on Vandenberg's odyssey from isolationism to internationalism was Walter Lippmann's response when Arthur Vandenberg Jr. asked him after Vandenberg's death to comment on his father's contribution to the nation. Lippmann found it in the speech of January 10, 1945:

> When a sudden and tremendous change of outlook has become imperative in a crisis, it makes all the difference in the world to most of us to see a man whom we have known and trusted, and who has thought and felt as we did, going through the experience of changing his mind, doing it with style and dash and in a mood to shame the devils of his own weakness. I would argue at the bar of history . . . that his spiritual experience . . . was the creative element which made his other political powers so enormously effective.[57]

Was this the conversion experience that changed the course of Vandenberg's life? The pattern of his behavior between Pearl Harbor and the delivery of "the speech" suggest that his "conversion" was a gradual process, as his son observed, having "evolved slowly in the Senator's thinking over a long period, but by the spring of 1943, it was well established." Vandenberg himself seems to have been surprised by any equation of his address with a conversion experience. His own reflections suggest that he did not realize that "he was taking off" into a new era, important as he hoped his speech would be.[58]

By labeling his address "The Need for Honest Candor: Clarification of Our Foreign Policy," the title and subtitle used in *Vital Speeches of the Day,* Vandenberg felt at the time that he was sending a message to the president, who was about to leave for the conference with Churchill and Stalin at Yalta. There it was expected that the three leaders would flesh out the proposals from the Dumbarton Oaks Conference. The "candor" to which he repeatedly referred throughout his talk centered on the importance of unity among the three allies in winning the two wars and then assuring that the United Nations would be the guarantor of a lasting peace. Many newspapers used the immediate war aims for their headings. Failure in these goals would lead to "the curse of World War Three." Unity was threatened by unilateral actions on the part of Britain and the Soviet Union, to which the United States, by its silence, appeared to acquiesce. America feared unwisely that disunity would follow if Roosevelt discussed publicly the different interests of the Allies. Vandenberg was annoyed that "there seems to be no fear of disunity, no hesitation in Moscow when Moscow wants to assert unilateral war and peace aims which collide with ours. There seems to be no fear of disunity, no hesitation in London when Mr. Churchill proceeds on his unilateral way to make demands often repugnant to our ideas and ideals." His reference was to Stalin's proposed partition of Poland and Britain's actions in Greece. Vandenberg questioned why "we must be the only 'silent partner' in this Grand Alliance."[59]

"Silent" was his description of the administration's failure to articulate its own objectives in founding the Atlantic Charter and the United Nations, and for this he blamed the president. On the other hand, he praised Roosevelt for indicating in his annual message to Congress that he wanted to use America's influence to prevent "temporary or provisional authorities in the liberated countries" from blocking "the eventual exercise of the peoples' right freely to choose the government and the institutions under which as free men they are to live." With respect to military cooperation against the revival of German or Japanese militarism, he felt that the president, as commander in chief and without referring action back to Congress, "should have instant power to act, and he should act." Vandenberg then urged the next big step: to "authorize the ultimate international organization to review protested injustices in the peace itself."[60]

Vandenberg was not advocating a world government. He wanted to ensure that in pursuing international cooperation the United States would not find itself endorsing an unjust peace, an outcome he had worried about over the past year. He felt that the president muddied the issue, unwittingly deprecating the rights proclaimed in the Atlantic Charter and the Declaration of the United Nations through "his recent almost jocular, and even cynical, dismissal of the 'Atlantic Charter' as a mere collection of fragmentary notes." Roosevelt's offhanded comments at a press conference two weeks before had "jarred America to its very hearthstones. It seemed to make a mere pretense out of what has been an inspiringly accepted fact. . . . It seemed to suggest that we have put too much emphasis upon a fighting creed which did not deserve the solemnity which we have been taught to ascribe to it." And at a time when Stalin and Churchill were deprecating the Atlantic Charter, "the President's statement was utterly devastating in its impact." The senator did add, though, that, to his credit, Roosevelt "has since sought to repair this damage. I hope he has succeeded."[61]

Yet disillusionment with the Allies and with the administration's responses to their unilateral actions was not the theme that the world heard. Rather, it was this assertion: "Let me put it this way for myself: I am prepared, by effective international cooperation, to do our full part in charting happier and safer tomorrows." Less audible was his caveat: "But I am not prepared to permanently guarantee the spoils of an unjust peace." Does this declaration, then, mark the embrace of an internationalism that was to mark the last decade of Vandenberg's life?[62] The context of the address does not bolster this interpretation.

The answer lies not in the text of the speech itself but on the glosses the nation—and Vandenberg himself—placed on the address. Certainly, it was not intended to quash his doubts about the wisdom of Roosevelt's wartime leadership any more than it terminated his criticism of executive power at the expense of the Senate.

In fact, the hectoring tone of the speech seems directed more to warning an unreliable president against the wiles of the European allies in the forthcoming Yalta Conference than to claiming a faith in internationalism. Would Roosevelt once again bypass Congress and the American people in secret deals he might make at Yalta? Vandenberg obviously did not trust Roosevelt to protect American interests in the way Churchill and Stalin would advance the interests of their countries.[63]

Two months later, after the Yalta agreements did nothing to assuage his concern about secret deals affecting American sovereignty, the senator restated the points he had made in January, emphasizing that it was in America's self-interest "to join in organizing permanent justice in a free world of free men." He said again that "our oceans no longer protect our ramparts." But in affirming cooperation with other nations he emphasized that "I am not joining in any movement to submerge our independence in a world state. I am talking about co-operation between nations which retain their essential sovereignty. But one of the attributes of sovereignty is to relinquish voluntarily whatever segments can be traded for something more valuable to us. That is all we should be asked to do if international peace co-operation is launched on the right basis."[64] This was a mixed message. In a single paragraph he celebrated American independence and identified its limitations.

As the speech took on a life of its own, Vandenberg discovered potential benefits that he may not have appreciated while laboring over his speech in January. In a March 1945 article for the *Saturday Evening Post*, he perceived that the speech shed the "isolationist" label by stopping the incessant name calling that sullied the debate over neutrality before Pearl Harbor: "I should like to say in passing, that I wish we could quit calling names. It does not help the peace effort in America to scream 'isolationist!' at every citizen who did or 'Warmonger!' at every citizen who did. What happened on a black Sabbath in December 1941 changed everything. I know of no so-called 'isolationist' who has not faithfully supported the war effort from that hour to this. It has usually been an anti-isolationist who has kept this theme alive." Dulles found another benefit in the address: "His proposals are not sporadic but coalesce with and push forward a preexisting Republican program."[65]

But the primary impact of the address centered not on the executive-legislative tensions or on Vandenberg's suspicions about Roosevelt's trustworthiness or the importance of America standing up to its allies in the making of peace. Rather, it was on the implications of "cooperation" that transcended its immediate application to permanent demilitarization of the Axis powers. Vandenberg was praised for his advocacy of cooperation between the parties in America as well as with the world through a new United Nations organization. The real surprise to him as well as to his readers was his now-dominant role of leadership in the framing of a bipartisan foreign policy that followed in the Truman administration. It may have been a minor theme in the speech, but it ultimately overwhelmed every other message the senator intended. As Ernest Lindley projected, "If a single speech can convince the world that the United States does not intend to revert to isolationism after the war, Senator Vandenberg's on Wednesday should do so. Its importance grows as its text is more widely read and analyzed."[66] Arguably, close analysis of the text would not justify this prediction. But the interpretations it spawned made it a milestone if not the turning point in Vandenberg's evolution from isolationism to internationalism.

6

The Conversion Experience, 1945

If the celebrated speech of January 10, 1945, did not transform Vandenberg into an internationalist who had truly left isolationism behind, then a case may be made that his appointment as a delegate to the conference in San Francisco to draw up the UN Charter did make him a true believer in a new order. Remembering Woodrow Wilson's mistake in dispatching to Versailles in 1919 a delegation that lacked a genuine Republican representative, the president on February 28 appointed a delegation that was as inclusive as possible. Among the members were Harold Stassen, former Republican governor of Minnesota and currently a navy commander, Dean Virginia C. Gildersleeve of Barnard College, two congressmen—Sol Bloom (D-NY) and Charles A. Eaton (R-NJ)—and two senators—Tom Connally and Arthur Vandenberg. Secretary of State Stettinius would head the delegation.[1] Much as with the Committee of Eight, this was a balance intended to remove charges of partisanship in the fashioning of a new league of nations. While no current isolationists were represented, the presence of the Democratic chairman of the Senate Foreign Relations Committee and the most influential Republican spokesman on foreign policy, both strong defenders of Senate prerogatives, was expected to silence the voices of critics.

That the president considered him for such an important role seemed to Vandenberg an obvious recognition of his position as the Senate's leading Republican spokesman on foreign affairs. This masterful stroking of the senator's ego demonstrated that the artful president had not lost his magic in dealing with adversaries as well as adherents.

There is no doubt that Vandenberg was pleased with the invitation and fully confident that he could make a difference in serving the nation's interests. But could he trust the president to give him a free hand at the conference table? Here was the rub. Memories of Roosevelt's persistence in elevating the presidency above the Senate combined with the president's secretive ways inhibited an immediate acceptance of the invitation. Assistant Secretary of State Breckinridge Long certainly exaggerated Vandenberg's hatred of Roosevelt by repeatedly dwelling on it, but he was accurate in identifying the suspicion that characterized the senator's instinctive reaction to any Roosevelt initiative.[2] When Vandenberg expressed his sorrow over the president's death on April 12, 1945, he accompanied his respect for the loss of "a truly great and gallant spirit" with notice of his flaws and criticism of the president's physician, Admiral Ross McIntyre, for allowing the dying man to run for a fourth term.[3]

His response to Roosevelt's invitation was gracious and cautiously positive in saying, "I take the liberty of inquiring what specific commitments, if any, would be implicit in my acceptance of this designation; and whether I might feel that it will not violate your commission or your expectations . . . if I freely reserve the right of final judgment upon the ultimate results of the Conference."[4] These were not pro forma queries; he was not playing hard to get. The senator had serious problems with the vague promises of the Dumbarton Oaks Conference and with the present Soviet stance on Poland. He made special mention of the need for "justice" to be an integral part of the new charter.[5]

The initial State Department response, while Roosevelt was still en route home from the Yalta Conference, was evasive. Not until March 3, when the president assured him of "free expression in the delegation," was Vandenberg fully satisfied. Roosevelt even encouraged Vandenberg, in what turned out to be his last conversation with him, to persist in his strong language about Soviet misbehavior in central Europe.

Actually, the senator had made his decision to accept the invitation before his interview with Roosevelt. He recognized the reality of the world situation and the futility of objecting to decisions at Yalta that had been approved by the American and British governments. If no effort were made to achieve a new world order, he feared that the Soviet Union then would be in complete possession of everything it wanted. So if he would be guaranteed the "untrammeled freedom" to express his own views in

San Francisco that the administration promised, then "I think I am called upon to put my head in the noose and take my chances." In this debate with himself Vandenberg did imply an appetite to take up the challenge appropriate to his new role in the arena of foreign policy, although he did not confess to it. He also displayed his hopes for a peaceful postwar world, which coexisted with his anxieties about Soviet aspirations and the administration's response to them.[6]

THE MENTORS: JOHN FOSTER DULLES

Notwithstanding his personal history as a successful editor and legislator, Vandenberg was understandably nervous about engaging in the world of international politics. Assured as he was of his primacy in the Senate, where he could identify and expose weaknesses in the administration's management of foreign affairs, he was not confident in his role as leader in the field. Membership in the Senate's Committee on Foreign Relations did not make him an authority in the field and certainly not a policy maker. He needed someone to guide him through the thickets of diplomacy, and he found an experienced mentor in the person of John Foster Dulles, with whom he had forged a friendship during the presidential campaign of 1944. There was no better model than Dulles, whose experience as a diplomat went back to The Hague Conference of 1907, where the eighteen-year-old grandson of Benjamin Harrison's secretary of state, John W. Foster, served as secretary to the Chinese delegation. In World War I he was counselor to the U.S. delegation to the Reparations Commission at Versailles at a time when his uncle, Robert Lansing, was Woodrow Wilson's secretary of state. In the interwar years he was an active international lawyer, serving as well as chairman of the Federal Council of Churches' Commission on a Just and Durable Peace. Small wonder that Vandenberg looked to him for advice on his way to the San Francisco conference.

Vandenberg made his dependence explicit when he wrote to Dulles on February 17, 1945, that "I wish you were going to be with me at San Francisco (if I go). If you want a job as 'Advisory Counsel' I prayerfully petition your occupancy in the room next to mine at Frisco (maybe). . . . I should like to feel that I can lean on you throughout the enterprise (if it happens.)" After the senator finally accepted the invitation, he continued "to hope that *you* will be with me from start to finish—officially or otherwise." He followed up this idea with the secretary of state at the first meeting of the delegates. Each delegate was granted a staff of two, and "I privately told Stettinius I want to take John Foster Dulles as my lawyer." Stettinius replied that while he had "great respect for Dulles," the "President greatly dislikes 'Tom' [Dewey] and Dulles and that it might be obnoxious." Roosevelt had not forgotten the 1944 presidential campaign. The secretary raised the alternative of having Dulles as adviser to the entire delegation in his capacity as head of the Federal Churches' Commission on a Just and Durable Peace.[7] When it seemed unlikely that Vandenberg's or Stettinius's proposal would materialize, Dulles professed that he preferred "to have no special status at San Francisco. For several years now I have, in various non-official capacities, worked for the creation of a world organization, dedicated to securing a just and durable peace. I think that if I continue in that way it will best serve the general cause we all have at heart."[8]

But Dulles's wish to have no official status quickly melted in the face of Stettinius's "desire, concurred in by the President," to have him act as general adviser to the U.S. delegation at the San Francisco conference. "After reflection" he changed his mind. He did not want to appear too eager. There is no doubt, however, that Dulles was as pleased as Vandenberg was by his inclusion in the delegation. As he told the senator, "I know that you have wanted it and pushed for it, and I am deeply appreciative of the confidence in me which has been evidenced by your attitude."[9] Given the frequency of his contributions to the proceedings, he would have been unhappy to sit on the sidelines while the debates went on without him at Stettinius's penthouse suite at the Fairmont Hotel.

Dulles responded to Vandenberg's requests for advice quickly and with full support of his intentions to see to it that the principles of "justice" would be central to the work of the delegates. He cheered the senator with such statements as: "To my mind such progress toward justice is the heart of peace. A league to enforce the *status quo,* particularly the kind of status we now know we shall get, would be the surest road to war. If you can be instrumental in avoiding that danger, you will have made an immense contribution." Two weeks later Dulles went into detail about how to improve the language of the proposals from the Dumbarton Oaks Conference. In that letter to Vandenberg he warned against preventing the council from taking up such matters as the western boundary of Soviet Russia on the grounds that it was a purely domestic matter. Dulles fulfilled his promise of providing a revised statement on possible amendments to the Dumbarton Oaks proposal over the concept of justice, and he also offered much more.[10]

Vandenberg was appreciative of Dulles's expertise in the language of diplomacy, especially when it was in accord with his own judgments. As he wrote on February 22, "Once more you give me courage and stimulation by your agreement with my point of view." He was grateful to Dulles for giving him "precisely what I want." And on March 6 he gushed, "I cannot begin to tell you how much I appreciate your cooperation."[11]

Vandenberg and Dulles were in lockstep by the time the San Francisco conference opened. They had listened to Senator Warren Austin's objections to their positions on expanding the authority of the Security Council. Austin favored "the original idea of limiting the principal functions and powers of the Security Council to 'primary responsibility for the maintenance of international peace and security.'" He preferred to leave responsibility to the General Assembly, "the natural organ of the proposed organization to vest with the power and responsibility for laying down rules." Vandenberg dismissed Austin's reservations with the observation that his viewpoint "always did and it always will lack 'imagination.'"[12]

The death of Roosevelt on April 12, 1945, just two weeks before the conference was scheduled to open, invigorated the Michigan senator. He knew Harry Truman as a colleague and hailed his response to the question of the conference being postponed. Truman resolved it immediately and positively. Unlike Roosevelt, who had planned to attend, Truman would leave its leadership to Secretary of State Stettinius. A courtly personality but not a forceful one, the secretary permitted the two members of the Senate Foreign Relations Committee to dominate the U.S. delegation. In his frequent absences they served as chairmen of the delegation. Nevertheless, Vandenberg recognized Stettinius's strengths as well as his weaknesses: "He is the *best* 'General Manager' I ever saw. He *gets things done*. But that is about all he can do. There needs to be a stronger hand in charge. Moreover, he does *not* have a seasoned grip of foreign affairs. He rarely contributes to our policy decisions."[13]

The Michigan senator came to realize that he had a good feel for foreign relations. The collaboration between Dulles and Vandenberg continued. Occasionally the senator felt the need for advice that Dulles could supply. Dulles was still the mentor when at a meeting of the U.S. delegation he explained to Vandenberg the distinction between "attack" and "armed attack." He noted that the distinction was made deliberately to cover the Monroe Doctrine.[14]

Still, it was obvious that as the conference proceeded Vandenberg appeared to be the crucial figure in San Francisco. The Canadian diplomat Lester Pearson forecast before the conference ended that Vandenberg and Stassen might well be the most influential members of the U.S. delegation: "They outrank in ability and in popular appeal Senator Connally, Congressman Bloom, and Congressman Eaton." Pearson was convinced that as a leading Republican, Vandenberg was perhaps the most important single influence in Congress for ensuring that the repudiation by the president in 1919 would not be repeated in 1945.[15] Given his years in the Senate, President Truman knew the importance of winning over his former colleagues and recognized Vandenberg as the Republican who held the key to the votes in the Senate.

Vandenberg understood the reasons for the deference he received from the president and his secretary of state. The senator made frequent references to the significance of producing a charter that the Senate would accept. It was important to have specific language rather than the broad terms of the Dumbarton Oaks proposals. Lacking specificity "lends dangerous weight" to critics who deny that the power is already implicit. He was thinking of critics in the Senate who had already indicated this as their line of attack on the charter. Skeptics asserted that the Dumbarton Oaks proposals "will freeze the post war world in a rigid pattern created by expedient decisions made during the war." Vandenberg added that he was in a "peculiar position," representing the minority side of the Senate, where votes had to be produced for the ratification of the charter. When Soviet foreign minister Vyacheslav Molotov asked if the other American delegates agreed with Vandenberg's views, Stettinius confirmed that they were unanimous in their support.[16]

Awareness of his status humbled Vandenberg as well as empowered him. It also highlighted contrasts between him and Dulles. As the conference proceeded, Vandenberg the politician emerged as more important than Dulles the technician. On his proposal regarding revision of treaties, Vandenberg was surprised that Molotov could even doubt that he was speaking for his entire delegation. Molotov had to understand that review of treaties was indispensable if the charter was to get through the Senate.[17] There was no need to consult Dulles in asserting his views. Dulles was able to dissect the details of a treaty with more expertise than Vandenberg, but the vital issue of winning the nation's backing was outside Dulles's sphere of experience.

Vandenberg did not uniformly agree with Dulles. Notwithstanding Dulles's familiarity with the arcane points of international law, the senator did not hesitate to disagree with the lawyer's memorandum arguing for the exemption of the Monroe Doctrine from a Security Council veto. While the senator agreed with the special status of the Monroe Doctrine, he did not accept Dulles's reasoning. Vandenberg complained that "Mr. Dulles' point of view reduced itself to the principle that we have the right to do anything we please in self-defense."[18]

Dulles often was at a disadvantage in explaining his positions in a political context. He was an outsider. He was uncomfortable defending himself against the charge that he had been an isolationist in the past, even a member of the America First organization. To a soldier in a field hospital at Fort Bragg in 1944 he protested that he had worked with Woodrow Wilson, shared his ideals, and was disappointed when the United States did not join the League of Nations. He had devoted his life, he insisted, to establishing an international order, notably through the Federal Council of Churches. Earlier in 1944 the columnist Marquis Childs had reported on his putative connections with the America First group. Dulles admitted that Edward N. Webster, a prominent client of his law firm, had asked advice on legal steps to incorporate a New York branch of that organization. When he learned that he was reported to be one of its counsels, "I at once got in touch with Mr. Webster and told him that he must not make such statements as I had made it clear that I did not want to be identified, directly or indirectly, with America First."[19] Understandably, he wanted to be free from the taint of any connections with such an isolationist group in the middle of World War II.

The charge, however, dogged him throughout the year. In denying columnist Drew Pearson's implication he had contributed $500 to the America First organization, Dulles had to admit that his wife, "who was and is quite a pacifist, took an interest for a time" in the organization and did make a $500 contribution. "I only knew of this vaguely, but I did know that she attended one or two of their meetings and asked me to go with her, which I declined to do." Pathetically, he asked how anyone who knew of his personal history "could reasonably think that I could be an isolationist or 'American Firster' in deed or in spirit."[20] As a senator who never apologized for his prewar isolationism, Vandenberg was not confronted with this problem.

Dulles's skin may have been too thin for political life, as his unhappy few months in the Senate revealed when Governor Dewey appointed him to fill a vacancy in 1949. In matters political Vandenberg was clearly the senior partner. But their relations remained close, with the senator advancing Dulles's candidacy at every opportunity. No one was more persuasive than Vandenberg in getting the president to appoint Dulles in 1950 as a consultant to the State Department, partly on the understanding, as Secretary of State Dean Acheson told Senator Herbert H. Lehman (D-NY), who defeated Dulles in a special election, that Dulles would not be a candidate for the Senate.[21]

THE MENTORS: WALTER LIPPMANN

Another major influence on Vandenberg as he moved more deeply into international affairs was that of Walter Lippmann, arguably the most influential American political philosopher in the twentieth century. He was also a journalist, roosting in such prominent newspapers as the *New York Herald Tribune* and later the *Washington Post*. Vandenberg was comfortable with journalists and always regarded himself, with good reason, as one of them. He had forged intimate relations with a few, most notably James Reston of the *New York Times*.

Lippmann was of a different order, a thinker about foreign relations who extended the relatively narrow boundaries of Vandenberg's vision. It is not a coincidence that Arthur Vandenberg Jr. turned to Lippmann after his father's death to give an answer to the question "What will history show to have been the contribution of Senator Vandenberg in the evolution of the United States from a basically isolationist country in 1940 to our present-day position of world leadership?" Wisely, Lippmann recognized that it was too early for history to judge the senator's role, but as noted in chapter 5, he penned a personal judgment of a man who in changing his mind could move a nation.[22]

Their initial contacts were confrontational. Lippmann, five years younger than Vandenberg, had long been a power in American public life, and to challenge him, as the senator did over the Patman bonus bill in 1935, took some courage as well as initiative. Vandenberg may have praised Lippmann for his "clear-thinking mental apparatus," but he still misspelled the columnist's name in two letters written in that year. There was no meeting of the minds at this juncture, certainly not over the propriety of the Patman bill, which would pay what Lippmann regarded an excessive amount of money to veterans. Vandenberg was supportive; Lippmann was not.[23]

Intimacy did not come quickly. Although there was increasing mutual respect between the two as war enveloped Europe, tensions mounted over Vandenberg's Senate resolution calling for abrogation of the 1911 treaty with Japan. The senator disputed Lippmann's charge that his resolution "was the longest step on the road to war since 1915." He made his case for a new and more effective treaty. Lippmann was not convinced. He not only repeated the charge but labeled Vandenberg "a pacifist and isolationist." In response, Vandenberg asked his old friend Carl Saunders, editor of the *Jackson (MI) City Patriot,* "to keep after him." The senator declared, "It is frankly amazing to me that Lippmann will misstate this record and then misrepresent it."[24]

This storm was blowing over even as they wrangled about Japan. War in Europe had forced both men to come to terms with America's position. Neither wanted American involvement in the European war and both understood the necessity of changing the arms embargo. Lippmann wanted Vandenberg to use his influence in the Senate to lift the embargo on arms but keep it intact for shipping and finance. Vandenberg disagreed; he voted against the repeal in its entirety. But he shared Lippmann's conviction that "we should avoid getting into a situation where intervention in the European war is even to be considered as a practical possibility."

And Vandenberg would agree with Lippmann's insistence on building up America's defenses, including a two-ocean navy.[25]

As the war approached an end, questions regarding the postwar world drew the two together. Vandenberg read with much more appreciation than he had before the war the wisdom he found in Lippmann's daily columns. He hoped that Lippmann's advice to the administration "would have *some* effect on the powers that be," as he joined with the pundit in urging the removal of the presidential powers as commander in chief as an issue in the Dumbarton Oaks proposals: "Why jeopardize 99 percent of this great adventure in organized security by stubbornly and blindly insisting upon asking for the final one percent of totalitarian power which you do not need and which you would not dare to use in any major crisis if you had it?" To give the president a "blank check" would energize opponents of the proposals.[26] Lippmann's authoritative voice was important to a still-fledgling player in foreign affairs who in the past had been adamant about the abuse of presidential authority.

By the summer of 1944 they were closely allied. There was no problem then with the spelling of Lippmann's name when Vandenberg addressed him as "My Dear Walter." Their bonding helps to explain biographer Ronald Steel's crediting Lippmann as the author of Vandenberg's celebrated speech of January 10, 1945. Its thrust certainly fitted the columnist's views. But it is an exaggeration to claim that Lippmann also supplied the text; the senator took too much pride in his own words as he pounded them out on his old typewriter. Moreover, the wording of the speech lacked the elegance Lippmann's prose would have provided. The pundit, who was not immune himself to the lure of public acclaim, faulted the senator for his ostentatious vanity, even as he exploited it. At a reception at the Mayflower Hotel as accolades were being showered on the senator, Lippmann saw him strutting around "just like a pouter pigeon all blown up with delight at his new role in the world."[27]

Before Vandenberg left for San Francisco, there was a mild dispute between them over what Lippmann called "Senator Vandenberg's Thesis": whether political decisions made during the war should be reviewed in the new world organization. The answer was yes, but Vandenberg did not want to discuss specific proposals publicly until the American delegation in San Francisco had considered them. Essentially, they were in complete agreement on a distinction between peacemaking and peacekeeping. The senator maintained that "Dumbarton Oaks must be held to the latter character. I totally agree. Indeed, I think it is desperately important that the country should not mistake the San Francisco limitations. They have nothing to do with specific peace settlements."[28] Vandenberg's concern that Lippmann could misinterpret his position reflected the importance of Lippmann's imprimatur.

It did not matter that they did not always agree. Vandenberg's antipathy toward the Soviet Union, reinforced by its treatment of Poland, did not accord with Lippmann's putative acceptance of a Soviet sphere of influence in Eastern Europe in 1945. But if the journalist felt the senator was excessively influenced by the hard-line ideas of W. Averell Harriman, the wartime U.S. ambassador to the Soviet Union, this was a temporary breach. It was repaired not only by their common reaction to Soviet behavior in 1946 and 1947 but by Lippmann's views about the 1948 presidential election. He preferred Vandenberg to Dewey or any other Republican aspirant. Where they were most closely allied was over their advocacy of the Atlantic alliance and their concerns about its militarization, a linkage that they both deplored.[29]

Lippmann was an enduring influence on the senator, and Vandenberg in turn influenced the pundit after World War II. It was not simply an effort to flatter a powerful politician that induced Lippmann to tell Vandenberg that his speech on April 27, 1948, was "pitch perfect." It "makes me wish more than ever that you could speak with full authority for the United States."[30] As with Dulles, there was not always perfect harmony between Vandenberg and his mentor, but he profited from the relationship. Indeed, it may be claimed that the profits were mutual.

PREPARING FOR SAN FRANCISCO

After receiving satisfactory responses to his reservations about accepting the president's invitation, Vandenberg gladly joined the delegation. The administration gave him what he wanted—freedom to express his own views, and presumably those of his party, and the addition ultimately of John Foster Dulles as adviser to the delegation. The senator would attend in his new capacity as a factor in the shaping of a new world order. His spirits were buoyed by the positive reactions he received to his amend-ments to the Dumbarton Oaks proposals.

But almost immediately, his old suspicions of the president's duplicity and of the wiles of Soviet diplomacy surfaced in the preliminary meetings of the American delegates before they flew off to San Francisco. What went on at Yalta was the crux of Vandenberg's problem, and yet it was not one that could be managed simply by public exposure. It was all the more difficult since a primary subject of Soviet manipulations at Yalta was Poland, a country whose cause Vandenberg had long championed out of respect for justice as much as for the votes of ethnic Poles in Michigan elections. As he told his friend Frank Januszewski, editor of Detroit's *Polish Daily News,* "I have not altered my view respecting Poland—both for her own precious sake and as a 'symbol.' I could get no greater personal satisfaction out of anything more than from joining—aye, in leading—a public denunciation of Yalta and all its works as respects Poland." But what deterred him was the fear that by indulging his passions he might endanger the cause of world peace that was the objective of Dumbarton Oaks and the San Francisco conference. If his actions should "dynamite the new Peace League," neither Poland nor the allies would benefit. While he would do his best to right the wrongs of Yalta he must respect the reali-ties of the Yalta decisions, particularly the "stamp of approval" from both Roosevelt and Churchill.[31]

Vandenberg did tell the editor that "I could have *refused* to sit as a Delegate at San Francisco as mute protest against what has happened." But if he had done that he would have lost any chance to redress the in-justice done to Poland. Januszewski responded that some of his friends would have preferred that he reject the president's invitation, but he sup-ported the senator's decision to accept and participate in the delibera-tions and accept compromise when necessary. But Januszewski insisted that "Yalta was not a compromise: it was an unconditional surrender." He hoped that with the Michigan senator at the conference the question of Poland would be kept open.[32]

He need not have worried about Vandenberg's continuing commit-ment to Poland's cause. Yalta was a red flag that would have impelled him to action whether or not Poland was the central issue. Despite the cautionary note he had articulated about recognizing the reality of the situation on the ground in Europe, the senator could not refrain from leading an attack on Roosevelt's "baffling secrecy which leaves us eternally uncertain of what 'deals' have been made." At a meeting with the delegates on March 23, the president surprised them with the information that Stalin had asked for six votes in the General Assembly to match Britain's six for the British Commonwealth. Roosevelt seemed to take pride in having talked Stalin into accepting three, instead of six, votes, in return for which the United States would also have three votes. This secret deal infuriated Vandenberg, if only because the nation was supposed to have had full knowledge of the arrangements the allies had made at Yalta. Moreover, this deal highlighted Britain's six votes in the assembly compared with only half that number for the United States. It was no surprise that Churchill signed off on this decision. Roosevelt asserted that the delegates, of course, were free to do as they pleased, since no formal commitment had been made, although he noted that he would vote for the deal if he were a delegate. The president was only adding salt to the wound.[33]

Vandenberg was sure that "this will *raise hell*." He was referring to the Senate, but he was ready to raise hell personally. He was offended that there had been no discussion with the delegates on the subject. The more he thought about the deal with Stalin for extra votes, the more agitated he became. It was unfair to smaller nations as well. The senator told the press on March 29 that "I would deeply disagree with any voting proposal . . . which would destroy the promised sovereign equality of nations in the Peace League's Assembly. . . . This applies as much to extra votes for us as for any other nation." The president's action implicitly committed the United States to supporting the three votes for the Soviet bloc, despite what Roosevelt said to Vice President Truman about the delegates being free agents with respect to the three additional votes. Truman appeared "flabbergasted" when he heard from Vandenberg that the delegates were free only to reject the three extra American votes.[34]

The senator faced a quandary. He would lose whichever course he followed. He responded to a correspondent who was worried about the effect of the San Francisco conference on the Republican Party: "If representatives of the Republican Party had declined the President's invitation, it would have been just about equivalent to committing suicide in public." He admitted that he wished he "had never been invited because the assignment inevitably becomes constrictive even though I did not accept until I had a warrant for free action." Given the goal of establishing a successful world organization, he felt it was his duty to meet his new obligations as best he could.[35]

Vandenberg may have exaggerated the risks he was taking. At least, they did not seem to faze him. As soon as he became a delegate, he intended to be heard at the conference and to place his own stamp on the proceedings. This initially took the form of eight amendments to the Dumbarton Oaks proposals, as revised by Dulles. The most prominent of them was the addition of a paragraph to Chapter 8, Section A: if the Security Council found that "any situation which it shall investigate involves injustice to peoples concerned it shall recommend appropriate measures of adjustment which may include revision of treaties and of prior international decisions." He was particularly concerned with the principles of justice and human rights, which were addressed in five of his eight amendments.[36]

He convinced his colleagues and the State Department to include the word "justice" in their proposals at the session and to give the General Assembly jurisdiction over measures to foster justice and human rights.[37] Getting these additions incorporated into the charter may have been less important to him than the opportunity to have his views aired and attended to. Rather than worrying about adverse political repercussions, he seemed to relish the prospect of challenging both the administration and the Soviet Union in San Francisco. And he seemed to enjoy the enmity of the Soviet press as much as he did his conflict with Roosevelt. Leo Pasvolsky, the State Department's Russian-born Soviet expert, assured him that Soviet press attacks "would not make him 'persona non grata' with the Russians. . . . Not at all—they respect a fighter—they liked to 'be told.'"[38] True or not, Vandenberg never seemed to mind being a target.

Parenthetically, he had doubts about the sincerity of the British ally regarding postwar boundaries. Britain did not need to make an explicit agreement with the Soviets to "make a shambles of the Atlantic Charter." Foreign Secretary Anthony Eden told him personally that no arrangement was made on boundaries: "All Britain had to do is to silently acquiesce in the present territorial aspiration voiced at Moscow. . . . We may well discover (too late) that we were not sufficiently specific when the President laid out our primary partnership with our Allies."[39]

The senator was prepared to challenge both Roosevelt and the Soviets before the delegates convened in San Francisco. He had made his displeasure with Roosevelt's policies public on March 29 after the *New York Herald-Tribune* broke the story about the "extra" votes in the assembly. The upshot was reluctant acceptance in San Francisco of the Soviets' three extra votes and rejection of the offer of three for the United States, a moral position that Vandenberg felt took off some of the curse from Roosevelt's behavior at Yalta.[40]

THE SAN FRANCISCO CONFERENCE, APRIL 25–JUNE 26, 1945

The primary objective of the conference was to flesh out the bare bones of the Dumbarton Oaks recommendations. After the opening ceremony at the San Francisco Opera House, the delegates were divided into four commissions, each devoted to a section of the Dumbarton Oaks proposals, and twelve committees, each dealing with specific subjects. To provide order, a steering committee composed of the chairmen of each delegation was created, but an executive committee of fourteen effectively directed daily activities. In addition to the formal arrangements there was the informal but more powerful evening meetings of the Big Four delegates on the Security Council (Great Britain, the United States, the Soviet Union, and China). As host nation the United States presided over these gatherings, where the most important issues were decided.[41]

As the opening day for the conference drew near, the senator was uneasy about the Soviet attitude. How serious was its commitment to the concept of a world organization? Two signs were not positive. One was an insistence in the first week of April that the Soviet-controlled Lublin government be Poland's representative in San Francisco, and ultimately in the new league, to the exclusion of the London-based government. A second source of skepticism about Soviet interest was the downgrading of the conference by the assignment of the young diplomat Andrei Gromyko, instead of Foreign Minister Vyacheslav Molotov, as a delegate.[42] Still, it was obvious that the Russians did not want to leave the world stage to the Americans. Molotov did go to San Francisco.

The issue of Polish representation was more difficult but the Soviets backed off from their demands during the first week of the conference, presumably in the face of the strong objections of Secretary of State Stettinius. He was backed by the furious warnings of Senator Vandenberg that "if any such action had been taken it would have wrecked *any* chance of American approval of the work of the Conference." It was the Senate's approval that concerned Vandenberg: "I was sitting directly behind Stettinius. I told him *this* move *must* be *killed* at once and in the open. I sketched out a quick, brief statement and handed it to Stettinius." He went on to note that Molotov was amazed at the passion the Americans expressed. The Soviet foreign minister ultimately acquiesced in a motion from the Belgian foreign minister, Paul-Henri Spaak, postponing a decision until a new Polish government, more democratically represented, was organized. This success convinced the senator that "we have to stand our ground against these Russian demands and *quit appeasing Stalin and Molotov.*"[43] Vandenberg's tentative optimism in the first week of the sessions was undergirded by the position President Truman took on the future of the conference.

President Roosevelt died on April 12, less than two weeks before the conference was to convene. He had planned to attend and speak. Vandenberg was relieved both by Truman's quick decision to have the conference proceed as scheduled and by his decision to stay at home and leave the running of the American delegation to Secretary of State Stettinius. Truman lifted Vandenberg's spirits by declining "even to wink at a surrender to Stalin on his demand for representation here for the Lublin Poles."[44]

Truman had been a colleague of Vandenberg in the Senate and, while not an intimate, was on good terms with the Michigan Republican. The president shared his views on the Soviet Union. Vandenberg rejoiced that "FDR's appeasement of Russia is over. We will 'play ball' gladly with the Russians and 'give and take' because we *must* have unity for the sake of peace *but* it is no longer going to be all 'give' and no 'take' so far as we are concerned." Stettinius then said to him, "*If you* had been talking about Poland to Molotov not even *you* could have made a stronger statement than Truman did."[45] In light of this praise it was not surprising that Stettinius received higher marks for his leadership from Vandenberg than from other members of the U.S. delegation or from the press.

Vandenberg had a right to be pleased with himself. He was a powerful figure in San Francisco. He and Connally had left Washington together to bipartisan acclaim, as senators "on both sides of the aisle were getting to their feet, clapping their hands in violation of Senate rules."[46] The two leaders would share the chairmanship of the U.S. delegation when Stettinius was absent. The common hope for success where Woodrow Wilson had failed did dampen to some degree their denunciations of the USSR. They did not want to have the Soviet delegation walk out of the conference. The future of the new world order was at stake.

It was a heady experience for Vandenberg. The ceremonial plenary meetings of the conference were at the ornate San Francisco Opera House, but the most important activities were at the elegant Fairmont Hotel, where Stettinius occupied a luxurious penthouse suite. Vandenberg's office and suite were on the fourth floor of the hotel, where he not only had a front-row seat at a critical moment in history but was himself a key player in the drama that unfolded. He was chairman of the Committee on Regional Arrangements.[47]

There was never any doubt about his enjoying the "daily battles," a term he used regularly in his diary. When he first met Molotov in Stettinius's penthouse in a private conference on April 27, Molotov flattered him, "greeting me with a very genial smile and said he 'knew all about me.'"[48] The senator took this remark as a compliment concerning his vigorous defense of America's interests and his combative positions regarding Soviet ambitions. The first combat was over Soviet demands for rotation of the presidency of the conference among the permanent members of the Security Council. Molotov preferred to have four chairmen, symbolizing, according to Vandenberg, Russia's obsession with equality. British foreign minister Anthony Eden brokered a compromise, establishing four rotating chairmen, but with Stettinius as chairman of the chairmen.[49] Although the Russians claimed victory, in reality the United States had its way; Stettinius was in effect the head of the conference. It was the appropriate place for the host nation.

But this was just the opening skirmish. Vandenberg was certain that the Soviets were trying to attack the West piecemeal, as Hitler had done, with Poland as their first prize. The concession of three votes for the Soviet bloc—Roosevelt's unfortunate concession at Yalta—would have to be accepted, but nothing more. White Russia and the Ukraine would join the new league, as promised, but whether they would be seated at this conference, as demanded by the Russians, was another matter. Vandenberg feared a new Munich if further concessions were made. But following Truman's instructions, the delegation planned to vote for their seating despite the senator's warnings. This was the logical consequence of U.S. acceptance of the three Soviet republics in the United Nations. Vandenberg's was the lone negative vote in the U.S. delegation, in opposition to his colleagues.[50]

That the Soviets were violating the understandings reached at Yalta was obvious; they were determined to keep the territories they liberated and occupied during World War II under their control. It was equally obvious that they were outnumbered in San Francisco and at a disadvantage in advancing their agenda. The three extra votes, even combined with those of their Czech and Yugoslav colleagues, were dwarfed by the votes of the forty-five other states, the vast majority following the positions of the Western powers. Soviet isolation was particularly evident in the controversy over the three extra votes for its bloc.

The U.S. delegation's agreement to seat White Russia and the Ukraine, with Vandenberg as the lone dissenter, was not the end of the matter. Stettinius had to be sure that the Latin American bloc would go along with the American arrangement. But the twenty republics imposed their own terms in exchange for their votes. They asked that Argentina be admitted to the General Assembly. Predictably, the Soviets objected on the understandable grounds that Argentina had delayed declaring war against Germany—a prerequisite for membership in the UN—almost to the end and that Fascist elements in its government accounted for a pro-German stance. Although the Soviet position found some sympathy among the delegations, Argentina was admitted in plenary session by a vote of thirty-two to four, whereas White Russia and the Ukraine were accepted unanimously. Latin American support for Argentina was based less on a sense of regional solidarity than on unhappiness over being taken for granted by the United States. Canadian diplomat Escott Reid was annoyed at what he considered the pettiness of so much of the wrangling. He felt that "things were badly handled during the first week—silly fights over chairmanships and Argentina, on the latter of which the Russians put the western powers badly in the wrong."[51]

As for Vandenberg's role, he modestly disclaimed the credit that newspapers were bestowing on him as the key figure in confronting and defeating Molotov over Poland and Argentina. The *Washington Times Herald* reported that "it looks as if the entire history of the conference may revolve around a battle of wits between these two men—it is the hand of Vandenberg that is generally discerned in US moves on [the] Conference chessboard." He dismissed this accolade by saying that "this isn't true. But I *have* had my part in it." But he could not conceal a note of satisfaction in being identified as the essential leader of the U.S. delegation. Presiding over the delegation's full press conference the next day, with—as he noted—"about 600 newspapermen" in attendance, he admitted that "some decisions have been made which were repugnant to me. But these events cannot be segregated into air-tight compartments and judged exclusively on their own merits. They must be weighed in connection with the *total* situation." He was not going to let the conference fail over what he ultimately felt were lesser issues. The framing of a charter for the United Nations was too important to allow the Soviet-American conflicts to doom the mission.[52]

Yet conflicts continued to threaten the conference. They were not limited to Americans and Russians. They also involved nations outside the circles of power. The veto power of the Big Five (the Big Four plus France) was a persistent grievance to the smaller nations and often exacerbated differences between the United States and the Soviet Union. Members of the British Commonwealth led the protests, with only modest results. Escott Reid, representing Canada as a middling power, was particularly exercised over the solidarity of the Big Five in using their veto power to override the choice of the General Assembly. The smaller powers included the Americans as their antagonists, even though the Russians were usually the greater offenders. Reid made the point that "life with the Russians is difficult, but life without them would be impossible."[53]

Controversy over the veto divided America from Russia throughout the sessions. For the Soviet Union the veto was its vehicle for survival in a hostile atmosphere, and it fought to defend its use at every opportunity. The Yalta agreements were clear on the authority of the permanent members over enforcement of Security Council decisions but ambiguous over procedural matters. Just what was procedural was the question. Led by Australian foreign minister Herbert V. Evatt, the smaller nations feared that a permanent member of the Security Council could block discussion of disputes. Stettinius carried Truman's message to permit freedom of discussion in the Security Council, with only the decision to act subject to the veto. The Russians wanted the veto to include even preliminary discussion and investigation of disputes by the Security Council. Vandenberg felt that "the 'veto' is bad enough under *any* circumstance. But when it can stop the whole process of peaceful inquiry, it becomes, at this point, utterly indefensible." The senator backed the "bitter fight" of Canada, Australia, and New Zealand to "change the 'veto' in this *one* particular."[54]

Among the most sensitive issues bothering Vandenberg was how to preserve the Monroe Doctrine—now expanded to cover the hemisphere by the Act of Chapultepec, signed in Mexico City on March 18, 1945—from being affected by the veto. The sanctity of the Monroe Doctrine had long been an article of Vandenberg's personal faith, alongside the constitutional powers of the U.S. Senate. The charter would legitimize regional organizations, but could collective action by the Pan American Union succeed if its acts could be vetoed in the Security Council? There was also the danger that other regional groups might subvert the goals of the UN if they formed aggressive blocs. Vandenberg's answer, applauded by the Latin American states, was that "we do not propose to desert the 100-year old Monroe Doctrine, the 50-year old Pan American Union, and the recent Act of Chapultepec, but that we do not propose to give regional arrangements any such supremacy as will destroy the unity of the world organization and invite a general break-up of the world into regional groups."[55]

To satisfy the Senate's probable insistence that Chapultepec be protected in the event that it was not specifically included in the charter, Vandenberg noted that "the Senate (with my approval) will attach an interpretation saying that we construe the language to specifically include Chapultepec." He concluded that the best course to follow would be "to use the general language in the Charter (so as not to invite a lot of other regional identifications some of which would be obnoxious), then to pass a Delegation Resolution notifying the Senate of our interpretation."[56]

The ultimate solution lay in Article 51 of the charter, affirming the inherent right of collective defense if an armed attack occurred against a member nation, until the Security Council took the necessary measures to maintain international peace and security. Political scientist Philip Briggs believed that "the inclusion of article 51 in the United Nations Charter had allowed Vandenberg to maintain his strong nationalistic position regarding existing American regional commitments, while at the same time supporting collective security and internationalism." Article 51 was for Vandenberg, therefore, "the perfect compromise." As the North Atlantic Treaty was being framed in 1948, the senator saw Article 51 as "a new formula under which the United Nations Charter can be *made to work without* Charter amendments which manifestly are unattainable under existing UN circumstances and membership. . . . It is a formula which faithfully lives *within* the Charter but *outside the veto*."[57]

But this harmonizing of the Monroe Doctrine with the charter did not resolve other problems at San Francisco, notably whether Big Five members could veto even discussion of a question brought to the Security Council. Andrei Gromyko, representing the Soviet Union after Molotov returned to Moscow, left the United States with a dilemma. How much could the United States concede to have the Russians sign the charter? As Vandenberg put it, "My view is that we *must* get a Charter whether Russia likes it or not. It is desperately important that she should sign. But it is no less important that *we* should not stultify our souls."[58]

Stettinius, speaking for the White House, then asked Connally and Vandenberg what they thought of having Ambassador Harriman in Moscow ask Stalin if he would be satisfied with the conference simply recording "the different interpretations which we put on the Yalta 'veto' formula." The assumption was that Stalin would not yield on his veto stand. "I instantly replied that it was impossible," Vandenberg wrote, "that it would not only leave the vital Charter question in doubt but also actually would give Stalin the very 'veto' for which he is contending; and that it would be a 'climax of humiliation' for the United States. Connally (less vigorously) agreed." So did Stettinius and the State Department. The United States faced down the Soviets, and Vandenberg exulted on June 7, "*America Wins!* The 'Veto' Crisis broke Today—and it broke *our* way." The Soviets would not stand in the way of hearing discussion of any dispute brought before the Security Council.[59]

The Soviets, however, were not finished with their demands. With the veto issue in the Security Council settled, they sought to limit the assembly's authority to engage in unrestricted discussion. Their proposal failed by a vote of forty-two to zero, with Russia abstaining. Vandenberg proudly noted in his diary that that it was his initiative that was instrumental in giving the assembly the power to discuss and recommend regarding "'the peaceful adjustment of *any* situations, *regardless of origin,* which it deems likely to impair the general welfare, etc.' This is *my* paragraph—and the basis for my claim that we are proposing to make the Assembly 'tomorrow's town meeting of the world' (a phrase which is constantly being quoted and which seems destined to *live*)." His insistence that all sections of the charter be open to debate prevailed. The Soviets conceded on June 20. Vandenberg felt that his success justified the importance of standing up to the Russians.[60]

The San Francisco conference was never solely a contest between the Americans and the Russians. The smaller nations, as noted, intended to be heard, and they were heard. They were unhappy with the veto power in the hands of the Big Five, but this was a power that both the Soviet Union and the United States demanded. Despite Vandenberg's deeply felt objections to the veto in general, he would not recommend any action that conceivably could infringe upon the Senate's constitutional authority in matters of war and peace and on the status of treaties or upon the ultimate veto powers of the five permanent members of the Security Council. He can properly claim authorship of the charter's Article 14—the Vandenberg amendment—that contained the General Assembly's right to recommend measures for the peaceful adjustment of any situation, regardless of origin. Yet there was a caveat in this article, referring to Article 12's limiting the General Assembly's power to make recommendations with respect to questions under consideration by the Security Council.[61]

This was the basis of his opposition to New Zealand's proposed unlimited right of the assembly to consider anything within the sphere of international relations, eventually phrased—because of a Soviet demand—as "within the scope of the present Charter." Vandenberg feared that allowing concurrent authority to two organs would change the whole concept of Dumbarton Oaks and require the rewriting of the charter. It was also an example of consensus between two major powers at the expense of the smaller powers.[62]

As the conference drew to a close, Vandenberg reiterated that the assembly had "no power to review treaties and none was ever intended." He believed that if this were permitted, "it would have meant interminable debate." The most he would concede was the right of the General Assembly to review "CONDITIONS" that might necessitate revising some treaty terms—"that is to say, the power to RECOMMEND the revision of CONDITIONS."[63] His language should have been vague enough to forestall any Soviet criticism; the Russians would not disagree with this limitation on assembly powers. Vandenberg never fully recognized that this position was not in the spirit of his frequent perorations against the veto. But it was in keeping with his conception of America's national interest.

POSTSCRIPT TO SAN FRANCISCO

The San Francisco conference, adjourning on June 25, produced a mixed record. The differences between the United States and the Soviet Union remained unsettled and always potentially toxic. The smaller nations had no choice except to accept the decisions of the Big Five, particularly over the veto. And while they generally lined up behind the United States, it was not always an easy alignment. They were well aware of the limits of solidarity with the Americans. Their objections would have been more vigorously expressed had the Soviets not appeared to be a more dangerous adversary. Vandenberg understood their concerns, but he also recognized that these concerns had to be subsumed under the imperatives of American national interest, whether it be the defense of the Big Five's veto or any other concession that might jeopardize passage of the charter in the U.S. Senate.

Yet the mood on the part of the American participants at the end of the two months of deliberations in the San Francisco conference was one of exhilaration, and for Vandenberg this mood increased as the summer of 1945 went on. The conferees felt that they succeeded in fleshing out the relatively vague recommendations of the Dumbarton Oaks Conference. The senator envisioned the opening of a way to a new world order. Writing in the New York Times a few months later, he confessed to wondering "during the first week or two how it could be humanly possible for any consolidated point of view to issue from such piebald forms." Crisis after crisis followed from debates over the Yalta voting formula, but they all passed despite being "lugubriously greeted by the press as representing the imminent breakup of the whole adventure. But a unanimous report emerged. The United Nations remained united." He admitted that there were compromises that were inevitable in any such body. It took two months of continuous contact, staying at the table until they reached an agreement—none of the preceding wartime conferences had this advantage.[64]

The summer of 1945 was a euphoric time for the senator. The bitter strife with the Soviets was set aside at this time. Instead, he showered praise on his colleagues. He began with the chairman of the U.S. delegation, Secretary of State Stettinius, "who has done a magnificent job. Without his 'drive' we should have been here for two more months." He was serious in his regard for the secretary's performance and expressed his regret when the president announced his replacement as secretary of state on July 8, although the fact that he was going to be replaced was known before their return to Washington. James F. Byrnes, Vandenberg's former Senate colleague from South Carolina and most recently a Supreme Court justice, was his successor. Vandenberg was particularly upset by the abrupt and ungracious way Stettinius was shunted aside to an inferior post as a delegate to the new world organization, from which he resigned in November 1945.[65]

With only a touch of condescension he commended the navy commander and former Minnesota governor Harold Stassen as "one of the ablest young men I have ever known." He paid tribute to Dr. Leo Pasvolsky, special assistant to the secretary of state, for his encyclopedic knowledge of Soviet affairs. He reserved his most extravagant praise for Dulles, "the most valuable man in our entire American set-up. I do not know what we should have done without him."[66]

Vandenberg and Connally returned to Washington on June 28, to be greeted with the same emotional response from the Senate that they received when they left for San Francisco on April 20. Senators from both parties rose in violation of Senate rules to applaud them on both occasions. Vandenberg had seconded Connally's promise to work on a nonpartisan basis, without illusions that "the conference can chart the millennium." Now Connally could claim that the promise was kept. Packed galleries shared the excitement of the senators. A brass band met the delegation as it arrived at National Airport. And when Connally and Vandenberg entered the Senate chamber arm-in-arm, the contrast with the experience of Wilson returning from Paris in 1919 was striking.[67]

Appropriately, as chairman of the Foreign Relations Committee Connally addressed the Senate first on June 28, declaring that "the Conference provided a system of collective security without imposing a superstate." He did not claim to have brought home a perfect document, but the charter represented "a significant beginning. . . . The eyes of the entire world are centered on what we do here. . . . The world charter of peace is knocking at the doors of the Senate. We shall not turn it away." Vandenberg matched Connally's hopes in his own speech the next day, praising his rival for allowing the minority representatives "to play our full role in the deliberations. . . . He was a tower of strength."[68]

Vandenberg's sentiments about the promise of the charter were fully expressed in his heartfelt report to the Senate on June 29: "I have signed the San Francisco Charter. I believe it represents a great forward step toward the international understanding and cooperation and fellowship which are indispensable to peace, progress and security. If the spirit of its authors can become the spirit of its evolution I believe it will bless the earth. I believe it serves the intelligent self-interest of our own United States which knows, by bitter experience in the Valley of the Shadow of two wars in a quarter of a century, that we cannot live entirely unto ourselves alone."[69]

The wording contains the usual florid rhetoric, but it also expresses the essence of Vandenberg's conversion to internationalism. He "would support the ratification of this charter with all the resources at my command." Despite obvious "infirmities" in the document, "I shall do it because peace must not be cheated of its only collective chance." In light of his frequent denunciations of the Yalta formula and Roosevelt's collaboration with the Soviets in producing it, he denounced the charter's serious mistakes yet was ready to say that "there is no other plan available. . . . In any effective organization for peace and security in the world as it is and as it's going to be for some time to come—whether we like it or not—the Great Powers must assume special and particular responsibilities . . . there is no other way." So the afterglow of San Francisco encompassed the Soviet Union, at least in the summer of 1945.[70]

Inevitably, critics would call on Vandenberg to defend his putative justification of the Yalta concessions. To the editor of a suburban Detroit weekly on August 29, he claimed to "have no illusions about the San Francisco Charter. I agree that the ultimate answer largely depends upon the Soviets' attitudes. I also agree that there are numerous phases of the peace settlements which I do not like and which offend my sense of justice." But having admitted these caveats, he was "unable to see that any of these situations argue against a trial of the San Francisco Charter which—regardless of all these other anxieties—is the best promise that the world has ever had for the creation of international security." This was the message that he had given to the Detroit Economic Club a month before: the charter "represents a great, forward step toward the international understanding and co-operation and fellowship which are indispensable to peace, prosperity and security."[71]

Given the harmony that prevailed in the Senate following the return of the delegates, it is not surprising that Connally would convene hearings as quickly as possible. He justifiably assumed that the hearings, open to dissenting witnesses, would be quickly completed with ratification to follow. He was correct in his assumptions. Still, there could be obstacles ahead. Vandenberg reported to Dulles some of the scenarios he had heard, including "the *possibility* that Hawaii, Alaska, and the District of Columbia might become some sort of statistical wards for the new international organization." The *Chicago Tribune,* hostile to the charter and a consistent adversary of Vandenberg, used these examples of hidden threats to America's sovereignty.[72]

While he felt that Dulles "will smile (perhaps noisily)" at such a distant prospect, the advocates of the charter could not ignore the potential conflict between the constitutional requirement granting Congress the exclusive right to declare war and the president's authority to decide whether the use of force fell within his own constitutional prerogatives as commander in chief. "But," he added, "it seems to me that we have substantially met this dual problem (involving the constitutional functions of both the President and the Congress) if we clearly make the Delegate the statutory agent of both Congress and the White House."[73]

These concerns did not materialize in the hearings, which began on July 6 and concluded on July 15, opening with Leo Pasvolsky's detailed commentaries and closing with Dulles's expert observations as an international lawyer. Vandenberg intervened only rarely, such as when a hostile witness challenged Roosevelt's agreements at Yalta or to emphasize Dulles's role in winning Bishop Bromley Oxnam's approval of the charter. Oxnam was president of the Federal Council of Churches.[74]

The hearings were only a formality. Such opposition as did surface ranged from witnesses who saw the charter as a Communist plot to those who condemned it as insufficient and incomplete. What mattered to Vandenberg and Connally was the invisibility of isolationists and other Senate critics. All but two senators voted to ratify the charter. Vandenberg celebrated on July 28: "The battle is over . . . by a vote of 82 to 2! . . . It really was an amazing outcome."[75]

It was also his personal victory. With justifiable self-satisfaction he wrote to his wife that "everyone now seems to agree, I could have beaten the Charter if I had taken the opposite tack. I must confess now that it is all over, that I am very proud to have been at least one of its fathers." By inserting "at least" into his confession, he displayed false modesty. He knew that he was a central if not the controlling figure in San Francisco and was the key to the Republican vote in the Senate on July 28. He reveled in the power he enjoyed. More than that, his experience in San Francisco had changed his life. From this time until his death in 1951 he identified himself with the United Nations and its charter. Not that he was without qualms about the organization's future: "Heaven only knows whether the Charter will 'work.' I *think* it will. If not, *nothing* would."[76]

If a specific time can be identified for Vandenberg's conversion to internationalism, it would not be the trauma of Pearl Harbor in December 1941 or the impact of his speech in January 1945. Rather, June 1945 is a better fit; it is the point when he came to recognize both the primacy of the United Nations in America's future and his own role in making that future possible. Notwithstanding his many reservations, his appointment to the American delegation elevated his sense of his importance to the success of the San Francisco conference. He quickly put his own stamp on the charter in the form of the familiar Vandenberg amendments that had characterized his contributions to Senate proceedings in the three terms he had served as a Michigan senator. The United Nations, and especially its charter, became his property over the next five years.

Arguably, his conversion met Acheson's sardonic and only superficially accurate description of his "political transubstantiation" that required his personal touch before it become "a true doctrine worthy of all men to be received."[77] Helping to align American foreign policy with the terms of the UN Charter was a manifestation of his conversion.

George C. Marshall (*third from right*) shakes hands with Senator Tom Connally of Texas, as Senator Arthur Vandenberg of Michigan (*left*), President Harry S. Truman (*second from right*), and James Byrnes (*far right*) look on, on the occasion of Marshall's swearing in as secretary of state in the Oval Office, January 21, 1947. (National Park Service, Abbie Rowe, courtesy of Harry S. Truman Library)

The signing of the UN Charter in San Francisco, 1947. President Truman, Secretary of State Edward Stettinius Jr., and Connally stand at left while Vandenberg signs the document. (Bentley Historical Library)

Vandenberg (*in bow tie*) and General George Marshall (*in light-colored suit*) step off a plane, being met by Truman and George Marshall. (Bentley Historical Library)

Senator Arthur M. Vandenberg, Republican of Michigan, relaxing, March 1939.
(Harris & Ewing, photographers, Library of Congress)

1940 GOP hopefuls in Washington, D.C. The American Society of Newspaper Editors dinner at the Willard Hotel on April 21 commanded a goodly crop of forty possibilities, and here a few on the GOP side talk with William Allen White, Emporia, Kansas, editor and president of the society. *Left to right:* White, Senator Robert A. Taft of Ohio, Thomas E. Dewey, and Vandenberg. (Harris & Ewing, photographers, Library of Congress)

Vandenberg wades through piles of newspapers as he relaxes at home during the evening, July 17, 1939. The senator liked to keep his hand on the pulse of the nation by reading newspapers. (Harris & Ewing, photographers, Library of Congress)

Members of the delegations to the United Nations Conference on International Organization gather for a discussion. At the extreme left is James C. Dunn, U.S. assistant secretary of state, an advisor. The others, all delegates, are (*left to right*): U.S. Representative Charles A. Eaton; U.S. Representative Sol Bloom; Vandenberg; U.S. Senator Tom Connally; former French prime minister Joseph Paul-Boncour; the Earl of Halifax, British ambassador to the United States; U.S. Secretary of State Edward R. Stettinius Jr., chairman of the U.S. delegation; Andrei A. Gromyko, Soviet ambassador to the United States; and V. K. Wellington Koo, Chinese ambassador to Britain. The conference opened April 25, 1945, in San Francisco. Representatives of fifty nations met at the parley to set up the structure of a world security organization. (U.S. National Archives and Records Administration)

Secretary of State Dean Acheson (*right*) discusses the Far East at a prolonged session of the Senate Foreign Relations Committee, January 10, 1950. Talking with the secretary during a recess in the hearing are Vandenberg (*left*) and Connally (*center*), chairman of the committee. (U.S. National Archives and Records Administration)

Vandenberg (*center*), with Senator J. William Fulbright (D-AR) (*left*) and Senator Thomas C. Hart (R-CT) (*right*), looks over a transcript of the vigorous speech he gave in the Senate on June 29, 1945. (U.S. National Archives and Records Administration)

Vandenberg (*left*) and Connally, as part of the Committee of Foreign Affairs of the U.S. Senate, meet to discuss NATO, April 27, 1949, in Paris. (New York Times Photos/U.S. National Archives and Records Administration)

7

The Senator as Diplomat, 1945–1946

Vandenberg's commitment to the United Nations was tested in the year following the San Francisco conference, when he spent 213 days at conference tables, primarily discussing the translation of the charter into reality, at the first meeting of the General Assembly in London, three times in Paris for the Council of Foreign Ministers, and at the second session of the General Assembly in New York at the end of 1946. Despite frustrations Moscow posed at every opportunity, despite his suspicions of the selfish interests of the Allies, and despite his annoyance with some of the tactics that the American delegation adopted, he emerged with greater conviction than before about the necessity of the UN's role in keeping the world's peace.

Inevitably, the euphoria arising from the San Francisco conference and the subsequent rapid ratification of the UN Charter in the Senate faded by September 1945. The problems facing the United States as it worked with the victorious Allies in shaping the United Nations organizations were daunting, as the senator knew they would be. But the challenges notwithstanding, Vandenberg was eager to accept President Truman's invitation to be a delegate, along with Senator Connally, to the first session of the United Nations General Assembly in London in January 1946. He told British newsmen upon his arrival in Southampton in January 1946, "I really had no right to come here for the Assembly, but having helped at the birth of the United Nations in 'Frisco, I wanted to be in on the christening. And I have a desperate feeling that this is the only thing left to save the world."[1] His words told readers how important his experience was in San Francisco and also how important he was in carrying out the message of San Francisco.

Even before he sailed to Britain he was aware of the challenges facing the nation, and those challenges had multiple origins. Primarily, they stemmed from his concerns that the Soviet partner was not only unreliable but hostile to America's objectives and hence subversive of the goals of the UN Charter. He envisioned problems with the Soviets over the future of Poland, Greece, Turkey, Iran, and particularly Germany. None of these fears was new. Conflicts with the Soviets at San Francisco were never settled, and they would revive in even more toxic form as the major powers tried to set ground rules for operating the new organization. Months before Winston Churchill popularized the term "iron curtain" to define the imprisonment of Eastern Europe, Vandenberg charged that "the iron curtain must be lifted in this world if there is to be any safe existence for humankind hereafter."[2]

He won notoriety in the Soviet press for the intensity of his criticism of Soviet policy. In 1947 an article in the *Saturday Evening Post* encapsulated his reputation among Communists with the title "Russia's Pet Whipping Boy." He had become "one of Moscow's pet villains, ranking between Winston Churchill and the Vatican." When Vandenberg learned that Soviet radio had devoted a solid fifteen minutes to denouncing him, his response was to say that "only the Pope has been similarly distinguished." It was unlikely that he was unhappy with the attention the Kremlin paid to him as its arch antagonist. The senator used Soviet hostility to bolster his reputation as a solid ally of Polish democrats. He speculated to the newspaper publisher Frank Januszewski when running for reelection in 1946 that "an eloquent and overwhelming rebuff to the Communist pledge to liquidate me next September would be the most powerful message that Polish-Americans would send to Moscow or to Warsaw."[3]

At all times, however, the senator was careful to avoid advocating a permanent break with the Soviet Union. The future of the United Nations required a continuing connection, as positive as possible, for its survival. "It is obvious that UNO (in its present form)," he asserted in April 1946, "depends upon the temperature of the Soviet-American relationship. I do not despair of these relationships if we say what we mean and mean what we say. . . . I would sum it up in two words—'friendly firmness.' We cannot blame Moscow for thinking it can 'push us around' because this is precisely what happened during the war in all the Stalin-Roosevelt contacts."[4] It was understandable up to a point for Roosevelt to appease the Russians, given his fear that they might withdraw from the war and make a separate peace with the Nazis. Vandenberg himself sought a long-term agreement with the Soviets to prevent the reemergence of German militarism. That proposal was featured in his seminal speech of January 10, 1945.

But almost as a reprise of his observations in San Francisco, he deplored the "lessons we then taught the Russians to believe, namely: that 'appeasement' was a cardinal factor in our attitudes toward the Kremlin. I feel quite sure that when Russia learns that the 'appeasement days' are over . . . that we intend to be equally just to Russia herself when 'justice' is on her side—she will realize it is not impossible for us to learn to live together in reasonable amity despite the inevitable rivalry between our ideologies." Only his consistent conviction that "collective security is the only hope of the world" kept his pessimism in check about the aims and tactics of the Soviet adversary.[5] The fate of the UN was too precarious to be sacrificed by Russian defection from the organization. He deplored this need to accommodate the Soviets, a consequence of Roosevelt's putative appeasement of Stalin at Yalta and at other summit conferences during World War II.

CONTENDING WITH SECRETARY OF STATE BYRNES

Rather than blame the circumstances that created tensions between the United States and the Soviet Union, Vandenberg put much of the responsibility on the Truman administration and on Secretary of State James Byrnes for their unwillingness to stand up to the Russians. As a former colleague in the Senate, Byrnes appeared to Vandenberg as too typical a politician, comfortable with the compromises politicians make. It did not help the two men's relations that the Michigan senator felt Stettinius to have been unfairly treated and summarily removed from his post as secretary of state in favor of Byrnes. Not that he disliked Byrnes, at least not before they went to London. As he told his wife, "Jimmy Byrnes is a grand guy (for any *other* job down here.) But his whole life has been a career in compromise. . . . Just as we have, at long last, got Russia to understand (through Stettinius) that we occasionally mean what we say, Stettinius gets the axe and Jimmy (who helped surrender at Yalta) comes back in!"[6]

Byrnes began his tenure as secretary of state on the wrong foot. Even though he was appointed just a few days before leaving with the president for the Potsdam Conference on July 16, he should have found time to consult key senators. Vandenberg was further miffed, as was his Democratic counterpart, Tom Connally, by Byrnes ignoring them in the development of a joint Anglo-Canadian-American proposal on international control of atomic energy. Byrnes also failed to consult with them in planning American policy at meetings of the Council of Foreign Ministers at London and Moscow in December 1945.[7] They were subsequently appalled at Byrnes's intention to share scientific information with Russia in the course of setting up an atomic commission under UN auspices. Vandenberg noted that the Committee of Foreign Relations, along with members of the Atomic Bomb Committee, were "opposed to giving any of the atomic secrets away unless and until the Soviets are prepared to be 'policed' by UNO in respect to this prohibition."[8]

Meeting with the president on December 11, 1945, Vandenberg and his colleagues on the Foreign Affairs Committee were distressed to see the contents of the mission Truman had assigned to Byrnes. It confirmed their fears that the secretary would be giving away too much without reciprocal concessions from the Soviets. Four consecutive steps were to be taken, with "inspection" and "control" left for last. The plan felt all the more deplorable when it seemed that the president failed to grasp its implications. Vandenberg felt that the Byrnes formula had to be stopped. Vandenberg and his colleagues understood that the course the president and secretary of state were following reflected their refusal to play "atomic diplomacy." Still, to Vandenberg this behavior was a continuation of the appeasement that he hoped had ended in San Francisco.[9]

There were other factors at play, including the administration's surprising disrespect for the prerogatives of the Senate. Beyond all other considerations was an election in 1946, when Michigan voters might disapprove of their senator's attachment to a flawed atomic policy. The pall that fell over the State Department's relations with the Senate also affected other significant areas of foreign relations. Vandenberg knew that his Republican colleagues would not support a postwar loan to Russia but feared that if Congress granted Britain an urgently needed loan and then denied one to Russia then the United States would have "made further cooperation among the Big Three practically impossible (which, incidentally, would be the end of UNO)." He was willing to take that risk "regardless of logic or mathematics or other *rational* considerations. I have a feeling that we ought to 'go along' with this loan for the sake of some nebulous affinity which the English speaking world must maintain in mutual self-defense." He was as good as his word. The Senate approved the loan on May 10, 1946, by forty-six votes to thirty, after Vandenberg gave his approval. But he was right to worry about reactions in Michigan. His vote in favor of the British loan was unpopular with his constituents.[10]

The senator's dissatisfaction with the administration's policies might have jeopardized his acceptance of an appointment on December 21 as a delegate to the UN General Assembly meeting in London, scheduled for January 10, 1946. Opposed as he was to Byrnes's atomic initiatives, he notified the president that he would "resign rather than run counter to these instructions."[11] His conversion to a bipartisan policy to champion the cause of the United Nations was a primary factor in his acceptance of the assignment. Duty to the nation and devotion to the UN transcended, or at least modified, his party loyalties. As he put it on the eve of his departure for London, "The fact remains that I am reluctant to leave at this particularly difficult moment. I would not think of it if I did not have a deep conviction that—regardless of all domestic troubles—nothing is remotely comparable to the importance of stopping World War III before it starts if this is humanly possible." Because the UN was the only hope for the development of "international peace, security, and justice . . . it is my first duty to see this through."[12] His sense of his own importance in solving atomic and other problems combined with a patriotic duty to keep him involved in the conduct of American foreign policy.

In London Vandenberg worried about whether the firmness of Byrnes's objections to Soviet violations of the Yalta agreements, particularly with respect to a free Poland, seemed justified. The Soviet promise of equality between the London-based Polish government and the Soviet-controlled Lublin government was never kept. It was British foreign minister Ernest Bevin rather than Byrnes who condemned the Soviets, a fact that annoyed the senator. Elections were rigged to guarantee victory of the Lublin government. Even more ominous was the arrest of London Poles who returned to their homeland. There were minor successes in London. Despite a Soviet veto, Stettinius, no longer secretary of state but head of the American delegation to London, submitted a resolution to the General Assembly seeking removal of unwanted troops on foreign soil. The British and French voluntarily accepted the terms of the resolution and removed their troops from Syria and Lebanon.[13] But this was small consolation in light of Soviet obstruction.

Vandenberg was always concerned about the United States giving away atomic information before adequate safeguards were in place. He was troubled by Byrnes's acceptance of separate stages in the new UN Atomic Energy Commission's progress toward control of the atom. Presumably "the successful completion of each [stage] will develop the necessary confidence of the world before the next stage is undertaken." The result of this arrangement was that the issue of safeguards would not be reached until the first three stages—exchange of information, control of atomic energy, and elimination of atomic weapons—had been settled. The senator dissented. He foresaw that an exchange of information might be made before a system of effective inspection had been achieved. His mistrust of Soviet motives was obvious. This was not the intention of the agreement in Moscow, which incorporated a declaration of the United States, Britain, and Canada made in Washington on November 15, 1945. To overcome Vandenberg's suspicions, the official gloss on these four stages claimed that there was no intention to direct the commission to deal with the four subjects separately and the commission was left free to consider each subject in any order it saw fit. So the State Department assured Vandenberg.[14]

In his recollections of this issue Byrnes told of inviting Vandenberg and Connally to dinner. When Vandenberg expressed doubts about the safeguards provided for in the atomic resolution, Byrnes pointed out that the language of the draft was "precisely that agreed upon in the previous November by Prime Ministers Clement Attlee, Mackenzie King, of Canada, and President Truman." Moreover, he reminded them that he and Connally had been present when the statement was made public and had approved it. Vandenberg then admitted that the newspaper story emanating from Moscow had misled him. Byrnes was convinced that "if

Vandenberg had been with us in Moscow there would not have been any misunderstanding on the subject, and from that day to the end of my service as Secretary I insisted upon his accompanying us to every international conference. Senator Connally and I had no serious differences with him."[15]

Vandenberg did not share Byrnes's memories. He returned from London no more satisfied with the secretary's conduct than he had been before he left. As for Connally, he was aligned with Vandenberg, not with the secretary of state The Michigan senator's speech on January 27, 1946, offered his impressions of the UN meeting in London to the Senate. He felt that his reactions were important enough for him to address his colleagues before Connally returned from London. Prolix as ever despite his intention of presenting "a brief report," he returned to Washington "with no illusion that automatic peace awaits the world just because the machinery of the United Nations is now in gear." Although he noted that in the thirty-seven days that the General Assembly met the delegates gave life to the charter, until then "a scrap of paper," he warned against a resumption of power politics—by the United States as well as by the Soviet Union. But he clearly singled out the Soviets as obstructing the work of the UN and asked the question raised throughout the world: "What is Russia up to now?" The answer "has a vital bearing on the destiny of the United Nations." He noted that the two contending ideologies must learn to live together in harmony but only "if the United States speaks as plainly on all occasions as Russia does; if the United States just as vigorously sustains its own purposes and ideals upon all occasions as Russia does; if we abandon the miserable fiction, often encouraged by our own fellow travelers, that we somehow jeopardize the peace if our candor is as firm as Russia's always is; and if we assume a moral leadership we have too frequently allowed to lapse."[16]

There was no doubt about the implied criticism of the secretary of state. Vandenberg's praise of Senator Connally for his "sterling services in" London did not extend to Secretary Byrnes, whose name was not mentioned in the speech. He conspicuously omitted Byrnes's role at the General Assembly even as he praised Bevin and Georges Bidault, the French foreign minister, as well as Connally. Even his antagonist, Andrei Vishinski, the chief Soviet delegate to the UN, earned the sobriquet of "brilliant."[17] A week later Stettinius noted that "Vandenberg is pretty sore on not being taken into camp a little more, not only in London but in Washington too. He and Jimmy are not getting on all too well. . . . I think it is a two-edged sword. Van always talks collaboration. He says collaboration at present is just being told about it right before it goes into the newspaper. . . . In his private talks he does not think well of Truman but blames Jimmy for this lack of cooperation."[18]

But the estrangement was coming to an end, after Byrnes seemed to acknowledge Vandenberg's reproofs the following day by denouncing Soviet aggression in language as strong as the senator's had been. Byrnes included the statement that "if we are to be a great power, we must act as a great power." Vandenberg praised his "evangelical speech." And less than a month later in Grand Rapids he endorsed "the new American approach which was voiced in the most courageous candor of our own Secretary of State Byrnes. I hope it is not too late. I applaud and sustain him in this new vigor."[19] From March 1946 until Byrnes's retirement in January 1947, bipartisanship in foreign policy flourished in the persons of Senator Vandenberg and Secretary Byrnes.

CONTROLLING THE ATOM

A primary source of Vandenberg's unhappiness over Secretary Byrnes's conduct of American foreign policy in 1945 was his position on the atom bomb. Controlling the atom seemed to the senator to be the most compelling issue facing the nation. It affected all the major challenges of the day as he saw them—the necessity of investing atomic control in the United Nations, the dangers of sharing atomic information with the Soviet adversary, and the inadequate leadership of the Truman administration in managing the problem.

Vandenberg's anxiety may have begun when he visited the White House before leaving for the San Francisco conference and noted Roosevelt's copy of his own speech of January 10, with his words heavily underlined: "If World War III unhappily arrives, it will open new laboratories of death too horrible to contemplate." Roosevelt then gestured toward the speech with the remark, "Senator, you have no idea how right you are, but you'll discover before the year is over." Although Vandenberg knew nothing of the atomic bomb at that moment, its revelation at Hiroshima and Nagasaki in August 1945 forced him to look at the implications of what he had theoretically considered too horrible to contemplate and fixed in his mind the indispensable potential the United Nations had to address the consequence of atomic power.[20]

The senator, as usual, did not retire into contemplation. He took action, always keeping in mind that the genie unleashed at Hiroshima threatened the very existence of civilization. His actions took three interconnected forms. First and foremost was his judgment that the United Nations was the only appropriate controller of the atom. Second was that the transfer of control from the United States to the United Nations must be accompanied by a system of constant inspection. This requirement reflected his fears that the Soviets in the UN would acquire new knowledge about the bomb unless the transfer was carefully managed. Third was his continuing worry both about the temptations in Congress to politicize the issue and the inability of the Truman administration to cope with Russian machinations. Vandenberg's concerns about the State Department's weakness in dealing with the atomic problem in the United Nations was at the heart of his quarrels with Byrnes in the fall of 1945 and the winter of 1946.

He was relieved to see an end to the bickering among congressional committees that would have oversight of atomic energy and was pleased to be the author of the resolution that established a special committee on atomic energy to settle the jurisdictional issue in the Senate. The senator subsequently supported the goals of the United Nations Atomic Energy Commission. He told a Michigan correspondent in March 1946 that "the use of atomic energy for military purposes should be *conclusively* prohibited everywhere." But to effect this result, care had to be taken to limit information about the American monopoly until a system of inspection would protect America's national security.[21]

In the fall of 1945 Vandenberg felt that the joint committee would coordinate legislative and executive plans and stop the congressional "rush to get somebody's pet bill reported." He had to navigate between the claims of the Military Affairs Committee, speaking for army interests in protecting atomic secrets, and the torrent of advice from the scientific community, much of it emanating from the Atomic Scientists of Chicago.

The scientists insisted that sharing the secrets of the bomb with the world would be a means of avoiding an armament race.[22]

This conflict over whether atomic power should remain a military weapon or be applied to peaceful civilian uses was seemingly settled by the Senate's appointment of Brian McMahon, a young and forceful Democratic senator from Connecticut, as chairman of the select committee. His bill, S. 1717, submitted on December 20, 1945, conformed with the president's judgment that the entire program should be under civilian control with a government monopoly of materials and facilities. Despite vigorous objections from Secretary of War Robert P. Patterson and the military's allies in Congress, the president repeated his support for civilian control in his State of the Union address of January 14, 1946, along with his hope that the United Nations would develop instruments to tame the atom.[23]

Vandenberg was as eager as McMahon to maintain civilian control of atomic energy and was even more supportive of the UN's role in the process. But McMahon was upset by the senator's amendment to his bill that would set up a military liaison board, putatively duplicating the proposed Atomic Energy Commission. The bill permitted the board access to all matters before the commission as well as the right to consult with the commission whenever it wished. Additionally, if it failed to reach an accord with the commission, the board would have the right of appeal to the president on any action by the commission that affected national defense.[24]

It was doubtful that Vandenberg was seeking to subvert the McMahon bill by inserting the military's imprimatur in a way that would diminish civilian control. Vandenberg's professed concern was that America's atomic secrets must be maintained until appropriate safeguards against their misuse were assured. He wanted the military to have a voice in determining the nation's atomic policies. In correspondence with Walter Brooks of the Association of Philadelphia Scientists, he claimed to have no pride of authorship "in the so-called 'Vandenberg Amendment.' You can change its language to suit yourself so far as I am concerned—just as long as those who are charged by our Constitution with responsibility for national security shall have an *advisory* chance to function." Earlier he asserted that he "was under 'no pressure from the Military.' I never consulted the Military. They never consulted me."[25]

McMahon was the lone dissenter on the special committee when the vote was taken on March 12, 1946, to accept the Vandenberg amendment. McMahon was afraid that the military liaison board was a long step toward undermining the principle of civilian control of atomic energy. The Connecticut senator was not alone in his opposition. The scientific community backed McMahon's position, while Secretary of Commerce Henry Wallace initiated a vitriolic campaign against Vandenberg's action to, as he put it, deliver the nation to "military fascism."[26]

Vandenberg was perplexed over McMahon's reaction to his amendment. His response to critics—excepting Wallace, whose accusations went beyond the bounds of reason—was to counter misperceptions about the problem of the atomic bomb and his views on the subject. First he tried to make it clear to a Michigan correspondent that the bomb itself could not remain a permanent secret. Nor was it a secret in 1945. Britain and Canada "have been our atomic partners and are in possession," he noted in November 1945, "of *all* the information which we have upon the subject." Moreover, U.S. scientists had pointed out that any other nation could develop the bomb within a few years, "whether we like it or not." Therefore, he argued, the only sensible course for the United States was to develop, through the United Nations, "a system of complete world-wide inspection which would guarantee to civilization that *no* nation (including ourselves) shall use atomic energy for the construction of weapons of war." Vandenberg compromised his admirable self-denial, however, by telling his correspondent that "if it were at all *possible* to keep this secret in our own possession indefinitely, this would be my first and emphatic choice because we *know* that America will not use this devastating weapon for aggressive purposes."[27] Despite his continuing devotion to the United Nations, his pride in American exceptionalism could in 1945—and later—trump his internationalism.

Vandenberg felt it necessary to correct the editor of the *Baltimore Sun* when he accused him of succumbing to military control over peacetime management of atomic energy. The senator protested that he had led the battle that sidetracked congressional attempts to do just that. As the author of the Vandenberg amendment, he disclaimed any military pressure or consultation with the military: "Under the Vandenberg Amendment this Military Committee will have no powers at all, in the sense of exercising affirmative authority." Its one function was to make recommendations to the civilian commission when matters of national security were involved. He maintained that the "proposed Military Liaison Committee cannot itself interfere with the functioning of the Civilian Commission. It cannot challenge civilian control. It can *only* advise the President that some contemplated action by the Civilian Commission threatens the national security. Only the *President* can act."[28]

Satisfying critics was not an easy task. To critics on the Right he had to admit that placing the atom under centralized government control violated the principles of free enterprise. But, he asked a Michigan businessman, what choice was there? "The use of atomic energy for destructive purposes is the greatest hazard that ever threatened civilization in general and the American way of life in particular." There had to be a government monopoly on fissionable material until dependable safeguards were developed. As he wrote to another Michigan businessman, the McMahon bill along, with his amendment, might be called "'socialistic' or 'totalitarian.' But whatever it is called, I hope that it accomplishes a *totalitarian* control of atomic energy for the time being."[29]

To critics on the Left, particularly those in the scientific community, his professed conviction that civilian control would prevail was questioned: "Actually, would not this board of review hold up all decisions of the civilian commission? Would not the board place an intolerable burden continually on the President? Would it not harass the civilian commission until only men who would go along with the military would be on the commission?" Vandenberg dismissed these questions as unrealistic. If the committee tried to harass the commission, "I should expect the President to change the personnel of the 'Liaison Committee' in twenty minutes. At any rate, I have that much confidence in *any* President of the United States." Although the senator failed to quell the scientists' opposition, he accepted the compromise language proposed by University of Chicago chemist Thorfin R. Hogness allowing military consultation that would not infringe upon the functions of the civilian commission.[30]

Other issues arose to plague the senator in his self-selected role as guardian of the Joint Committee on Atomic Energy. Vandenberg was surprised to learn in the summer of 1947 that President Roosevelt had made an arrangement with Churchill at the Quebec conference in 1943 barring the use of the atomic bomb without Britain's consent. Aside from resentment over such an obligation itself, he was disturbed by the possibility that atomic materiel stored in Britain might fall into Russian hands in the event of a war in Europe. Meeting with Secretary of the Navy James Forrestal and Undersecretary of State Robert A. Lovett in November 1947, he also learned that the United States would share with Britain access to uranium from the Congo. Lovett assured him that Britain's influence with Belgium and South Africa was a major factor in securing uranium from those countries.[31]

Vandenberg was upset about the extent of atomic information that was shared with the British, while the British were equally upset over the limits of the exchange. The issue was resolved in 1949 only after Vandenberg opposed the administration's position that Anglo-American partnership included sharing information on weapons, although there would be no consultation with the British before deciding to use the bomb. An agreement had been reached in 1948 whereby Vandenberg, with the support of Senator Bourke B. Hickenlooper (R-IA), a member of the Special Committee on Atomic Energy in 1945 and then chairman of the Senate section of the Joint Committee on Atomic Energy, got rid of the FDR-Churchill accord. All Congo oil would go only to the United States. Given the state of the Cold War in 1948, Britain's acceptance of the American position was an acknowledgement of its dependence on the United States for economic and military assistance.[32]

This Anglo-American tussle diverted Vandenberg's attention from his primary reason for involvement in atomic affairs: the provenance of the United Nations as the guarantor against the destruction of civilization by the atom bomb. Even more of a diversion was the important selection of a chairman of the Atomic Energy Commission. The nominee was David E. Lilienthal, a dedicated New Dealer and object of attack in the past as chairman of the Tennessee Valley Authority (TVA). Inevitably, as chair of the symbol of the New Deal's centralization of power, he was vulnerable to Republican criticism. Vandenberg himself was not immune to the taint of socialism that Republicans associated with the TVA. Yet he backed off from his initial demands that the Military Liaison Committee members attend all Atomic Energy Commission meetings after Lilienthal showed the impracticality of that approach. Vandenberg followed a familiar pattern. He would raise formidable objections at first, then subsequently rethink their application and finally come around to the witness's point of view. Without fully suppressing his reservations about the New Deal background of the nominee, Vandenberg took on his colleagues in defending the appointment. Lilienthal appreciated that Vandenberg and Connally had "'put their money' on the UNO idea."[33]

It could not have come as a surprise to Vandenberg that the business community was unhappy with the Lilienthal appointment. A close Michigan friend wired him that it would be better to have "in this position someone whose past record and known views are not so avowedly sympathetic to government ownership. . . . He is a conspicuous advocate of all the New Dealism which are anathema to me." The senator's response made negative views of Lilienthal irrelevant as he explained his hopes for international control of the atomic bomb: "Until we have completed the peace treaties and until we have negotiated a competent international agreement to outlaw the use of atomic energy for destructive purposes, it is absolutely vital—in my opinion—that 'public ownership' and 'public control" of atomic policy be as completely airtight and foolproof as it is possible to make it."[34]

At the hearings before the joint committee Lilienthal experienced a constant torrent of abuse from Senator Kenneth McKellar (D-TN), a longtime personal enemy whom Lilienthal had antagonized by rejecting his attempts to exercise his patronage powers in the TVA. McKellar's attacks ranged from accusations of Communism to questioning Lilienthal's patriotism. Tinged as these accusations were with anti-Semitism, Vandenberg was revolted by McKellar's prejudices. He considered the charge of Communism a "fantastic fabrication, highly remindful of the 'lynch law." McKellar's excesses probably helped to secure a favorable recommendation from the joint committee by a vote of eight to one. In light of the overwhelming support Lilienthal received from the scientific community, Vandenberg feared "wholesale retirements of our scientists from our atomic organization if Lilienthal were to be rejected."[35]

He was as strong in his defense when the nomination reached the Senate floor. But he had not anticipated the near unanimity of his most influential Republican colleagues against the appointment—Styles Bridges (R-NH) because of his feelings about public power, Wallace White (R-

ME) over Lilienthal's dictatorial behavior with the TVA, and Kenneth Wherry (R-NE) on any charge he could think of. Vigorous as Vandenberg's defense of the candidate was, he recognized that there were a few "juvenile communists" in a minor branch of the TVA. And he was aware that the Acheson-Lilienthal report on atomic energy did not include a ban on a UN veto—an omission subsequently rectified in Bernard Baruch's changes when he became a U.S. spokesman on the UN Atomic Energy Commission. Yet the Michigan senator remained firm in his backing of Lilienthal even in the face of opposition from Senator Taft. In a speech to the Senate on April 3, 1947, he noted that after seven weeks of "utterly exhausting" committee hearings, "I have been driven to the belief that logic, equity, and fair play, and a just regard for the public welfare, combine to recommend Mr. Lilienthal's confirmation in the light of today's realities." He won over seventeen Republicans to defeat a motion to send the nomination back to committee, which would have resulted in Lilienthal's rejection.[36]

Vandenberg's chivalrous support of Lilienthal was only partly motivated by the unfairness of his critics. The primary motivation lay in his belief that the appointment was in the national interest. But partisan prejudices were never wholly eliminated. In 1949, when the question of lax security in the Atomic Energy Commission arose, he displayed less enthusiasm about the chairman's leadership qualities. As a member of the joint committee chaired by Senator Hickenlooper, he was quick to dismiss the familiar charge of mismanagement but had reservations about Lilienthal's management abilities. It bothered him that government educational grants in the atomic field had been extended to students with Communist ties. He subsequently supported a Republican recommendation to limit Lilienthal's reappointment to two years.[37]

In the International Arena

What began in San Francisco in the spring of 1945 expanded into a new role for the Michigan senator. He saw himself as the defender and publicist for the United Nations, positioned to serve as an advocate for the new organization in the U.S. Senate and as a diplomat in the peace process, helping to repair the shredded fabric of a devastated Old World. He could not escape this role, and no matter how much he protested, he did not want to. Throughout 1946 he was engaged as member of the U.S. delegation, first at the initial meeting of the UN General Assembly in London in January, then as adviser to the U.S. delegation to the Council of Foreign Ministers in Paris through two sessions from April to July 1946, and then on to New York in the fall for the final session of the Council of Foreign Ministers. He did not resist the president's reappointment of him as a U.S. representative at the second session of the UN General Assembly, which met in September.[38]

While these activities absorbed the majority of his time, they did not indicate neglect of his responsibilities as leader of the Republican minority on the Senate Foreign Relations Committee and on the Senate floor. He had no problem with his priorities. His mission was not only to project his views of American foreign policy in international forums but also to explain them to the Senate. Once he had changed his judgments of Secretary Byrnes, he was a vigorous defender of the secretary's leadership and made the bipartisan character of his position fully evident to his Senate colleagues.

Given his belief in his special contributions to the creation of the United Nations, he took a leading part in discussions with the State Department about the extent of U.S. commitments in negotiating agreements concerning Article 43 (which made armed forces available to the Security Council) before his departure for Paris in April to ensure that the United States would not bear an unreasonable share of the expenses of future operations taken under the authority of the Security Council. He joined Senator Austin in efforts to convince Latin Americans that the Monroe Doctrine was unaffected by U.S. membership in the United Nations. Not incidentally, Vandenberg "emphasized that great progress had been made in getting the United Nations accepted by the American people."[39]

At this same meeting he urged that the atomic bomb be excluded from weapons of a proposed U.S. contingent. He was sure that the question would sooner or later be raised on the floor of the Senate. Although he believed that the UN eventually would acquire the bomb for its own use, this was not the time to raise the issue. It would be premature to take such action until the UN Atomic Energy Commission had made its proposals for international control. In light of Soviet obstruction over the atomic issue, this could be a long wait, despite his ultimately optimistic conclusion.[40]

Vandenberg's cautious approach to implementing the UN Charter was fully justified by his experiences at the Council of Foreign Ministers. Plunging into the thickets of diplomacy, he found the Soviets blocking U.S. initiatives at every turn. Whether the conflict was over the disposition of Italian colonies, excessive reparations demanded by Foreign Minister Molotov, or the future of Trieste, the senator vented his spleen about Russian behavior. He enthusiastically cheered Byrnes's new defiance of the Soviets, having forgiven him for giving away so much in the Moscow meeting in the fall of 1945. There was little room for new U.S. concessions.

In addition to Molotov's persistent demands, Byrnes, Vandenberg noted, had to cope with such American Russophiles as Secretary of Commerce Henry Wallace and Senator Claude Pepper (D-FL), who regularly condemned American policy for being too severe with the Soviet Union and seemed to have more sympathy with Soviet positions than those of their own country.[41] But it was the Russians who tested Vandenberg's temper. He appreciated Byrnes's new but strong resolve to avoid any more appeasement. "No more Munichs!" Vandenberg asserted in his diary. "If it is impossible for us to get along with the Soviets on such a basis, the quicker we find out the better. America must behave like the *Number One World Power* which she is. Ours must be the world's moral leadership—or the world won't have any."[42]

When confronted with firmness, Molotov would occasionally yield, even though there would be little change in Soviet behavior. That the situation remained the same was less important to Vandenberg than the foreign minister's understanding that "the 'appeasement' days are over." The putative U.S. need for appeasement went back to the time when Roosevelt worried about the Soviets leaving the war and making a separate peace with the Germans. Stalin and Molotov now knew they could no longer "'write their own ticket'" in these international meetings.[43]

Postponing action on issues more important than the boundaries of Yugoslavia and Italy, such as the role of Germany in the postwar world, was an inevitable if unsatisfactory conclusion at the two sessions of the Council of Foreign Ministers in Paris. The Anglo-American approach to dealing with Germany as a whole fell victim to France's requirement that the Saar be permanently under France's control and to the Soviet effort to sow dissension among the Western allies. Vandenberg expressed his frustration over the management of the German question in his endorsement of Bevin's observation on July 10 that "we are all agreed that Germany must be administered as an economic unit. We are all agreed that this is not being done today. At least we must settle our *current* disagreements. Let us deal with our short-term problem at once." The senator concluded that Bevin "offered a general paper on the subject. Molotov offered a general paper of his own, and the session rose—in complete confusion."[44]

When Vandenberg returned to Washington in July to present a report on the Council of Foreign Ministers' progress in Paris, he did not fail to relate to the senators the techniques the Soviets used to block reasonable resolutions of boundary disputes. Using Trieste as an example, he pointed out the unfairness of Yugoslavia's claim to the city, which had been part of Italy for twenty-five years. The Soviets constantly disputed the justice of Italy's claim on the basis, among others, that Yugoslavia was one of the Allies throughout the war, whereas Italy was an Axis enemy until military defeat turned it into a belated cobelligerent—"when, I hasten to add, her sacrificial contributions to allied victory were loyally immense." Given the principle of unanimity under which the Council of Foreign Ministers operated, Vandenberg reported that a compromise was inevitable, at least on this issue. There would have been no settlement had not the idea of a free territory of Trieste been conceived.[45]

That Vandenberg himself was deeply involved in this contest was demonstrated by this speech to the Senate on July 16, 1946, decrying the way the Trieste issue was handled. The decision on the future of Trieste should have been made by all the Allies who had fought the war, together with the "advice of the General Assembly of the United Nations." While the Michigan senator always presented an American position on every issue relating to the peace process, he never forgot the importance of the role the United Nations should play. He would have preferred that Trieste have gone to Italy but praised the secretary of state for accepting a compromise that would protect "human rights and fundamental freedoms beneath the seal of the United Nations."[46]

He concluded his speech with a melancholy recognition that the German question was less open to compromise, let alone solution. The cleavage between the great powers was wide, and "the basis of trouble is the fact that the Potsdam Agreement divided Germany into four air-tight compartments, preventing the exchange of goods or communications, or even ideas." Vandenberg then reminded his colleagues of the many failures at Yalta, particularly the abandonment of Poland to Communist control: "I have made vigorous and repeated protests on this score, and I shall continue to do so, despite the bitter attacks upon me which have emanated not only from official Warsaw but from official Moscow, and from the integrated Communist press all around the world." By engaging in debates in Paris he had personalized the West's contest with the Communist world, placing himself at its center.[47]

Despite the oppressive atmosphere in Paris, Vandenberg did not leave the rostrum on a note of pessimism. He summed up by noting that the major powers had agreed on treaties to end the war with Italy, Hungary, Romania, Bulgaria, and Finland: "It took many weary months to reach this agreement. The important point is that an agreement has been reached. Peace thus gains in stature." As for the failure of negotiations over the future of Germany, "the prospect is no darker than it was on other occasions." It is worth noting that he believed that "peace hangs chiefly on three factors which are inextricably interwoven." One of them was obvious—finding a bridge between East and West. The other two reflected the senator's mutually dependent core convictions—the success of the United Nations' operations and its ultimate outlawing of "atomic bombs and kindred instruments of sudden and overwhelming mass destruction."[48]

As the acknowledged voice of the Republican Party on foreign affairs, Vandenberg was the engine for the national consensus behind Secretary of State Byrnes's foreign policy. From a skeptic in 1945, the Michigan senator had become a cheerleader for a reformed secretary of state, who vigorously opposed Soviet obstructionism on the international scene. When the president reappointed Vandenberg to serve at the September session of the General Assembly of the United Nations, he felt a duty to accept. This sense of duty, reinforced by Secretary Byrnes's pleas, sent him back to Paris in September to participate in the completion of peace treaties with the former enemies of World War II—absent Germany and Austria—under the aegis of a twenty-one-nation conference. The peace treaties with Italy, Bulgaria, Hungary, and Romania were not reached until the end of the year in New York. Vandenberg and Connally took credit for the Senate's confirmation of the Italian treaty by a vote of seventy-nine to ten in the Senate. The other treaties were ratified by voice votes. Secretary Byrnes made a point of crediting Vandenberg for the adoption of a joint Anglo-American resolution in the face of Soviet opposition whereby the Big Four (Great Britain, the United States, the Soviet Union, and France) and the riparian states affirmed the principle of free commerce and navigation of the Danube.[49]

But while Vandenberg was in Paris, Secretary of Commerce Henry Wallace delivered a speech on September 12 in New York's Madison Square Garden that threatened to unravel the bipartisan foreign policy fashioned by the competitive partnership of Connally and Vandenberg. Much of Wallace's speech was familiar. He had condemned U.S. policy toward the Soviet Union as too harsh, lacking understanding of Russia's problems. This was familiar to Vandenberg as well, since Wallace had attacked his amendment to the McMahon bill in support of a military liaison board as opening the way to "military fascism." But Wallace's fierce attack seemed primarily directed against the Republican Party as anachronistic, doomed like the dodo to extinction, yet damaging to the cause of world peace if the party assumed power briefly on its way to extinction. Making matters worse was the president's apparent approval of the speech when he saw an advanced copy.

The secretary of state threatened to resign unless Truman silenced his secretary of commerce. Byrnes claimed that keeping Wallace in the Cabinet after he broke a promise to abstain from engaging in matters of foreign affairs left the world confused about America's policies and left bipartisan relations in tatters. He reminded the president that "you and I spent 15 months building a bipartisan policy. We did a fine job convincing the world that it was a permanent policy upon which the world could rely. Wallace destroyed that in a day." Truman forced Wallace out of the Cabinet the next day.[50]

Of all the participants in this drama, Vandenberg was the most vulnerable. He had staked his career and his position in the Republican Party on working with the administration to fashion a policy that would preserve world peace through the instrument of the United Nations, which he helped to create. Yet his press statement following the Wallace speech reflected sadness more than anger: "Although differing in some points, most Republicans have been glad to join most Democrats, thus presenting a united American front to the world. . . . But the situation equally requires unity within the administration itself. We can cooperate with one Secretary of State at a time."[51]

This relatively mild reaction may have been a by-product of their formerly good, if not intimate, relations during Wallace's vice presidency. They had been neighbors at the Wardman Park Hotel. Ten days after the Madison Square Garden speech Vandenberg's closest political friend, John Foster Dulles, echoed the senator's unruffled reaction. He wrote to the Yale economist Irving Fisher, "Wallace has fine aspirations and many good ideas. When, however, he gets down to applying, them he is apt to be unrealistic. . . . His Madison Square Garden speech was an illustration of how, when he has to apply his general principles, he goes astray."[52]

Unlike Dulles outside the political arena, Vandenberg had reason to worry about the effect of the Wallace speech. An election was coming up in two months, and many Republicans chafed at being tied to Vandenberg's bipartisan course. It curbed attacks on the Truman administration, which could limit the Republicans' expected victory at the polls two months later. Wallace appeared to have exposed the fragility of the Republican collaboration with the Democratic administration on foreign affairs. The senator had to weigh not only his dedication to the primacy of the UN in American foreign relations against his fellow Republicans' need to distinguish the party from the Democrats but also the fate of his own candidacy for reelection. He made his decision to stay the course. The impact of his experience in San Francisco was too profound for him to repudiate bipartisanship, even at the cost of his Senate seat.

His delicate relationship with Senator Taft, the dominant figure on the domestic scene within the party, had to be part of the calculus. There was an informal understanding that Taft would leave the party's foreign policy to Vandenberg, but it was always brittle and susceptible to disruption. The primary problem inevitably was Vandenberg's conversion to internationalism, and with that to the necessity for close cooperation with the Truman administration. The Republican party, by contrast, was never converted to bipartisanship; it had taken all of Vandenberg's powers of persuasion since San Francisco to neutralize this visceral opposition.

While Taft recognized the changing postwar mood in the nation, his relegation of foreign affairs to Vandenberg was always qualified. When the Michigan senator reluctantly but definitively sided with the administration on a loan to Britain in 1946, Taft had eighteen Republican senators in opposition on his side; Vandenberg managed to secure seventeen. This was an impressive success, sufficient in combination with Democrats to secure the loan.[53]

In public Taft did his best to demonstrate his alliance with Vandenberg, but his approval was not always credible. When Taft congratulated his rival for successful management of the Paris conference, he exaggerated Vandenberg's role, perhaps to compensate for his reservations. Writing to the Michigan senator, he supposed "there may be some differences as there always are, but I approve without qualification your whole position as far as I know it." Qualified though this endorsement was, Vandenberg chose to see it as a vote of confidence: "I deeply appreciate the spirit in which you have written" was his response. "It is typical of a relationship between us which—despite whatever differing opinions we may occasionally hold—will *never* amount to serious disagreements." "Courteous suspicion" was how one reporter described the relationship. Taft could rationalize his acceptance of Vandenberg's ambiguous role by crediting him with "finally forcing [the administration] to abandon the policy of appeasing Russia."[54]

THE ELECTION OF 1946

No matter how tenuous the solidarity over Republican foreign policy may have been, it did not deter Vandenberg from keeping faith in bipartisanship—even through a critical election period. His leap into the world arena had not been casual; he believed that his presence in Paris was indispensable in the campaign against Russian expansionism. In fact, he was convinced that the Kremlin had identified him "as the evil genius behind this new American attitude," as he told Howard C. Lawrence, a loyal promoter of his presidential candidacy in 1940. He was grateful for renomination to the Senate, despite his giving his international responsibilities priority over his duties to his state.[55]

Given this mind-set, he could not resist returning to Paris in June and again in September and traveling to New York for the UN General Assembly. In New York he combined his zeal for fair treatment of former enemies with awareness of his own parochial interests, notably Finnish voters in Michigan. He sought to reduce the size of Finland's reparation payments by claiming that $300 million was too heavy a burden for a country with "her record of scrupulous fidelity to fiscal obligations."[56] His constituents would go to the polls two weeks later.

Vigorous as his championing of the United Nations was in the Senate and in the press, he was just as vigorous in his defense of U.S. interests at UN meetings. He was particularly exercised at the General Assembly meetings in New York in November 1946 over the excessive costs the majority of its members would impose on the United States. Initially the State Department had placed a ceiling on its contributions of 25 percent of the total cost of the UN's administrative budget. But recognizing the financial plight of most of the member nations, the United States was willing to raise its financial contribution.

While acknowledging the organization's needs, Vandenberg insisted the issue was not what the United States could afford to pay "but what is right and wise and just as between partners in this common enterprise." He also reminded his fellow American delegates to the General Assembly that "it was an old dictum that taxation without representation was unjust." He said he would note that for his British colleagues.[57]

His patriotic sentiments as well as a sense of his own importance kept him from campaigning in the fall. As he put it to Kim Sigler, Michigan's Republican candidate for governor, "I want to make every contribution to the campaign within my power. Unfortunately, however, I am afraid that these opportunities are going to be much too limited because of the unavoidable obligations of my own public service. By fortuitous circumstance I happen to be one of a very few men who are engaged at the heart of things in the liquidation of the war and in the creation of permanent peace."[58]

It is hardly surprising that he put the Wallace controversy quickly behind him as he prepared to return to the UN General Assembly. In a letter to his campaign headquarters in Michigan he noted that he "should like to make *one* broadcast from Detroit or Grand Rapids," but it would not be partisan, unless there was a personal attack on him. He would just "report on the peace situation generally without reference to politics. . . . I shall certainly not make a broadcast under the Republican National Committee." Actually, he felt that his approach would be good politics as well: "I believe we would have everything to lose and nothing to gain but one last-minute speech which stripped our campaign of its absentee, non-partisan character."[59]

Vandenberg knew that his enemies would take advantage of his absence from the hustings and accuse him of abandoning his post. The most vociferous critic was the *Chicago Tribune,* whose publisher, Colonel Robert R. McCormick, had been an adversary over the years. There was no doubt about the newspaper's influence, particularly in western Michigan. Vandenberg's embrace of a bipartisan foreign policy was an unforgivable offense to the publisher. Some of the opposition served him well, notably the shrill voices of the Left, Henry Wallace and Senator Pepper, whose hostility was a reminder to Republican loyalists that their senator was not a hostage to the Left. If the Democratic National Committee should attack him, he would respond. But not otherwise: "Let's not throw away our advantage. The people are not dumb. Anyway—I'm not going to get my work for peace bogged down into politics. Politics are important, but *peace is indispensable.*"[60]

The senator was fortunate in facing a lackluster campaign by his Democratic opponent, whose support from his party was equally lackluster. Vandenberg's decision not only to limit his speeches before Michigan audiences but to ensure that when he did speak—to the state's American Legion or to a University of Michigan audience in August during a brief respite from Europe—both were nonpolitical and in support of the administration's foreign policy. While he did no campaigning in his home state, he used the vehement attacks from Moscow and from New York's Communist *Daily Worker* to remind correspondents of his nationalist credentials.[61] It could not have escaped notice that leading Democrats with whom he had worked for the past year and a half raised no voices against his reelection.

This covert claque of Democratic friends did not extend its influence to the Democratic National Committee, which was actively promoting its candidates for the Eightieth Congress. The senator was bemused by the contradictory message the Democrats dispatched to him. In a long letter to the committee's chairman, Postmaster General Robert E. Hannegan, he observed that "on the *same* day that I receive President Truman's commission as an American Delegate to the second session of the General Assembly of the United Nations—a commission which says that he 'reposes special trust and confidence in my integrity and ability'—his Party's National Committee, at the request of his Party's State Committee, sends two of its most prominent orators . . . into Michigan to seek *my* Party's defeat and *my* defeat in particular." He accused the Democrats of doing what he refused to do: namely, politicizing foreign policy.[62]

In this letter to Hannegan, sent just a week before the election, he wrote that fellow Republicans had criticized him for unwittingly encouraging a one-party system with the potential of destroying American liberties. His bipartisan approach to foreign policy, "it has been argued . . . helps the 'ins' to keep the 'outs out.' Unquestionably, there is a powerful argument to be made along these lines—*particularly if and when the majority party takes 'foreign policy' into election politics.*" He warned the Democratic Party leader that "if I am defeated it is the *Administration's* 'foreign policy' which really takes a licking because I am so closely identified with it. Yet if I *win*, I may contribute to a major *political* defeat for the Administration. So the Administration loses in *either* event." When he then asked, "Is bipartisan foreign policy permanently possible?" he implied that it could be if the Republicans played by the same rules he had followed. The two-party system had to be maintained, and areas outside foreign policy remained legitimate subjects of debate.[63]

Vandenberg's gamble paid off. Republicans gained a majority in both chambers of Congress. In Michigan the senator's victory was overwhelming. He won by a margin of 567,647 ballots, the second-largest majority of his career, and he judged the result to be an "unmistakable endorsement of the united, bipartisan foreign policy through which we are striving for national security and for world peace with justice." Three days later at the United Nations he could assure its members that "regardless of what political regime sits in Washington, you can count upon the wholehearted cooperation of the government of the United States in striving through the United Nations for a system of mutual defense against aggression and for organized peace with justice in a better, safer world."[64] The nation, he believed, had confirmed his vision of a world threatened by the atomic bomb and by the division between the democratic West and the Communist East. Salvation lay in the new United Nations, which he had helped to create and which became a bedrock of his internationalism.

Vandenberg would replace Connally as chairman of the Senate Foreign Relations Committee and become president pro tempore of the Senate as well, filling the vacancy in the office of vice president. As the Eightieth Congress began its sessions, Vandenberg was devoted to the work of the United Nations, more important to him than the always insecure bipartisan relations with the Democrats. Disappointments at the UN notwithstanding, he continued to believe there was no other instrument to keep world peace.

8

The Senator as Statesman, 1947–1948

Vandenberg's stock was never higher than it was at the beginning of the first session of the Eightieth Congress in January 1947. Without expending any time or energy in campaigning, he had won reelection to the Senate by a surprisingly large margin. He was now more than spokesman in foreign relations for the Republican Party; he was chairman of the Senate Foreign Relations Committee as well as president pro tempore of the Senate in the absence of a vice president. His position was thus a testament to the wisdom as well as the success of his particular brand of bipartisanship. He preferred to use the term "unpartisan" to avoid the political connotations of the word "bipartisan."[1]

His ascension to chairman of the Foreign Relations Committee was carefully managed. He had Senator Taft, the party leader in domestic affairs, concede him primacy in foreign affairs, albeit with some ambivalence. Recognizing the sensitivity of the relationship, the Michigan senator made a point of asking the president to include the Ohioan in any congressional conference of fundamental and far-reaching importance because of his position as chairman of the Republican Senate Policy Committee. He also wanted Taft's approval by letter before introducing foreign policy measures for debate on the Senate floor. Given Taft's instinctive resistance to much of the Truman's administration's foreign agenda, these were sensible gestures on Vandenberg's part.[2]

He was equally diplomatic, although more confident, in dealing with Senator Arthur Capper of Kansas, the ranking member of the Foreign Relations Committee, who was almost twenty years his senior. Vandenberg made his move gracefully. Immediately after the election he apologized to

Capper for "allowing—without denial—the general newspaper prophesy during the last year that I would become Chairman of the Senate Foreign Relations Committee under a Republican regime. I should have talked with you about this many months ago. I am afraid that I assumed— without any right to do so—that you would not care to take on the burden of this particular assignment." He admitted that in light of their long friendship he "took it for granted that you would wish me to serve in the Chairmanship."[3] Vandenberg was right. He knew that the Kansan preferred the chairmanship of the Agriculture Committee, but he was disingenuous in suggesting that he was surprised by the newspaper speculations. That he was dealing with a fellow journalist made his apology all the more palatable to his senior colleague.

Having anticipated and disposed of problems in his relations with Republican colleagues, he could turn to his concerns about the centrality of the United Nations in American foreign relations, reasonably, if not fully, assured of continued cooperation with the president and Secretary Byrnes. He was less certain of former Republican isolationists who were understandably alarmed by Soviet behavior at UN meetings, as reported by the Michigan senator himself. In two letters to Colonel Alton T. Roberts, a prominent member of the American Legion in Royal Oaks, Michigan, he expressed his shared frustration with Russian abuse of the veto power in the Security Council. But he could not go along with the Legion's recommendations for a fundamental reconstruction of the UN Charter: "It would break the U.N. if undertaken now or in the immediate future." He felt there was "no practical hope of writing a new [charter] if we are unable to find a way to fully utilize our existing possibilities."[4]

Moreover, there was another reason for caution in dealing with the veto. He recognized its value to America's national interest. Although he felt that the potential use of armed force was appropriately inherent in the charter, "I seriously doubt whether the American people will ever be satisfied to let a majority of the Security Council virtually order us into war without our specific consent." This was his reason for asking the American Legion to "go slow" in its demand for a suspension of the veto. Vandenberg's alternative was to seek "suspension of the veto *only* in respect to Chapter VI [of the charter,] which deals with pacific settlement of disputes." While it was unlikely that the Soviets would accept this compromise, it reflected his conviction that the national interest would never be in conflict with the vital purposes of the UN and its charter.[5]

No matter how provocative he found Soviet behavior, Vandenberg knew that the future of the United Nations depended on an ongoing relationship between East and West. At a radio symposium in Washington on January 19, 1947, he spoke for the nation as well as for himself when he said that the United States "was prepared to live and let live," despite ideological differences. Nevertheless, "we can neither condone nor appease conquest, we must require reciprocal fair play on a two-way street. . . . I am cautiously hopeful for the future but I would not relax our vigilance for one split second." Yet, he continued, "there might have been serious turmoil in this world if it [the United Nations] had not existed."[6] There was a schizophrenic quality in his references to the Soviet Union and the United Nations. On the one hand, he never shrank from chastising the Soviet adversary when its actions jeopardized the future of the organization. On the other hand, he had to sound a positive note if the UN was to remain functional.

Straddling this divide was not easy, as he discovered when he tried to reconcile the interests of two important ethnic lobbies to the need for patience in dealing with the limitations of the UN. Both the Polish and Jewish constituencies had spokesmen in Michigan in the newspaper world, a factor that facilitated close connections with the Michigan senator, who never forgot his many years as a journalist. To the editor of Detroit's *Polish Daily News* he regularly offered assurances of his steadfast opposition to the Communist regime in Warsaw and his continuing condemnation of the decisions at Yalta. At the same time he had to counsel patience in America's confrontation with the Soviets in the United Nations. To the editor of Detroit's *Jewish News,* he constantly repeated his allegiance to the Jewish cause in Palestine while refusing to urge any American unilateral initiative that would create excessive disharmony among America's allies in the UN.

His language in letters to both friends was supportive but cautious, with an eye on the interests of both the United States and the United Nations. He was firm in telling Frank Januszewski that he "*never* suggested to you that you should approve the Yalta Agreements. . . . What I *have* advised you is that you and your friends should *concentrate* on *immedi-*

ate problems in which there is some chance for *immediately* helpful action. There is no *immediate* chance to revise the basic formula in respect to Poland." Similarly, in the course of an extended correspondence with Philip Slomovitz, he empathized with Slomovitz's anxieties about the current crisis in the Palestine situation: "I share these anxieties—not only in respect to the successful conclusion of our hopes for partition but also in respect to the far wider implications . . . to the national security. . . . I am opposed to any unilateral action by the United States on our own responsibility. The problem has been transferred to the jurisdiction of the United Nations and *there* it must be settled."[7] Whether the problem lay in the past, as with Poland in 1945, or in the future, as with Palestine, Vandenberg tried to balance America's national interests and the UN's interests with those of the concerned parties, and for the most part he succeeded.

THE LIMITS OF BIPARTISANSHIP

The senator needed all the powers of his office and of his legislative experience to persuade his Republican colleagues to share his objectives for the nation. The agreement with Senator Taft to concede leadership in foreign affairs was always tentative. Vandenberg's relations with Tom Connally, the minority leader on the Foreign Relations Committee, were closer than those with the Ohio senator, his opponent in the campaign for the Republican nomination in 1940. The rivalry with Taft was never far beneath the surface. On the other hand, Vandenberg had willing allies to effect his objectives, including fellow Republicans on the Senate Foreign Relations Committee who shared his views, such as Henry Cabot Lodge Jr. of Massachusetts, H. Alexander Smith of New Jersey, and Alexander Wiley of Wisconsin. And, as was evidenced in the press he received, he could bask in the praise that friends at the leading American newspapers bestowed on him. Above all, Vandenberg's mastery of parliamentary procedures would advance his agendas.

Yet there was an element of unreasonable optimism in his contribution to a symposium sponsored by the National Broadcasting Company at the beginning of the Eightieth Congress. His response to the question "Are we making progress toward world peace?" was positive because of the United States' "firm, friendly candor" with the Soviet Union. With a bow to the United Nations, he thought "there was no longer any partisan politics in the fixed and united American foreign policy, with which we shall fully cooperate with the United Nations in support of collective security in the effort to stop World War Three before it starts." He saw this as "a Republican policy, a Democratic policy and an American policy. Certainly that will be the Republican program." He had confirmed this belief in a speech at the Cleveland Council on World Affairs a week before when he claimed that "partisan politics, for most of us, stopped at the water's edge. I hope they stay stopped—for the sake of America—regardless of what party is in power." Whatever differences remained on foreign policy, "they should not root themselves in partisanship."[8] This was the language of wishful thinking that he frequently employed.

THE RIO PACT

In the same address in Cleveland Vandenberg disclosed a clear dissent from bipartisan foreign policy, at least in areas outside Europe. He specified Latin America and China as objects of his critical attention. The former, with the Monroe Doctrine at its heart, had been much on his mind since the San Francisco conference that established the United Nations Charter. In fact, his concerns with hemispheric solidarity were manifested before he entered the Senate.[9] The United Nations should be involved in pressing Argentina to purge itself of the last vestiges of Nazism, he argued. If the hemisphere could not be unified, Communism would move in.[10]

The senator had an opportunity to deepen his involvement with Latin America when the president appointed him and Senator Connally on August 1, 1947, as delegates to the Inter-American Conference for the Maintenance of Continental Peace and Security, to be held in suburban Rio de Janeiro.[11] He recognized the potential incompatibility between his recent duties as a delegate to the UN and the obligations of a U.S. senator. He had written to Eleanor Roosevelt earlier that year that "having participated in the United Nations in helping to *make* the decisions, I am not a 'free agent' when I return to the Senate to function in my 'Congressional' capacity. Indeed, it *could* be a most embarrassing and difficult situation in the event that I did not approve of some decision made by the United Nations. I should dislike to *oppose* in Congress anything to which

I had given my consent (if only by reluctant acquiescence) in the United Nations."[12]

He went on to tell his former colleague in the General Assembly that "now against this argument . . . I am irrevocably committed to the achievement of peace and security with justice. It is my paramount and permanent interest in life . . . and I have no other wish than to dedicate them to this objective. So I am prepared to do whatever circumstances may seem to require; and if they seem to require my intimate participation in the work of either the United Nations or the Council of Foreign Ministers, I am quite ready to subordinate all other considerations."[13] On this basis he welcomed the opportunity to serve as a delegate to the Rio conference in the summer of 1947.

The conference, with its intention of updating the Monroe Doctrine, was long overdue, in his judgment, having been promised by Secretary of State Stettinius in 1945. The senator had been instrumental in securing acceptance at San Francisco of the UN Charter's Article 51 that legitimized such regional organizations as the Pan American Union. The article identified the inherent right of nations to collective as well as individual self-defense. The twenty-one American members of the Pan American Union had produced the Act of Chapultepec on March 3, 1945, declaring that aggression against any American state would be considered an act against all, with measures to follow, including the use of armed force.

In the course of the San Francisco conference Vandenberg had sent a stern letter to Stettinius expressing his dissatisfaction "with one phase of our proposal regarding 'Regional Agreements' and I am putting my viewpoint before you for immediate consideration before it is too late. If our European allies can be exempted from the jurisdiction of the Security Council, what can we say in defense of our action in requiring at the same time that Pan America must depend upon this new Peace League before it has demonstrated its adequacy, and must abandon its primary reliance upon inter-American relationships which are fifty years old and which were vigorously reasserted under our auspices at Mexico City within the last two months?"[14]

Vandenberg's complaint was favorably received. A month later he could claim that "we have found a sound, a practical formula for putting regional organizations into effective gear with the global institution.

. . . We weld these regional links into the global chain" under the auspices of the UN Charter's Article 51, as a guarantor of the defense of the American republics. He regarded this linkage as his special achievement at San Francisco. He took pride in the "precious inheritance of fifty years of benign history behind it."[15] Such was his sunny view of the history of the Monroe Doctrine, which in the wake of World War II appeared to be shared by most Latin American states. His protective if patronizing judgments about the status of U.S. relations with Latin America had not changed since 1945—or, for that matter, since the Theodore Roosevelt era. Small wonder that Vandenberg could relax in the friendly atmosphere of Petropolis in 1947.

There were decisions to be made before a new hemispheric treaty could be completed in Brazil, and the senator was in the midst of all of them. As spokesman for the U.S. delegation he successfully rebuffed Argentina's proposal to limit the treaty's application outside the hemisphere. And he took the initiative in backing a Peruvian proposal for the treaty to require an immediate cease-fire in the event of conflict between member states, even though the decision at Chapultepec made no distinction between aggression from a member or from a nonmember state. The Peruvian delegation wanted to make at least one last effort at peaceful settlement before action was taken. Given the need for Senate approval, Vandenberg accepted a provision that a two-thirds majority in favor of economic sanctions would be binding on all parties to the treaty. This was to make sure than no paralyzing veto could block action against an offender, as was possible in the UN Security Council.[16] He hoped to avoid even the possibility of the United States having the power singly to veto a Latin American proposal.

Vandenberg's eagerness to bring the Rio Treaty to the Senate for confirmation met no resistance in Washington. Secretary of State George C. Marshall was a strong proponent of the treaty. If anything would impede progress it could have been the senator's objection to the minimal UN role in the Rio Pact: "The thing I miss in your proposed text for Article 2," he wrote to Secretary Marshall,

is any direct reference to the fact that this proposed obligation is always subordinated to the Charter of the United Nations. I notice that when you come to Article 3 . . . you spell out the fact that it is 'subject to the provisions of Article 51 of the Charter of the United Nations.' I raise the question whether—in the same essential spirit—Article 2 should not spell out the fact that it is subject to the provisions of Articles 51, 52, 53 and 54 of the Charter of the United Nations. . . . I do not think we can be too scrupulous in preserving the overriding authority of the parent organization.[17]

Sensitive as he was to the Monroe Doctrine's role in America's foreign relations, he was even more sensitive to the vital importance of having every international obligation be in conformity with the charter.

Vandenberg's reservations about the terms of the Rio Treaty did not mask his impatience with the slow progress of the member nations in ratifying the document. By contrast, the U.S. Senate's Foreign Relations Committee, pushed by its chairman, had secured ratification on December 4, 1947. The Senate approved it four days later by a seventy-two-to-one vote. As Vandenberg had told Senator Taft, "I apprehend no controversy over the Treaty because it is distinctly in our American interest."[18] Subsequently, he was disappointed at the delayed ratification by too many Latin American members.

It took two more years before enough ratifications had been deposited, although the secretary general of the Pan American Union assured him that by October 1948 the treaty should be in place. Argentina finally approved it on June 28, 1950.[19] Vandenberg waited impatiently for a brief ceremony to "'tell the world.' It seems to me that it is a moment that could be used not only to underscore Pan American solidarity but also to underscore the utility of 'Regional Arrangements' under the U.N. Charter." The concept of regional arrangements could be applied to Western Europe as well. Vandenberg speculated in March 1947, "I am not certain . . . that it would not be worth looking at the possibility of regional alliances with a view to Europe. . . . I am firmly of the opinion that security is at the heart of the difficulties we are faced with."[20]

He told the Senate in December 1947 that in ratifying the Rio Treaty "we have translated pan-American solidarity from an ideal into a reality." Whether he was too confident in celebrating conformity between the regional arrangement that the Rio Treaty represented and the UN Charter was a matter that he did not have to study too carefully in 1947. To claim that the treaty was passed "with scrupulous regard" for the United Nations—acting strictly within Articles 51, 52, 53, and 54 of the United Nations Charter—was an assertion that he and the other framers of the North Atlantic Treaty had to back away from in 1949.[21] Articles 52 to 54—under Chapter 8 of the charter, "Regional Arrangements"—were subject to Security Council review, where the Soviet Union would have a voice and a vote.

THE CHINA CONUNDRUM

While Vandenberg found a few holes over Latin America in the "unpartisan" relationship he sought from the Truman administration, they were never deep enough to deter him from further cultivating his connection with the administration. By the time of the Rio conference, he had a new appreciation of the character of Secretary of State Marshall, who had succeeded an ailing James Byrnes in January 1947. Marshall, a five-star general who was credited as the architect of victory in World War II, awed Truman as well as Vandenberg by the power of his personality. Mrs. Vandenberg's personal relations with the general and his wife helped to cement ties between the two men. Bipartisanship was no problem with respect to the Rio Treaty.[22]

The administration's policies toward Nationalist China were another matter. The senator made a point of keeping his distance from those policies for a number of reasons. Not least was the Yalta factor. Just as he felt that Roosevelt had given away the freedoms of Eastern Europe at Yalta, so he believed Roosevelt had "sold out" Chiang Kai-shek's Nationalist government to the Communists. Long interested in Asian affairs, as far back as 1930, when, as a junior senator from Michigan, he championed early independence for the Philippines, Vandenberg had hopes for a Chinese victory against Japan in the course of World War II.[23] He was as disappointed in the corruption of the Nationalist government as the Truman administration was, but he differed with its recommendations for change, particularly its policy of bringing the Communists into the government.

Removing China from his bipartisan approach to the Democrats burnished his Republican credentials, which were inevitably weakened by his collaboration with the Truman administration on European and UN issues. He was able to demonstrate his independence from the administration dramatically in 1947 when the Foreign Relations Committee rejected Francis Biddle as U.S. representative to the UN Social and Economic Council. Vandenberg felt that that the council, "virtuously autonomous in their operations and in their budgets," "could be influenced by a person without the 'basic judgment' to restrain excessive spending," as he told Leon Henderson, chairman of the executive committee of Americans for Democratic Action. He denied any bias against Biddle, an attorney general in the Roosevelt administration and ardent New Dealer, noting to his friend, Harold Ickes, FDR's secretary of the interior, that he had supported "*scores* of them, just as I am *most happy* to report Mrs. Roosevelt as delegate to the General Assembly."[24] It certainly did not hurt his reputation within his party that a majority of the Foreign Relations Committee shared his belief that Biddle lacked the proper qualifications for the position.

Similarly, he held up the promotion of the China specialist John Carter Vincent to the post of career minister because of Vincent's record on China, although Vandenberg was "quite sure he is not a 'Red' (to use your word)," as he told a Michigan correspondent. He responded to a letter from Senator Styles Bridges (R-NH) asking him to reject Vincent's appointment, based "entirely upon the character of work he has done on the Far Eastern desk in the State Department." Although Vandenberg said he did not like Vincent's record, he wanted Bridges to "understand that I have *nothing* to present to the Committee from you as the basis for rejection."[25] When Vincent was assigned as minister to Switzerland Vandenberg was able to display his loyalty to the Republicans' China policy without forfeiting his reputation for moderation.

His dissociation of bipartisanship from the administration's China policies would also strengthen Vandenberg's ties with Senator William F. Knowland of California, a young ally in the bipartisan camp but also a vigorous defender of Chiang Kai-shek's China.[26] The steady decline in Nationalist fortunes, accompanied by a comparable increase in Communist influence, induced a sharper tone in Vandenberg's commentary on the China problem. He seemed to assign most of the blame for the Nationalists' plight to his own government. The Truman administration made a serious mistake in trying to fashion a coalition government with the Communists. Symbolic of the error was the Marshall mission to China in 1946 to help bring stability to Chiang's government. The general accepted the assignment as a good soldier who could not turn down the president's request. The mission ended in failure and frustration.

Vandenberg did not charge Marshall personally with the dismal results of the mission, but the general could not escape from involvement in the blanket dissent the senator repeatedly expressed about the mission. As he put it in a letter to a Michigan correspondent, "I have always vigorously disagreed with the China part of this Administration's foreign policy. I am one of those who believes that the anti-Communist stabilization of China is of vital concern to the intelligent self-interest of the United States. In my opinion, the disintegration of the Nationalist Government was at least partially due to this policy." To a Grand Rapids correspondent, he earlier had said that he had been "completely out of step with the Administration's China policy ever since we sought to force the Chinese Nationalist government to form a coalition with the Chinese Communists. I never knew of Communists who have joined a coalition for any purpose except to destroy it." It is not difficult to conclude that Vandenberg's long-standing anti-Communist positions, combined with his respect for Chiang Kai-shek personally, colored his perceptions of the administration's China policies. His attitudes seemed to presented a stark contrast with his bipartisan approach in other areas of the world.[27]

This judgment better fits the years after Communist China took over the mainland, leaving the Nationalists in control only of Formosa; it applies less well to the time when Marshall returned to Washington as secretary of state. While Vandenberg's condemnation of the administration's effort to create a coalition government and his mocking of the notion that Communists were essentially agrarian reformers were constant, his complaint that the administration failed to consult with him over its China policy is suspect. He had conversations with Marshall about helping Chiang's government from the outset of the secretary's tenure, even if he had not "had an opportunity as yet to 'talk this out' with our new Secretary of State. But I have had ample evidence from many important sources that my suggestion has powerful support among the *realists* who know something about the Chinese status."[28]

Subsequently, while his Senate colleagues were demanding access to the Wedemeyer Report—a result of General Albert C. Wedemeyer's survey of the Chinese situation in the summer of 1949—Vandenberg told Knowland that Marshall had given him a complete paraphrase of the report "and I was satisfied that its release would have been a serious blow to Chinese-American relations." Moreover, he had been consulted and had given advice about such sensitive issues as halting arms shipments to the Nationalists. On the strength of this information, historian James Fetzer claimed that Vandenberg took up a familiar position on China between the administration and its critics—performing "the broker's function."[29]

Throughout this period Vandenberg was well aware of Chiang's failures and their potential consequences. This knowledge lent credibility to the distance he kept from the administration's harshest critics. Withdrawal of the token American force in China, he asserted, would not be a signal of abandoning the Nationalists to the Communists: "This new American policy actually releases the Chinese Nationalist Government to 'clean out' the armed Chinese Communists."[30]

Vandenberg's hopes did not materialize. The new policy merely accelerated the pace of the Nationalists' fall. A year and a half later, writing to a correspondent in Saginaw, he was "forced to say that the Nationalist government has failed to reform itself in a fashion calculated to deserve continued popular confidence over there or over here. Under the circumstances, it is *not* an easy thing to chart an appropriate course of emergency action. But I assure you that the subject is receiving intense and prayerful attention."[31] The senator was not exaggerating the dilemma the country was facing with respect to Chiang Kai-shek's China. He understood that the Nationalists were primarily responsible for their own failures and that military or other aid would be wasted, probably ending up in Communist hands. Yet he repeatedly insisted on locating the root cause of China's downfall in the Yalta decisions in 1945. The mistakes made there were compounded by the Truman administration's misguided efforts to bring the Communists into a unity government under the illusion that they were essentially an agrarian party.

Despite all his forebodings, Vandenberg endorsed the extension of Marshall Plan aid to Nationalist China in 1948 through the Economic Cooperation Administration (ECA), despite all his caveats about how it would be used. The Marshall Plan, though intended for Western Europe, offered an opportunity for Republicans to tack on a China addendum as a challenge to the Truman administration. The senator earlier had declared his unhappiness with "any so-called 'Marshall Plan' which does not include China within its purview." When it was included, he boasted to a California friend that "I am proud to claim at least some part in forcing China into our ECA program one year ago."[32]

He was instrumental in the Senate's backing the China Aid Bill in March 1948, which included $100 million in military assistance in addition to $338 million in economic assistance. This aid did not translate into a commitment for U.S. military participation. And it was hardly a vote of confidence in Chiang, the generalissimo. After receiving Senator Knowland's gloomy report six months later, Vandenberg mourned that "China is lost" unless the United States increased its military aid.[33]

But Vandenberg had little faith in the usefulness of military aid. Writing to a Detroit correspondent in January 1949, he confessed that "the situation in China has disintegrated so rapidly that even those of us who have held this sympathetic view toward the Nationalist Government in China confront the grave question as to *how* any sort of American aid can be made effective and *not* be a waste of American resources."[34] The answer to his rhetorical query followed three months later. The Nationalists' war with the Communists ended in their defeat on the mainland when the Communists announced on December 8, 1939, the establishment of the People's Republic of China. The generalissimo took over Formosa as his new base.

Abandoning hopes for a Nationalist recovery did not mean that Vandenberg judged the Truman administration to be absolved for its failed China policies. Before the State Department issued a white paper in July 1949 presenting the history of American diplomatic actions in China, Secretary of State Dean Acheson and Senator Connally met in June with senior State Department officials to discuss following up Vandenberg's recent offer of "close liaison between the executive and Congress on Far Eastern Policy," which he made on the Senate floor a month before. It was too late; Vandenberg had not been involved in the drafting of the white paper, a mortal error on the administration's part. Getting "the Republicans in," as Connally recommended, should have been done earlier. At this point Vandenberg scoffed at the white paper's claim to be "a recital of facts," adding, "however, it 'adds up' to a defense of [the] Administration's policy in China. I do *not* agree with this policy. I think we virtually 'sold China down the river' at Yalta and Potsdam and in our subsequent official demands for coalition with the armed Chinese Communists." Without endorsing Chiang's continued belligerence from Formosa, he hoped all was not yet lost in China, but the most he could suggest was "an affirmative policy of vigilance and helpfulness in the Far East." He asked for a "new look" that would keep the Far East out of Soviet control.[35]

A "new look" was hampered by a "condition and not a theory in Formosa—and part of this 'condition' is that the Formosans themselves probably dislike Chiang Kai-shek's regime and are becoming critical even of our American position." But a more important concern was how to keep "another billion Asiatics out of the Soviet order." He worried that "while four hundred million Chinese have been drawn (at least temporarily) into the Moscow orbit, there still remain one billion people in the Far East who are still resisting Communist aggression; and whatever our policy *now* is to be, we must make sure above everything else that it does not alienate this remaining free billion. In my opinion, any *militaristic* action on our part in respect to Formosa could seriously jeopardize our successful contacts with India and Indonesia and Indo-China, etc."[36] Since encouraging further resistance from Formosa was not a serious option in 1950, Vandenberg sought to rationalize U.S. military inaction by looking at the larger picture in Asia. This did not placate the increasingly vocal China lobby in the United States, to which the Republican Party in general attached itself.

The one open path on which Democrats and Republicans would agree was to deny Communist China the Nationalists' membership in the UN and Chiang's seat on the Security Council. Vandenberg was in full accord with this objective in 1950, but he worried about using America's veto power to achieve this result. He felt that it would undercut the position he had steadfastly maintained at meetings—beginning at the San Francisco conference—on limiting the use of the veto on the Security Council, which had been so often abused by the Soviets. Secretary of State Acheson assured him that "we would expect that when the Security Council vote took place there would be a ruling by the presiding officer that the matter was procedural and not subject to veto."[37]

This cordial exchange suggests that Vandenberg's departure from bipartisanship over China had not severed connections with the Truman administration in 1950. His admiration for General Marshall, particularly evident as the general took over the State Department in 1947, had never diminished, no matter how critical he was of the administration's judgments. Although he had no reservations about rejecting Francis Biddle's appointment to the UN in 1947, he was more circumspect in handling R. Walton Butterworth's promotion to assistant secretary of state for Far Eastern affairs in 1949, despite the concerted efforts of Republicans to oppose his nomination. Butterworth personified the failed China policy that Vandenberg had criticized so frequently. Rather than outright rejecting Butterworth, Vandenberg voted "present" when his colleagues confirmed the nomination. His vote could be interpreted as a rejection of the China lobby embraced by so many in his party. He admitted to Senator R. Owen Brewster (R-ME) on the Senate floor that while he saw Butterworth as a symbol of a failed policy, "it is not quite so easy to assert what an alternative policy might have been. I concede that is far easier to be critical than to be correct."[38]

Vandenberg's grievance against the State Department was in part a by-product of the administration's unwillingness to confide in him over China as it had over Europe. Under Secretary of State Acheson he also missed the camaraderie that he had enjoyed with Byrnes, Lovett, and Marshall: "I dislike to say *anything*, however indirectly, which reflects on anything George Marshall ever did." It was the special relationship with Marshall that modified his complaints about the Wedemeyer Report and the white paper. The senator was never in a position to serve as broker between the parties, but Acheson was appreciative of his rebuke of Senator Taft for accusing the State Department of being "guided by a left-wing group who obviously have wanted to get rid of Chiang and were willing at least to turn China over to the Communists for that purpose."[39]

Bipartisan collaboration over China never materialized, but the goodwill between the senator and the Truman administration remained firm, as evidenced in their collaboration over aid to Europe in this period. It was also evident in Vandenberg's endorsement of Truman's stance on the Korean War. The senator was quick to tell the president that "I think you have done a courageous and indispensable thing in Korea," despite having "hitherto disagreed with our official attitude toward many phases of our Far Eastern situation." "Benched" as he put it, by what would be a terminal illness, Vandenberg wanted to be as helpful as he could be in this crisis. From his home in Grand Rapids, he reiterated his defense of the administration even though he noted to a constituent in October 1950 that "the Administration's Asiatic policies were at least partially responsible for the crisis which resulted in Korea." In both letters he expressed his belief that the war was also in defense of the UN Charter.[40]

The fate of the UN was always on his mind. In November 1950 he had written, "I think the Korean War was inevitable (under the circumstances) if the United Nations are to become in any degree effective against communist aggression. . . . Perhaps we could have avoided actual hostilities if we had been firm in notifying the communist aggressors that we would oppose any aggression in Korea as we have made it plain we will do in Western Europe."[41]

THE TRUMAN DOCTRINE

Undoubtedly, the administration's reactions to European crises at the same time that Communists were defeating the Nationalists in China were an important factor in preserving bipartisanship. In Vandenberg's eyes, the fate of Western Europe, threatened by Soviet aggression, trumped China's fate in East Asia. Just as Marshall was settling into his new post as secretary of state, he had to confront the unexpected challenge of Britain's retreat from empire—in India, in Palestine, and especially in Greece. There a civil war was in progress, and unless U.S. help was made available Greece could be lost to Communism. If Greece fell, Turkey's resistance to constant Soviet pressure could be fatally undermined. In six weeks' time Britain would terminate its aid to Greece. Such was the situation that appeared to confront the president and secretary of state on February 24, 1947.[42]

The timing of the British decision could not have been more inopportune. The Republican party controlled the Eightieth Congress and consistently displayed its reluctance to expand foreign economic aid. In fact, the newly empowered Republican majority seemed as firmly opposed to reducing tariffs as it had been to providing British loans. Senator Henry

Cabot Lodge Jr. likened the Republicans' approach to budget cutting to "a man wielding a meat axe in a dark room," who "might cut off his own head."[43] The recently installed secretary of state, George Marshall, was preparing for an extended meeting of the Conference of Foreign Ministers in Moscow when the news of Britain's decision reached Washington. The State Department's management of the problem then would be in the hands of Undersecretary of State Dean Acheson, whose relations with the chairman of the Senate Foreign Relations Committee had yet to be established.

It was at this moment that Truman, after no more than a private briefing with Vandenberg and other key legislators, enunciated what would be the Truman Doctrine with the flat pronouncement that "I believe that it must be the foreign policy of the United States to support free peoples who are resisting attempted subjugation by minorities or by outside pressures." This bold statement reflected the influence of George Kennan's eight-thousand-word telegram sent from Moscow to Secretary of the Navy James Forrestal in 1946. It was widely considered to be the origins of America's containment policy.[44]

Vandenberg's initial reaction to the shocking information was a reflexive resentment over the administration's failure to consult with him as chairman of the important Senate Foreign Relations Committee. As so often in the past, he conflated the prerogatives of the Senate with his own amour propre. His mood was not helped by Secretary Marshall's clumsy presentation of the State Department report to congressional leaders, with its depressing message that failure to help Greece and Turkey could set in motion crises in Italy and France. Concisely but drily, Marshall pointed out that in the past eighteen months the position of the democracies throughout the world had materially deteriorated. While Secretary Byrnes and Senators Connally and Vandenberg had been going from conference to conference trying to fashion Western solidarity in the face of Soviet expansionism, the Russians had been engaged in a systematic effort to encircle Germany and Turkey.[45]

Marshall's succinct summation failed to impress the legislators. Their queries that immediately followed centered on how much the effort would cost and whether the United States would simply be pulling British chestnuts out of the fire. It was Acheson who saved the day when he leaned over to Marshall and asked, "Is this a private fight or can anyone get in?" Acheson felt that Marshall had "flubbed his opening statement." He then proceeded to force his audience to recognize just what the stakes were if Greece and Turkey succumbed to Communism. Visibly moved, Vandenberg responded, "Mr. President, if you will say that to the Congress and the country, I will support you and I believe that most of its members will do the same."[46]

Vandenberg once again demonstrated his allegiance to bipartisanship. At a news conference immediately after Truman's address he stated that the "President's message faces facts and so must Congress. The independence of Greece and Turkey must be preserved, not only for their own sakes but also in defense of peace and security for all of us. In such a critical moment the President's hands must be upheld." Any other course would be dangerously misunderstood. The senator did not rule out examining the implications for U.S. global policy from Communist challenges "on many fronts." Nor did he ignore the need for conformity with the UN Charter, although he recognized that the UN lacked relief funds and had no agreements with member nations for military support.[47]

But once the emotions of the moment had dissipated, he had to confront the visceral opposition of Senator Taft and his allies, always suspicious of the administration's intentions. He also had to rationalize his own doubts. Monarchical Greece, after all, was no more democratic than Nationalist China. When the president presented his program of aid to Greece and Turkey on March 12, with a request for $400 million in both economic and military aid to those countries, Vandenberg had trouble making a specific response. To a Michigan correspondent who asked "whether there was any 'precedent' for the action we are taking in Greece and Turkey," he could not offer a definitive answer. It might be compared with the crisis at Munich in 1938, and so he concluded with a judgment that "Greece must be helped or Greece sinks permanently into the communist order. Turkey inevitably follows. Then comes the chain reaction which might sweep from the Dardanelles to the China sea."[48]

This uncomfortable conclusion was accompanied by long-standing complaints about the administration's failure to consult with the Senate. Less than two weeks after the president's address, Vandenberg deplored the administration's habit of never allowing "crises" to "reach Congress until they have developed to a point where Congressional discretion is pathetically restricted. When things finally reach a point where a President asks us to 'declare war' there usually is nothing left except to 'declare war.'"[49] The Greek crisis obviously revived memories of President Roosevelt's treatment of Congress. Given the circumstances, in which the president was as surprised as Congress by the sudden British decision to withdraw its aid to Greece, the senator's charge was exaggerated if not unfair. Senator Taft was equally disconcerted.

Still, Vandenberg had no choice but to accept and implement the president's action. As chairman of the Senate Foreign Relations Committee, he worked in tandem with the ranking Republican, Tom Connally, in hearings that began on March 24 to ensure that the hearings would move the program forward and indeed to make the nation's policy toward Greece and Turkey applicable to other peoples. When Acheson testified that the president had not stated that the United States would react to other situations just as it acted in the case of Greece and Turkey, Chairman Vandenberg seized the opportunity to clarify Acheson's testimony: "In other words, I think what you are saying is that wherever we find free peoples having difficulty in defending against aggressive movements . . . we do not necessarily react in the same way each time, but we propose to react." The senator upheld the principle of the Truman Doctrine without endorsing its military application.[50]

Vandenberg's immediate legislative reaction had been to invite his Senate colleagues to submit whatever questions they had about the president's program. He received some 400 questions, which he "boiled down" to 111 inquiries. This outpouring of queries testified to how consequential the issue was to the Senate.[51] For him no question was more significant than the one he posed to the administration. This concerned the omission of a specific role for the United Nations. The State Department's draft gave no advance notification to the UN of what the United States intended and how its actions conformed with the charter's requirements.

He should not have been surprised by this omission. After listening to the president's message on Greece and Turkey on March 12 he felt that "we should proceed as far as possible within the United Nations. But it is not practical at the immediate moment because the United Nations has no relief funds, and it has not yet concluded agreements with member nations for military support."[52] But when he examined the administration's draft bill, he interpreted the absence of advance notice to the UN as an understanding that the United States would proceed unilaterally, outside the terms of the charter.

The senator had sufficient warning about the difficulties the Truman Doctrine would create if the United Nations was excluded from the program. Passionate supporters of the UN expressed their dismay over the absence of a UN role. In his column on March 18, Walter Lippmann conceded that technically the United States was not obliged to consult the UN on the requests for aid, but "the heart of the United Nations Charter and the soul of the whole undertaking is the covenant to consult with the other members, particularly the permanent members of the Security Council, when an issue of international security and peace is raised. Undoubtedly, such an issue is raised here. . . . A full explanation, and a willingness to consider objections, would meet the obligations to consult."[53]

The UN issue was also a factor among the opponents of the aid to Greece and Turkey. The Left, with Henry Wallace as spokesman, decried the absence of UN involvement as just another proof of America's hostility to the Soviet Union. These critics charged the administration with militarism through its arms aid to Greece and Turkey. Unilateral action would bypass the UN and do damage to its role as keeper of international peace. The Right, led by the McCormick-Patterson press, saw military aid to Greece and Turkey as the road to war and the economic aid as a waste of American resources.[54]

That Vandenberg was sensitive to this criticism was obvious before he submitted his amendments. He and Connally had introduced an amendment to the Greece-Turkey bill as early as March 23, pointing out that since the United Nations was not in a position to provide aid, the United States' action to ensure the freedom and independence of those countries was in conformity with the principles of the UN. This essentially was the observation the senator had made immediately after the president's speech. The amendment stipulated that after the emergency was met, the UN might assume responsibility for implementing aid.[55]

This stopgap amendment was not enough. The crisis required a more explicit engagement with the United Nations, and the Vandenberg Amendment of March 31 sought to provide it. The amendment required the president to withdraw all aid if the purposes of the aid had been accomplished or if the Security Council, with the United States waiving its veto, and the General Assembly found that action had made the aid unnecessary. It did not matter that the amendment itself may not have been necessary; it showed the nation's deference to the authority of the charter. Given Vandenberg's transparent pride in the many amendments he had offered in the Senate over the years, this was an opportunity to correct the error that Acheson had committed in minimizing the UN's role in the aid program. As Vandenberg told the Senate on April 8, this was a defect that needed immediate correction: "The Administration made a colossal blunder in ignoring the UN."[56] Acheson was the "Administration" in this instance.

It was an unfair judgment, and Acheson in his caustic way responded in kind in his memoir. Vandenberg, he observed,

> was born to lead a reluctant opposition into support of governmental proposals that he came to believe were in the national interest. . . . It helps also if he can believe in his own little stratagems. One of Vandenberg's stratagems was to enact publicly his own conversion to a proposal, his change of attitude, a kind of political transubstantiation. The method was to go through a period of public doubt and skepticism; then find a comparatively minor flaw in the proposal, pounce on it, and make much of it; in due course propose a change, always the Vandenberg amendment. Then, and only then, could it be given to his followers as true doctrine.

Such was Vandenberg's approach as well to UNRRA during World War II and the Marshall Plan later in 1947.[57]

Acheson played along, crying out "peccavi" (I have sinned), and offered to pay for his sin by making the appropriate changes in the bill. His use of hyperbole more than matched Vandenberg's. The secretary's confession may have been necessary but his solution was not; Vandenberg intended to make the changes himself. The impact of the amendment itself may have been worth indulging Vandenberg's histrionics, even though Acheson dismissed them as "window dressing [that] must have seemed either silly or cynical or both in London, Paris, and Moscow."

Vandenberg's competitive partner, Tom Connally, seemed to agree with this judgment when he observed that "in order to get it [the bill] through, I had to accept Vandenberg's amendment that the UN could end the program" when it felt that further assistance was unnecessary. Joseph Jones felt that the amendment "took most of the remaining wind out of the sails of the United Nations issue," and Acheson admitted that "the amendment won over the bulk of the doubters."[58]

As important as any other factor in the passage of the Greek-Turkish aid bill was the effect of the Vandenberg Amendment on the Taft-led opponents who worried over the cost of the program. Vandenberg's initiative, with the help of his Democratic colleague Tom Connally, immobilized them. The invocation of the UN may have served as a fig leaf for the administration's program, and it worked. The Senate debate ended on April 8 with an impassioned speech by Senator Vandenberg, less than a week after the Senate Foreign Relations Committee reported its unanimous approval. The Senate passed the Greek and Turkish aid bill on April 23 by a vote sixty-seven to twenty-three. Its bipartisan character was reflected in the thirty-five Republican and thirty-two Democratic votes in favor of the bill. The bill became law on May 22 when the president signed it at the Muehlebach Hotel in Kansas City.[59]

The assumption that the favorable outcome of the debate over the Truman Doctrine was a serendipitous by-product of Vandenberg's ego has some merit but does not do justice to the senator. His demand for conformity to the principles of the UN Charter was genuine. It fitted the priorities he identified with U.S. foreign relations—assuring the Senate's proper relations with the executive branch, addressing the continuing threats from Soviet-led Communism, and, since 1945, linking U.S. foreign policies to the charter of the United Nations. Still, there was his residual discomfort with the military aspects of the Truman Doctrine, along with the open-ended commitment it seemed to imply.

The military aspect of aid to Greece and Turkey could not be avoided, despite successful efforts on the part of the administration and Vandenberg's Foreign Relations Committee to bury it under the economic program. Writing to Representative John S. Bennett (R-MI) on March 5, 1947, the senator blamed the Soviet Union for his having to couple military with economic aid: "The United Nations is not *yet* equipped with the military reserves contemplated by its Charter because Soviet Russia has stubbornly refused . . . to sanction agreements which are to be submitted to the member nations in respect to military reserves." Given the inability of the UN to perform this function, the Truman Doctrine was forced to take its place.[60]

But this was a topic subsumed in the spring and summer of 1947, under the rubric of economic aid to Western Europe. When Dulles in conversation with Lovett in August detected indications that the United States might ask the General Assembly for a mandate to send troops to patrol Greece's northern boundaries, he felt "it would be a reckless thing to do and contrary to the spirit, if not the letter, of the Greek Assistance Act." Moreover, he doubted whether Western European nations, then developing means of implementing the Marshall Plan, would back up a "more or less private, undeclared war between the U.S. and Russia, leading from what originally was a unilateral act." Only if a Soviet veto would nullify a Security Council proposal for a civilian commission to investigate conditions in northern Greece should the Security Council raise the right of collective self-defense under Article 51 of the charter.[61] It was a judgment Vandenberg would share.

THE MARSHALL PLAN

Economic, not military, aid dominated the first six months of the Eightieth Congress in 1947. While military aid evoked the image of engaging U.S. troops in a Greek civil war, this scenario was confined to ruminations of State Department strategists. Military aid, though embedded in the Greek-Turkish aid act, was difficult enough for the nation and Congress to accept. In the spring of 1947 it would apply only to Greece and Turkey.

Economic aid itself was at risk from the Republican majority that emerged from the congressional elections of 1946. When the Greek crisis intervened in February 1947, it diverted attention from Congress's efforts to reduce direct relief to devastated Europe through continuing contributions to UNRRA. These were to expire in 1947, until the president asked for their continuation with $350 million in new funds. The House cut the bill down to $200 million, but with the help of an ambivalent Vandenberg the original sum was restored. Emergency aid was then extended to a variety of countries—China; Italy, including Trieste; and Greece. These were countries of special interest to the senator. The aid also embraced Poland, with hopes of bolstering the influence of the remnants of Western-oriented Poles.[62]

The Foreign Relations Committee's efforts exacted a price: Vandenberg had warned that supplemental aid to UNRRA was the last foreign aid authorization he would support during the session.[63] He changed his mind in light of the implications of the Truman Doctrine. If his committee and the Senate also changed their minds, it was largely due to the anti-Communist thrust of the Truman Doctrine.

A comprehensive economic aid program on an ambitious scale was needed to revive a desperate Europe. Given the mind-set of a Congress intent on reducing the obligations of government and hostile in principle to continuing foreign aid, this idea was daunting. It turned out to be all the more challenging because, unlike the situation with the Greek crisis, there was no immediate Communist threat from Moscow to an individual Western European country, despite vocal Communist minorities in France and Italy. Yet if Europe were to be rescued from ultimately succumbing to Soviet pressure or to internal Communist subversion, then the United States would have to provide a means of reviving Europe's morale as well as its economy.

The Marshall Plan was a product of the deliberations of Undersecretaries of State William L. Clayton and Dean Acheson and George Kennan's policy planning staff. Charles E. Bohlen, like Kennan a Soviet specialist and at the time a special assistant to the secretary of state, drafted the final version. Acheson, a key aide to Secretary Marshall, and Clayton, head of the world's largest cotton brokerage, saw the plan as an extension of the purposes of the Truman Doctrine.[64]

While their deliberations preceded the Greek crisis, links between the Balkans and Western Europe appeared clear to the framers of the Marshall Plan. If the tribulations of Greece and Turkey were not to be replicated in France and Italy, where large Communist parties were flourishing, then the United States must help Europeans create economic conditions that would permit them to cope with the challenges of Communism. In his Delta Council speech in Cleveland, Mississippi, on May 8, Acheson delivered what the president called a "prologue to the Marshall

Plan." Rather than dwell on the menace of Communism, the secretary of state stressed the interrelation of food and freedom. The war against Communism "will not be over until the people of the world can again feed and clothe themselves and face the future with some sense of confidence. . . . European recovery cannot be complete until the various parts of Europe's economy are working together in a harmonious whole." Truman agreed. He saw the Truman Doctrine and the Marshall Plan as "two halves of the same walnut."[65]

The way in which the two programs complemented each other was not visible to those critics who worried about the military character of the Truman Doctrine. Walter Lippmann initially found irreconcilable differences between the Truman Doctrine as presented in March and the Marshall Plan as articulated in June, attributing them to the malignant influence of George Kennan's containment policy as expressed in his "long telegram" from Moscow in 1946. The pundit expanded on this theme in twelve pieces attacking the militant doctrine of containment. Kennan, the leading American expert on Communist Russia, blamed the imprecise language of his telegram for Lippmann's mistaken belief that he was "the author of precisely those features of the Truman Doctrine that I had most vigorously opposed."[66]

Vandenberg was not indifferent to the bellicose tone of the Truman Doctrine. He could share with his mentor Lippmann the perception that Truman's message to Congress was a hasty reflex action driven by the exigencies of the moment rather than a carefully plotted plan within the larger framework of U.S. foreign policy. Military aid to Greece and Turkey then was just a stopgap measure to plug Balkan leaks in the containment of Soviet expansion. In this context economic recovery was a secondary element. Lippmann found the Marshall Plan, unlike the Truman Doctrine, to be a more mature expression of the American aid to Europe after World War I, without the stigma attached to unpaid loans. With Europe contributing to its own rehabilitation, the Marshall Plan would present a combination of American idealism and self-interest. The United States would help to transform Europe, making it a partner rather than a ward and thereby bringing mutual economic benefits as well as establishing a shield against Communist advances. The military element in the Truman Doctrine would be minimized, although there would be an expectation that a rehabilitated and reformed Europe would be able on its own to cope with Communist threats. The scene was then set for Marshall's iconic commencement address on June 5, 1947, at Harvard University. Vandenberg had not been involved in the administration's preparations for the Marshall address, and this was a problem for the senator. Had he and his committee been consulted in the bipartisan manner that he had come to expect from the executive branch, he might have been less troubled by the costs of America's largesse in the weeks preceding June 5.

It was Acheson's seemingly extravagant plans for European reconstruction, divulged in his address on May 8 to the Delta Council, that disturbed Vandenberg, particularly after Senator Alben W. Barkley (D-KY), minority floor leader, a few days later told the Society for the Advancement of Science that the cost would entail "millions, even billions of dollars." This set off alarm bells. Both Vandenberg's ego and the status of the Senate were suddenly involved. He asked Marshall and Acheson if once again he was to be confronted with a massive foreign aid proposal without being consulted in advance—this time without the excuse of an unanticipated crisis. Marshall responded using just the right tone to appease Vandenberg's sensibilities. No such ambitious foreign aid package was intended in this session, but the secretary took the occasion to inform the senator that a major foreign aid program would have to be considered sooner or later, and when it was presented it would be carefully crafted.[67]

Marshall's response not only calmed the senator but intrigued him as well. When the secretary of state made his Harvard speech, the State Department had prepared the press for a proposal of large-scale economic aid that would be a product of a coordinated plan for Western Europe as a whole. Marshall's commencement address on June 5 did just that. In his low-keyed way the secretary of state made the point that American assistance would not be given piecemeal. For the aid to be effective would require coordination with the beneficiaries and assurance that they would be willing to break down barriers that had obstructed intra-European relations in the past. A program to help Europeans could not be launched unilaterally. The formal initiative had to come from Europe, and Europeans had to bear the basic responsibility for it. "The role of this country should consist of friendly aid in the drafting of a European program and of later support of such a program so far as it may be practical for us to do so. The program should be a joint one, agreed to by a number, if not all, of the European nations."[68]

Although Vandenberg believed that the administration had respond-ed to his concerns, he still had to deal with a Republican majority in the Senate determined to reduce taxes and cut government spending. The ad-ministration would have to do more to permit him to forge a partnership on the issue. Before the United States implemented Marshall's proposals, he wanted to be assured of what Europe's needs were and what impact meeting them would have on the U.S. economy. He would not use his in-fluence as chairman of the Senate Foreign Relations Committee and key spokesman on foreign policy for his party until the president appointed a bipartisan advisory council to gather the facts and offer recommenda-tions. As he pointed out to the White House on June 13, it was important to have open discussions about large-scale aid. "But they should not be misunderstood at home and abroad. At home they should not invite anxi-eties that we shall rush into imprudent and inadequately seasoned plans. Abroad, they should not be taken as evidence that our foreign friends can depend upon us as a substitute for depending on themselves. . . . Intelligent American self-interest immediately requires a sound, over-all inventory of our own resources" before undertaking new obligations.[69]

Nine days later the administration, anxious for the approval of the powerful chairman, announced the creation of three committees, one under the secretary of the interior to consider the capacity of American resources to accept the burden of large-scale foreign aid, a second under the chairman of the Council of Economic Advisers to consider the im-pact of such aid on the domestic economy, and—most gratifying to Van-denberg—a nongovernmental advisory council, headed by Secretary of Commerce W. Averell Harriman and composed of distinguished citizens from academia and the business world, to make an independent survey that would review the whole problem of foreign aid. This group would advise the president on the proper limits of the aid program.[70]

Vandenberg had emphasized to a Michigan correspondent prior to these actions that "it is said that my recent statement regarding the Truman-Marshall Plan for aid to Europe was an *endorsement* of the 'true religion.' On the contrary, it was the *first* public statement made which challenged *America* to 'look before she leaps.'"[71] Caveats aside, the admin-

istration's responses were sufficient for Vandenberg to give his imprimatur to the European Recovery Program (ERP) and the ECA. He took a
proprietary interest in their subsequent success.

Equally if not more important for the implementation of the Marshall Plan was Western Europe's reaction to the initiative of British foreign minister Bevin and his French counterpart, Robert Schuman, in
creating the Committee of European Economic Cooperation (CEEC)—
subsequently enlarged as the Organization of European Economic Cooperation (OEEC). The participating sixteen nations agreed to accept the
American conditions of self-help and mutual aid. By pledging to expand
their own economic targets and break down tariff barriers between European countries, they would advance the goals of the ERP. The Soviet
Union's refusal to join the effort helped smooth the way for congressional approval. A four-year package based on the credibility of European
beneficiaries was put together, with the total price originally at $29 bil-
lion, pared down to $22.4 billion after careful screening and ultimately
settled at $17 billion. Undersecretary of State Lovett heeded Vandenberg's
"suggestion that the words 'not to exceed $17,000,000,000' be eliminated"
from the proposed ERP legislation.[72]

Progress from the outline of a European Recovery Program to the
composition of an Economic Cooperation Administration, the agency
charged with administering the aid, had to contend with continued Republican attempts to restrict the authority of the administration's management of the process. Among the obstacles was former president Hoover's
recommendation that Congress scrap the ERP in favor of a $3 billon fund
for world destitution relief and a $1 billion loan to revive Europe's indus-
tries. Hoover's alternatives to the ERP reflected his experience in World
War I in administering a foreign relief program. Vandenberg replied that
the Marshall Plan required a four-year commitment to ensure the revival
and future unity of Europe. Nevertheless, Hoover's call had widespread
appeal in the Republican Party as it entered an election year.[73]

Raising the money required delicate management. It was a balancing
act for the senator. He had to cope with the resistance of many members
of his own party as well as the rivalry—and jealousy—of his Democratic
ally, Tom Connally, without appearing to be a mouthpiece of the Truman administration. He remained a critic as well as an advocate of the

administration, never forgetting that the ultimate objective of the ERP was not furthering bipartisanship but frustrating Soviet ambitions "by helping them [Western European nations] to rebuild an anticommunist, self-supporting society."[74]

He also had to assure himself of the compatibility of the ERP with the United Nations Charter. He admitted in June 1947 to Clark M. Eichelberger, executive director of the American Association for the United Nations, that since the UN could not resolve the problems of Europe, the ERP was a reasonable alternative, a position he had taken earlier with the Truman Doctrine. But he added, "I entirely agree with you that it is dangerous to continue the process of going outside and beyond the United Nations in meeting these international emergencies. But we are on the horns of a dilemma because it would be equally dangerous to fail in meeting the emergencies through a reliance on inadequate United Nations resources." He thought "it would be a disservice to the United Nations to give it a task which it could not fulfill." But if the Marshall Plan succeeded, it could strengthen the UN.[75]

That the future of the UN continued to be on his mind was demonstrated six months later when the senator opposed the administration's financial plans for constructing a new UN headquarters. Although he recognized that failure to show progress in the construction program that year could give critics evidence of the UN's disintegration, he was reluctant to ask Congress for funds to finance the project when he was seeking so many billions in foreign aid. He felt himself to be in an uncomfortable position, given that "psychology is important at this stage" of the UN's life. He did not want to signal that the new headquarters was not important to the organization's future. Yet he wondered how to "justify an extra, added drain upon our resources" for a job that "is *not remotely* in the 'emergency' class." He knew that the Senate would agree.[76]

Once he was sold on the ERP, Vandenberg was an indispensable ally of the administration. He was in the thick of the struggle for the ERP. But first he had to secure Senate approval of the interim aid bill. His zeal on its behalf was so strong that, as James Reston noted, the Democrats let him carry the load in the interim aid debate and take the criticism that appropriately should have been theirs. To his wife at the end of November he wrote of "a hectic day at the White House and the State Department.

... About 20 of us met in the Cabinet room this morning. The President is trying to discriminate between 'stop-gap' aid for France and Italy to keep them afloat until spring, on the one hand, and a permanent 'Marshall Plan' on the other. (It was this differentiation which I impressed upon Marshall last night as essential to any possibility of success.)"[77]

The special session of Congress convened on November 17, 1947, did provide enough funds to sustain the economies of France and Italy through the excessively cold winter of 1947, but not without difficulty. When an amendment was introduced to cut the authorization of the interim aid bill back to $400 million, Vandenberg considered this to be a blanket opposition to the program that included Senator Taft among its leaders. He compared it to "throwing a 15 foot rope to a man who is drowning 20 feet from shore." The Michigan Republican prevailed; the bill passed the Senate by a vote of eighty-three to six.[78]

It was not that he relinquished his role as chief spokesman for his party in foreign affairs. He remained a critic as well as an advocate of the administration. He protested in June 1947 to a Northwestern University professor that he was not responsible for the shaping of American foreign policy: "People seem to think I act as sort of a co-Secretary of State in connection with foreign policy decisions. This, of course, is totally erroneous." Bipartisanship applied only to the evolution of the UN and peace treaties in Europe. He noted to a correspondent a few months later that "Congress itself cannot take the lead in foreign relations because that is the President's job not only by Constitutional requirement but also by practical reality."[79] Yet his behavior, especially when he felt the administration failed to consult him, belied the secondary role he ascribed to the Senate.

Vandenberg's was often a decisive voice in the decision-making process, despite his disclaimers. Winning the backing of the business community, in his judgment, was indispensable for the success of the campaign. He told Undersecretary Lovett that it was "*vitally* important" for the administration to engage "four or five top-level business executives as . . . aggressive witnesses" before congressional committees. "Following your suggestion," Lovett responded, "I telephoned Judge Patterson [Robert Patterson, secretary of war, 1945–1946] in New York and requested that he and his group of proponents take immediate steps to line up the type of witness you have in mind and arrange to have them ready when the time comes."[80]

Vandenberg's imprint extended beyond propagandizing the Marshall Plan. He resolved the delicate issue of administering the program by having the respected nonpartisan Brookings Institution devise a solution. He convinced Marshall not to appoint an administrator of the ECA from inside the administration, and certainly not from the State Department. An independent administrator, free from the influence of the State Department, was the solution. Dean Acheson, recently retired as undersecretary of state, would have been just such an unsuitable candidate. And William L. Clayton, another well-qualified figure, was too intimately connected with the administration, despite his status as a business leader and favorite of the *Washington Post*. The senator advised Marshall of "the overriding Congressional desire that the ERP Administrator shall come from the outside business world with strong industrial credentials and *not* from the State Department." Vandenberg found the right candidate in the automobile executive Paul Hoffman, president of the Studebaker Corporation. Hoffman accepted the position at Vandenberg's insistence, saying that "he knocked all my defenses down and by the time I spoke to the President, I couldn't say no." At the hearings on the ERP in January 1948 Vandenberg vigorously defended the independence of the administrator against Connally's concerns about infringing on the powers of the president.[81]

The senator did not hesitate to chastise the administration for failing to provide sufficient details about how the aid would be applied under ERP. He told Secretary of the Treasury John W. Snyder that "it seems indispensable to the adequate information of ERP upon the floor of the Senate that we should have more definite information regarding a breakdown by countries in respect to the ERP program" in order to satisfy Congress's "responsibility for this enormous appropriation." Snyder tried to deflect this request with the argument that any breakdown of grants and loans between countries would "risk arousing very considerable and unwelcome comment in foreign countries." Nevertheless, Snyder understood that "this risk must be taken in the larger interest of successful presentation of the program to the Congress." The National Advisory Council, he suggested, would agree to supply some estimates to the State Department, "and I am sure that the State Department will communicate with you on this matter shortly."[82] Once again, Vandenberg was more a player than an adviser.

He used his legislative skills to translate the ERP into the ECA and to advance the program through his Foreign Relations Committee, the Senate, and ultimately the House in ways indispensable to the administration. He graciously ushered more than ninety witnesses—friendly and hostile—through hearings before the Senate Foreign Relations Committee from January 8 to February 3, 1948, with the strong support of Senator Connally. Vandenberg then navigated the hostile waters of the Republican majority in the House by convincing the administration to consider a dollar figure that the opponents of ERP could accept. When Senator Taft spearheaded opposition to a $5.8 billion authorization, based on Hoover's judgment that $4 billion was adequate for the first fifteen months, Vandenberg managed to maintain the authorization at $5.3 billion for a period of twelve months.[83]

The shock of the Communist coup in Prague in February and the subsequent sharpening of Soviet pressure on the West facilitated the course of congressional negotiations over the ECA. On March 1, 1948, Vandenberg delivered a heartfelt speech to the applause of both chambers of Congress, celebrating his committee's rewriting of the bill "to consolidate the wisdom shed upon the problem from many sources. It is the final product of eight months of more intensive study by more devoted minds than I have ever known to concentrate on any one objective in all my 20 years in Congress." On March 14 the Senate voted sixty-nine to seventeen to approve the program.[84]

Vandenberg's eloquence in the Senate and his persuasiveness in private conversations did not end the debate. Two months after the passage of the bill John Taber (R-NY), chairman of the House Appropriations Committee, proud of his reputation as a budget cutter, reduced the first-year appropriations for the ECA by 25 percent. Up to this time Vandenberg often had been annoyed and frustrated by his Republican colleagues but had kept his temper. Now he lashed out at the House, defying decorum to "argue that any such cynical reversal would be a major policy decision which should not be made through the back door of an appropriation bill. It should not be made at all." Understandably, he feared that the negative impact of this sudden change on the confidence of the Allies in America's word would undercut the effectiveness of the ERP. To Dulles he complained that "I do not know of how *any thing* could be more shocking or more subversive of every Republican *pretense* toward international cooperation. Mr. Molotov told Western Europe last summer not to make the mistake of 'trusting us.' Some of our distinguished colleagues seem bent on proving how right he was."[85]

"I beg of you," he pleaded to his colleagues, "—for the sake of the hopes by which free men live—that you give the ECA a fair chance." His plea succeeded in restoring most of the funds and—more important—the confidence of the Allies. Two months later he could confide to his friend B. E. Hutchinson his optimism about the future of the ECA: "I hope it will not be forgotten that ECA started from scratch about July 1st. It's been about 90 days. It took most of that time for Mr. Hoffman to organize 'his team.' . . . It is the best 'team' I have ever seen on a Government project."[86] In other words, it was his team.

It is tempting to overestimate Vandenberg's role in giving life to the U.S. effort to revive and reconstruct Western Europe. Others arguably had even more significant roles—Truman, Marshall, Acheson. Yet his estimate of his own contribution had merit. It was more significant than his championing the Truman Doctrine, largely because his vision of the ECA's future was grander than that of the Truman Doctrine—less vague and more altruistic. The ERP lacked the military emphasis that was attached to aid to Greece and Turkey. It spoke more to the idealism that so often animated the senator's views. In both cases he could rationalize a connection with the United Nations Charter, especially with respect to the Marshall Plan. But as the ECA was slowly coming into existence in 1947 and 1948, new challenges arose in the form of military assistance to a still fearful Western Europe. How efforts to meet these challenges could fit the terms of the United Nations Charter would become a primary problem in his approach to the North Atlantic Treaty Organization.

9

Charter and Treaty, 1948–1949

From 1947, when Vandenberg assumed the mantle of Republican leadership in matters of American foreign policy, until his hospitalization in the fall of 1949, the postwar world in Europe entangled him in conflicting emotions about the direction the United States should take. His polestar was the United Nations Charter; since his active participation in its composition at San Francisco in 1945, he had identified America's—and the world's—future with the success of this new international organization. His subsequent diplomatic experiences as a delegate to UN agencies and to meetings of foreign ministers confirmed the United Nations' indispensable role in the maintenance of world peace.

At the same time he saw this role jeopardized by a host of forces that included his own government and his own party as well as the enduring hostility of Soviet-led Communism to his conception of a new world order. Throughout this period the senator had to cope with the lingering isolationism of the Republican Party, which required the exercise of all his legislative skills and personal charm to keep in check. Concurrently, he had to be continually alert to the Truman administration's use of bipartisanship to compromise his position with his own party and—more importantly—to diminish the Senate's proper function in the management of the nation's foreign relations. But the most significant challenge was the Soviet Union's continuing pressure to control whatever parts of Europe it could and to advance its Communist system in those areas it could not control. In a world still reeling from the devastation of World War II, the Soviets regarded the UN as an instrument of American power that could inhibit Communist expansion. Vandenberg's abhorrence of

Communism and suspicion of Soviet policies were long-standing. He had opposed President Roosevelt's recognition of Moscow's legitimacy in 1933 and believed that his administration's softness toward Communism was at the heart of the regrettable concessions at Yalta in 1945. Yet Vandenberg was well aware that the United States must coexist with the USSR with some accommodation if the United Nations was to survive.

These were the sources of tensions that hung over Vandenberg's tenure as spokesman for his party in the loyal opposition to the administration in power. The electoral victory of the Republicans in 1946 provided Vandenberg with authority, as chairman of the Senate Foreign Relations Committee, to guide American foreign policy without being, as he noted frequently, a "co-secretary of state." How he juggled his objectives for the nation's foreign policies was a primary factor in determining their course in these critical years.

The Vandenberg Resolution

Looking back to 1947 one can claim that the Truman Doctrine was a by-product of the panicked reaction to Britain's withdrawal from the Balkans. To convince the country and particularly Congress, the administration had to frighten them into recognizing the implications of a Communist victory in Greece's civil war.

America, as the bulwark against the spread of Communism, would offer aid—military and economic—to free nations under siege. But the Balkans were not to be the focus of America's concerns in that year. The global reach of the Truman Doctrine was modified by caveats. The nation's focus was on economic, not military, aid for the more important area of Western Europe. The recovery and reorganization of Europe as envisioned by the Marshall Plan occupied center stage in Vandenberg's picture of America's place in the world. If successful, the European Recovery Program, morphing into the Economic Cooperation Administration in 1948, would serve a number of goals: reviving a Europe capable of resisting Soviet-led Communism, downplaying the need for a military response to Soviet aggressiveness, and displaying full conformity with the goals of the United Nations.

Vandenberg's embrace of an economic plan that would reform Europe, keep the Soviets at bay, and serve the interests of the UN did not include rearming Europe. The military dimension in the Truman Doctrine that had worried the senator was present in tandem with the economic element, even as the Marshall Plan was being devised. But Ernest Bevin and Georges Bidault, the foreign ministers of Britain and France, respectively, had signaled the inadequacy of economic aid by admitting that Soviet hostility to the West, expressed in the Communist parties of France and Italy, made a military response imperative. In their judgment only American participation, not just economic or even military aid, would provide the sense of security that Europeans needed for the ERP to deter Soviet aggression. To effect this result would require the United States to accept an entangling alliance in violation of its long tradition of isolationism.

The two foreign ministers would use the failure of the Council of Foreign Ministers to win the Americans over to their plans. The Soviet denunciation of the Marshall Plan and its intransigence over the future of Germany certainly awakened senior State Department officials to the possibility of just such an entanglement. After the collapse in December 1947 of the London meetings of the council, John D. Hickerson, director of the Office of European Affairs, told his subordinate Theodore C. Achilles, director of the Office of Western European Affairs, that "I don't care if entangling alliances have been considered worse than original sin since George Washington's time. We've got to have a peacetime military alliance with Western Europe. And we've got to get it ratified. It's your baby. Get going." Achilles attributed the language to fish house punch that Hickerson drank at the Metropolitan Club on New Year's Eve but agreed with the message he was delivering.[1]

Vandenberg was not a participant in the London sessions of the Council of Foreign Ministers or in any other European sessions after he assumed the chairmanship of the Foreign Relations Committee. Aside from the Rio mission in the summer of 1947, which was a happy diversion from his new duties, he stayed in Washington, burdened with responsibilities relating to the Truman Doctrine and the Marshall Plan. He turned down subsequent invitations to join U.S. delegations abroad. He declined Lovett's invitation to accompany the American delegation to a UNESCO conference in Mexico in November 1947 and Secretary Marshall's to the fateful Conference of Foreign Ministers in London in December. As for sending committee advisers to the UNESCO conference, he informed Lovett that "the continuous presence of the entire Senate Foreign Relations Committee is necessary in Washington and on the Senate job until the European aid programs are concluded."[2]

But there was no doubt about his familiarity with the problems raised by the Bevin-Bidault initiatives. Dulles kept him informed, first as the State Department's special representative in Paris to assure the French that their interests would be protected in the subsequent meeting in Paris and then as Vandenberg's representative with the foreign ministers in London. En route home from Southampton in December 1947, Dulles listened sympathetically to his shipmate Hickerson's conviction that only a military alliance could create sufficient confidence in Europe to restore the political and economic health of Western Europe. Dulles was impressed with Hickerson's argument and undertook to convince Vandenberg about the possibility of a commitment.[3]

That Vandenberg had been mulling the impact of the worsening relations between the Western democracies and the Soviet Union in the UN before the end of the London meeting was apparent in his linking of the Rio Pact to the European scene. The Soviet Union's maddening abuse of the veto power turned his attention to the position of the Rio Pact as a regional organization with the blessing of the UN Charter. He detected in the charter's explicit recognition in Article 51 of the "inherent right of individual or collective self-defense" a means of evading the Security Council's authority. In this context the Soviet Union could not exercise its veto power. He had found a way, as he informed a Kalamazoo constituent, "to circumvent the deadly 'veto'" and so "keep the United Nations vigorously alive for essential service even under adverse circumstances." He was not alone in this perception. Two weeks later he applauded the proposal of Hamilton Fish Armstrong, editor of the influential journal *Foreign Affairs,* to have the United States use Article 51 to make possible "protective actions" that would prevent the Soviets from exploiting the veto as a "tool to frustrate all efforts to lay a firm basis for peace and security."[4]

The concept of a European federation had been circulating throughout 1947, most notably in the concurrent resolution of Senator J. William Fulbright (D-AR) and Representative Elbert Thomas (D-UT) in March of that year, stating that "the Congress favors the creation of a United States of Europe within the framework of the United Nations."[5] Certainly, the deference to the United Nations would have appealed to the Michigan senator, but its lack of detail seemed a form of grandstanding that went beyond what Vandenberg or Democratic leaders would accept. Senate Minority Leader Alben Barkley (D-KY) observed with respect to economic aid that "while we may entertain the hope that that there would be a merger or amalgamation of the nations of Europe into one country, we cannot by implication make that a condition upon which we make this aid available." Vandenberg chimed in with his own reservations, fearing that any specific reference to political integration would be "a source of maximum embarrassment for at least a few of the exposed European countries."[6] The assumption of many of those sympathetic to European integration was that passage of an ECA bill would accelerate the process without the necessity of passing the Fulbright-Thomas resolution.

Vandenberg was pessimistic about the possibility of revising the UN Charter in light of Soviet behavior in the UN: "I would think that a *futile* U.S. Charter revision convention could be the worst possible thing that could happen to all our hopes. The fact of the matter is that most of the Charter difficulties would be very simply corrected by a *voluntary* change in the procedure of the Security Council regarding the use of the veto. So long as this is impossible, I see no present chance of arriving at a kindred result through revisionary compulsion."[7] He was also unhappy with a congressional resolution that would resolve the veto impasse by retaining the veto when pacific settlement of disputes was involved but would remove the veto in the Security Council from issues involving sanctions and the use of force. Obviously for different reasons, he lined up with the Soviet position at this point. He was concerned about the Security Council infringing on the constitutional powers of Congress to declare war. If the resolution removed the veto "only in case of armed aggression, it would allow others to tell us when we must go to war. It would push us out of the UN and leave it exclusively to Russia and its satellites."[8]

Despite the priority the chairman of the Senate Foreign Relations Committee gave to the passage of the ECA bill in 1948, circumstances in Europe forced him to focus on the rising Soviet threats to the West in the winter and spring, just as he was pressing the case for the ERP. The Soviet menace intensified throughout Western Europe in this period. While the

Communist coup in Prague in February was the most shocking instance, stalemate over Soviet policies in Germany, Soviet attempts to intimidate Norway, the continuing Communist war in Greece, and Communist uprisings in French and Italian cities all suggested that Soviet-led Communist activities had risen to a new level.

The West's reactions took a specific form—activation of Bevin's and Bidault's plans to lure the United States into a military alliance. The initial step was a stirring speech by Bevin on January 22, 1948, promoting a vision of a union of Western democracies, with Britain abandoning its traditional detachment from the Continent. The promise of such action, along with the activation of the self-help provisions of the Marshall Plan, seemed to be fulfilled on March 17 when Britain, France, and the Benelux countries concluded the Brussels Treaty, creating a Western Union (WU) that sought to coordinate their economic and military policies.[9] Its key provision would assure each member that if any one country should be the object of an armed attack, every other member, in accordance with Article 51 of the UN Charter, "will afford the party so attacked all the military and other aid and assistance in their power." The underlying purpose of the Brussels Pact, however, was clearly stated by former French premier Paul Renaud. Without U.S. participation, the Western Union "would be a mere outline with no substance and dangerous as well, since it would encourage illusions of non-existing strength."[10]

Europe's hopes were not immediately fulfilled. The United States did not join the Western Union. Its response was cautious. Aside from such enthusiasts as Hickerson and Achilles, the State Department's chiefs, Marshall and Lovett, were not ready to discard a long tradition of abstention from entangling alliances. Nor was the chairman of the Senate Foreign Relations Committee, one of whose anchors in foreign relations had been the Monroe Doctrine. Vandenberg feared that military aid would be a diversion from the aims of the ERP. Yet the fundamental argument of the Europeans could not be refuted. As the senator observed to a Grand Rapids friend in January 1949, the United States could not wait until economic stability returned to Europe before supplying military aid: "The basic question we have to settle is whether 'economic stability' can *precede* the creation of a greater sense of physical security. I am inclined to think that 'physical security' is prerequisite to the long-range economic planning which Western Europe requires."[11]

A way had to be found to provide the sense of security necessary for the ERP to succeed. While the Rio model offered a path to giving regional organizations legitimacy under Article 51, the United States obviously was not a logical candidate for membership in a European union. President Truman's reaction to the creation of the Brussels Pact was a dramatic address to Congress on March 17, 1948. It inspired the pact's authors to accept Bevin's observation, made two weeks before the treaty was signed, that "it seemed pretty clear that the Americans would, in fact, come in the long run, and recent events have made this all the more likely." The president's speech seemed to confirm this prediction, with Truman saying, "I am confident that the United States will, by appropriate means, extend to the free nations the support which the situation requires. I am sure that the determination of the free countries of Europe to protect themselves will be matched by an equal determination on our part to help them protect themselves."[12] Truman's language was ambiguous enough to encourage British expectations.

Two weeks after the president's speech a military alliance appeared to emerge from secret meetings held in the Joint Chiefs of Staff war room in the bowels of the Pentagon between American political and military leaders and their British and Canadian counterparts. Acting Secretary of State Lovett, Ambassador Lewis W. Douglas, John D. Hickerson, and Theodore C. Achilles represented the State Department at these "ultra ultra" sessions. Major General Alfred M. Gruenther, director of the Joint Staff, was the Defense Department's representative. These meetings, extending from March 22 to April 1, 1948, were so secret that one Pentagon chauffeur got lost trying to find the room. The secrecy surrounding these sessions itself created a problem. None of the other allies, notably France, knew that an alliance was in the works. But the State Department recognized the importance of winning the "concurrence of a few Congressional leaders, including Senator Vandenberg," and shared with them the position paper on the potential North Atlantic regional security arrangement.[13]

The obstacles to the security alliance envisioned in the Pentagon conversations were not easily overcome. Although America's membership in the Western Union was an untouchable subject, the administration encouraged Europeans to seek military integration along the lines of the Marshall Plan. Specifically, it endorsed the National Security Council's Directive No. 9 (NSC 9), on April 13, 1948, a promise of U.S. military aid if the Europeans came up with a coordinated defense system. This was not a sufficient commitment for the Allies, particularly for the British. They chafed over the secrecy imposed on the Pentagon proceedings. Nor were Europeans comforted by the removal of a military aid provision in the ECA bill. Despite the positive tone of NSC 9, it excluded American membership in the Western Union.[14]

What brightened the atmosphere was the Lovett-Vandenberg collaboration in setting the scene for a military arrangement that would be acceptable to all parties, European and American. They had come to know each other in their official capacities—Lovett as George Marshall's undersecretary of state and often acting secretary in Marshall's absence and Vandenberg, the most influential congressional figure, as chairman of the Senate Committee on Foreign Relations. They made an odd couple, given the larger-than-life personality of Vandenberg and the quiet, unobtrusive authority of Lovett. The Michigan politician-turned-statesman worked comfortably with the Ivy League–educated Wall Street banker–turned–diplomatist. They shared a vision of American leadership coping with the Communist threat by reviving and reforming a divided Western Europe. Not that their positions were identical; Lovett, though a Republican, served a Democratic administration and also served the particular interests of the State Department.

Theodore Achilles recalled that Britain's dissatisfaction with the lack of American initiatives after the Pentagon conversations induced the president to consider a direct military alliance with the Brussels Pact powers, warning the Soviets against any act of aggression toward the pact members. The Soviets' incipient Berlin blockade, following the creation of "Bizonia," uniting the American and British sectors of West Germany, increased a sense of urgency. But when Lovett raised the issue with Vandenberg, he "got a resounding [though ambivalent] 'No.' Why should Truman get all the credit." The idea appealed to the senator, but he suggested that, instead of an exclusive executive action, the Senate should ask the president to negotiate such an alliance. This would be in keeping with the bipartisan approach Vandenberg had been following since 1945.[15]

Lovett welcomed the Vandenberg suggestion, knowing how important the senator's voice would be in reversing the way American attitudes toward Europe had become fixed since the beginnings of the republic. A close working relationship with the Michigan senator would have other advantages. Involving the Senate in the process would reduce pressures from Europe for immediate results at a time when the Senate was absorbed in appropriations for the ERP.[16] The result was a partnership that had its origins in political expediency but quickly developed into a comfortable and productive fellowship, steeped in goodwill and mutual admiration. Vandenberg later mused nostalgically about Lovett's regular visits to his apartment, 500G in the Wardman Park Hotel. Over cocktails and cigars the two men hammered out documents that would become the European Cooperation Act and the Vandenberg Resolution (S. Res. 239). They enjoyed each other's company as they collaborated on texts that would satisfy all parties. Theirs was a connection the acerbic Acheson could never replicate.[17]

The Rio Treaty was both a model and an obstacle as Lovett and Vandenberg worked their way through the implications of U.S. association with the Brussels Pact. While Vandenberg always saw the Rio Pact as a regional organization that embraced the United States by updating the Monroe Doctrine, Lovett's willingness to apply the Rio Treaty without reservations to the proposed Atlantic security pact was unacceptable. The senator would not allow an automatic commitment to war based on incidents in Europe. The senatorial prerogative could be breached. This meeting with Lovett was also an occasion for Vandenberg to take the sting out of the military character of the proposed security arrangement. He would oppose in committee and on the floor of the Senate any U.S. obligation to the defense of the Western Union that would violate the terms of the UN Charter.[18]

Many of the final details were fine-tuned at Blair House on April 27, 1948. There Vandenberg called into question the administration's idea of the Senate adopting a resolution approving in principle a North Atlantic regional pact and then having the president call a convention of North Atlantic states, with the Brussels Pact members as its core. He felt that a conference should be called by the Europeans, not by the United States, and should take into account its relations with the United Nations. In recommending this path, the senator clearly emphasized the roles of both the Senate and the United Nations in association with a regional compact.[19]

Just one month after the first discussion at the senator's Wardman Park residence the resolution was ready for consideration by the Senate Foreign Relations Committee. Given the senator's concern for the future of the United Nations, it was not surprising that its charter featured prominently in the Vandenberg Resolution. Its preamble not only assumed the need for more effective use of the UN but went on to resolve that the Senate reaffirm the policy of the United States to achieve international peace and security through the United Nations. The resolution's key provision, in Paragraph 2, established the infrastructure for the membership of the United States in an enlarged Western Union: "progressive development of regional and other arrangements for individual and collective self-defense, in accordance with the principles and provisions of the Charter." Paragraph 4 specified Article 51 as provenance for the prospective regional association. Equally important was the requirement in Paragraph 3 that the United States' association with the organization would be "based on continuous and effective self-help and mutual aid." This seemed to signal a breakthrough in America's resistance to guaranteeing European security, but it was accompanied by Vandenberg's insertion of "constitutional process." The inclusion of Article 51 evaded a Soviet veto in the UN, but emphasis on the constitutional process evaded Europe's hopes for American membership in the new security arrangement. It preserved congressional authority over a declaration of war.[20]

Vandenberg's imprint was evident in every aspect of the resolution, and the president, behind the scenes, was pleased to see to it that it would be identified as a "Vandenberg Resolution." What better way of guaranteeing consensus in Congress? Even the wording of the resolution was Vandenbergian. No matter how verbose and grandiloquent he was in his many speeches, he was known as "one-page Vandenberg" for his insistence on reducing his resolutions to a single page. Lovett's staff, particularly Achilles, wrote the key paragraphs with the senator looking over his shoulder before typing the final draft on his battered portable machine. Achilles noted that Vandenberg wanted the resolution to be labeled "a Resolution of the Foreign Relations Committee" rather than the "Vandenberg Resolution." However, he could not have been displeased when the press and everyone else preferred the latter.[21]

Vandenberg's detractors—and even his admirers—usually belittle his contributions, often unintentionally. His parliamentary skills receive full appreciation, as does the enormous influence he exerted as the most commanding fixture in the Senate on foreign policy affairs. State Department official Joseph Jones and political scientist H. Bradford Westerfield both credited the senator with technical talents in winning legislative battles but were skeptical about his ability to conceptualize policies. Neither Acheson nor Kennan would contest this judgment. But Daryl J. Hudson, then a student at Georgetown University Law Center, took a different tack, pointing out that Russian scholar Adam Ulam claimed Vandenberg to be "as much as the secretary of state . . . responsible for the general direction of American policy."[22]

Lovett's recollections were more than an affectionate memory of their collaboration in 1948. He recalled taking copies of important cables to the senator's apartment and then working with him in developing positions.[23] Vandenberg was anxious to find evidence of Western Europe's commitment to building its own defenses in a collaborative way before the United States committed itself to reciprocal support. Membership in an expanded Western Union might be possible in the future, but no commitment to U.S. inclusion in this alliance should be made at this juncture. He impressed upon the administration the limitations of regional arrangements that would come under review of the Security Council and the veto power of its members. For this reason, Article 51 was an essential contribution to the resolution and, according to Hudson, made Vandenberg as much an author of Senate Resolution 239 as any member of the State Department.[24]

Vandenberg wasted no time in hurrying the bill through his committee and on to the Senate floor. The sooner he could make the resolution official, the easier it would be to deflect the many reservations critics both in Congress and in the press were bound to make. The most serious critics were often the most supportive of the senator's objective in upholding the authority of the United Nations.

Reshaping the UN to exclude the Soviets had some merit but would risk war without the backing of the General Assembly to ameliorate tensions. "I would think that a *futile* U.N. Charter revision would be the worst possible thing that could happen to all our hopes," Vandenberg told a Seattle correspondent in February 1948. Writing to his friend and colleague Senator Henry Cabot Lodge at the end of the year, he summed up his reasons against such dramatic changes in the UN. He asked for patience with the organization; it was only three years old. What would be the benefit of a formal statute forbidding its members to engage in wars? "It seems to me the realities are that if we cannot get Soviet and satellite cooperation in making the far more limited controls of the United Nations work . . . we could not reasonably expect Soviet cooperation in the conclusive controls of 'world government.' . . . Therefore, the question really boils down to this: are we ready to organize the world without the Russians, which is to say, against one sixth of the world which is Russian controlled? This one sixth may soon become nearer one fourth if China falls."[25]

This was not just a rhetorical question. He had an answer. Use Article 51, with the Rio Pact as a *"working model,"* he pointed out to the secretary of the Detroit Committee on Foreign Relations. But his preoccupation in May 1948 was not with fending off impractical reforms of the UN. Rather, he concentrated on the importance of Europeans showing the same willingness they had displayed in the wake of the Marshall Plan to emphasize self-help and mutual aid before the United States would complete a commitment to a new Atlantic union. This was the theme of his introduction to the Committee on Foreign Relations hearings on the Vandenberg Resolution on May 11, 1948. He opened the proceedings by underscoring the limits of America's association with a new security pact. He made it clear that "we are not presuming to have relinquished our constitutional function to give consent as well as giving advice to the President." He subsequently added that "there can be no open ended obligation of any sort whatsoever in respect to military assistance to Western Europe; . . . we must maintain our right of self-determination even as we grant it to others."[26]

Ten days later the Foreign Relations Committee voted unanimously to send Senate Resolution 239 to the Senate. He encountered little difficulty there, even when Walter George (D-GA), a member of the committee, questioned the wisdom of overextending U.S. commitments. The Georgia Democrat raised the question without opposing the resolution.

There was more agitation on the floor from both the Right and the Left. George Malone (R-NV) suspected a European trap to entangle Americans, while Fulbright wanted to insert a requirement of political unity into the resolution. Neither intervention prevented a Senate vote on June 11, 1948, that had only six negative votes. Fulbright and Taft abstained but did not vote against the resolution.[27]

THE PRESIDENTIAL ELECTION OF 1948

It was understandable if Vandenberg's haste in insulating his resolution from further debate was governed, at least in part, by the upcoming Republican convention in Philadelphia. It would also be understandable if he wanted the issue behind him as a successful prerequisite for his party's presidential candidacy. His appetite for the position had been demonstrated in 1940. His chagrin at being passed over in favor of the outlier Wendell Willkie was no secret. That 1948 was expected to be the year when the Republicans would return to the White House after sixteen years in the wilderness should have been a situation made to order for the Michigan senator. Without Roosevelt to contend with, the party saw Truman as vulnerable. Given the division within the Democratic Party between southern Dixiecrats and Wallace Progressives, along with the putative failures of the president himself in managing the economy, the press gave Truman no chance for success. *Newsweek* polled fifty leading pundits for its October 1948 issue. Not one journalist, including Lippmann and Reston, predicted a Truman victory.[28]

Despite the inducements, Vandenberg had no intention of seeking the presidency in 1948. It was not that he felt too old, although he mentioned this as a factor. Nor was it fear of defeat. His chances were better than those of his rivals in light of his accomplishments in the Senate. Rather, it was a genuine belief in the impact his Senate position had on the country and on his own legacy. From his Senate perch he could promote long-standing and recent goals, ranging from preservation of the Senate's prerogatives in foreign affairs to the advancement of the United Nations as the guardian of world peace. Not least of his reasons were his hopes for the future of the Republican Party, anchored to foreign policies he had framed.

Friends and enemies alike doubted his sincerity. But long before the convention met he was writing confidentially to a Detroit journalist "that I am not a candidate for the Republican Presidential nomination; that I do not intend to be a candidate; and that I do not wish to be a candidate. . . . There is nothing 'coy' about this statement. On the contrary, I mean every word of it."[29]

By speaking out clearly he hoped he could avoid any "draft movement." He failed to stop it. His stature in the state and in the country was too prominent to deter a Vandenberg boom. Michigan's was the most aggressive claque but his support was nationwide, especially among those who would stop a Dewey candidacy. The journalist Richard Rovere, writing in the May 1948 issue of *Harper's Magazine,* was puzzled as to why the Republicans endured "strife and discord in their search for a good candidate when all they have to do is draft a perfect candidate, Vandenberg, and call it a day."[30]

Arguably, the most impressive testimonials came from admiring Democrats. Former undersecretary of state Sumner Welles asserted that "good Democrat as I am, I must frankly say that in light of the crisis that is now looming I feel equally strongly that there is no other American who as President of the United States would be as well fitted as yourself to direct this Nation's foreign policy." A sharper-tongued Harold Ickes, Roosevelt's secretary of the interior, commented after the convention adjourned, "I don't know whether to hate you or admire you. From the very first you were my first choice for the Republican nomination, up to the very last, I firmly believed you would be the nominee. . . . But in any event, you out-Caesared Caesar in not only pushing aside the crown three times, but fifty times." He wondered if Vandenberg did not regret his "course a bit when the unutterable McCormick of Chicago [publisher of the *Chicago Tribune*] gave voice to the expression that 'Anyhow, Dewey was preferable to Vandenberg.'"[31]

Certainly, he was flattered by this groundswell of support, and he admitted he would have accepted a draft. But he knew this was unrealistic after Dewey's "unexpected show of strength on the first ballot," as he noted in his diary during the convention. Commenting on his decision to oppose his own nomination, the senator identified three reasons. First, he recalled the years he had spent in "fostering bipartisan unity in behalf of collective peace and security for us and the world. I considered it to be the dedication of my life. . . . I felt that its greatest danger in the critical days ahead was *not* in the White House but in the Congress." If ever he felt "some degree of *temporary* indispensability" it was to serve in the Senate at this time. Another reason—prescient in light of his death at the age of sixty-seven—involved his sense of age; he would be sixty-five in 1949, with the potential of replicating the misfortune of Woodrow Wilson's incapacity during the debate over the League of Nations. His final reservation stemmed from a conviction that in the new Republican House of Representatives he would be a divisive figure, given past legislative battles. Republican unity on a bipartisan foreign policy that he had put into the platform could be jeopardized if he were to become president.[32]

Vandenberg had no problem with Dewey as the party's choice. Dulles, after all, would be the next secretary of state, which meant that the causes he had worked for over the last three years would be in good hands. As he told a Detroit friend, "I am happy to say that the foreign policy planks in the new Republican platform are practically verbatim as I wrote them for submission to the Convention Resolutions Committee through Chairman Lodge. Without doubt Governor Dewey came closer to representing my viewpoints than any other Presidential candidates (with the possible exception of Stassen)."[33]

This was hardly a surprise. He worked to fend off isolationists' attempts on the convention's Resolutions Committee to "upset any sort of an enlightened foreign policy." With Dewey in the White House and Dulles in the State Department he looked forward "to the right kind of foreign policy for the next four (and probably eight) years." On the reasonable assumption that he would continue as chairman of the Foreign Relations Committee, he wanted the country and the world to know that his bipartisan policy would also continue. He issued a statement after a conference with Dewey and Dulles ensuring that "other nations which do not understand our political system should not be misled by our political campaign at home." As he told Dulles in July, "It is to be ever remembered that the next Republican Secretary of State is going to need Democratic votes in the Senate just as badly as the present Administration needed Republican votes."[34]

The bipartisan relationship with the Democrats still was a problem for his party that needed resolution, and Vandenberg clarified it for his colleagues. The foreign policies that he identified with himself—the Truman Doctrine, the Marshall Plan, and most particularly the diplomacy leading to a new alliance with Europe—were to be separated from the failed China policy of the Truman administration. Although the Vandenberg Resolution had opened the way in the summer of 1948 for an Atlantic treaty, there was no need to hurry it to completion. This could wait until a Dewey victory in November.

As the campaign grew more heated in the summer, Vandenberg's ability to distinguish the Republicans' foreign policy from the Democrats' was facilitated by the arrogance the Democrats displayed and by the errors they made. It was unseemly for the Democrats to claim all the credit for the results of bipartisan cooperation. Dulles was gratified in a chat with Lovett to learn that he and Marshall "were bitterly disappointed" in the Democratic Party platform. They thought that Truman had agreed to share credit with Vandenberg but "in the end the political advisers had written it their way." Vandenberg was repelled too by Truman's impulsive decision to send Chief Justice Fred Vinson to Moscow a month before the election to discuss major differences between the United States and the Soviet Union. Marshall's opposition on the grounds that this would subvert negotiations in Paris over the toxic Berlin crisis effectively squelched the idea, but it gave Vandenberg an opportunity to dismiss it as a "shot in the arm" for a failing campaign.[35]

Of all the offenses committed by the Truman campaign, the charge that the Eightieth Congress was the worst in history struck Vandenberg as the most outrageous. It was a feature of the Truman campaign. The senator was insulted. He complained to Dulles that "in the most important of all particulars (foreign relations) this is the *best* Congress in history. There is nothing remotely like it in the whole Congressional story for more than 150 years. . . . I think it is the most amazing record of constructive cooperation ever written in *any* Congress and I think it largely responsible for the country's substantial unity in its foreign policy voice, a 'unity' that may spell the difference between peace and war."[36]

It was not a subject he would put behind him easily. In a letter to Cornell University professor Curtis P. Nettels after the election he said that "my greatest criticism (among others) of President Truman's campaign speeches" was his failure to distinguish between domestic and foreign policies when he chastised the Eightieth Congress as "the second worst in history." The president was happy enough to claim all the foreign policy successes as his party's. The senator felt he had rebutted this smear in a nationwide address on October 4 when he reaffirmed the bipartisan policies in such a way that "Moscow can get no consolation from these results nor can it depend upon our disunity to 'divide and conquer.'"[37]

His resentment over Democratic tactics notwithstanding, Vandenberg had signaled in September, after conferring with Dewey and Dulles, that "regardless of political differences at home we are serving notice on the world that America is united to protect American rights everywhere through firmness in the right to seek peace with justice for ourselves and other peace-loving peoples of the world." There is no doubt about his sincerity. His telegram of congratulations to Truman on his unexpected victory spoke of closing "ranks behind the nation's chosen leadership."[38] As far as he was concerned they were already closed in the realm of foreign relations. There was little daylight between Vandenberg and the State Department as the nation committed itself to an Atlantic alliance in the summer of 1948.

THE NORTH ATLANTIC TREATY

Had Thomas Dewey been elected president in 1948, the North Atlantic Treaty might have been signed before the end of the year. Most of the provisions of a treaty were ready in September following the conclusion of the Washington Exploratory Talks on Security in July 1948—the talks that implemented the Vandenberg Resolution. Such was the reasonable expectation of the Republican leadership before the first Tuesday in November.

Truman's election upset the timetable and delayed the completion of the treaty until the spring of 1949. Delay was inevitable. A new team occupied the State Department. Marshall and Lovett, late but steadfast converts to an Atlantic alliance, retired in January. The new secretary of state, Dean Acheson, not only had to establish a facsimile of the relationship with Vandenberg that Lovett had managed so well but also had to become fully knowledgeable about the state of negotiations since his departure in

June 1947 as undersecretary of state. In the Senate the wary collegiality between Vandenberg and Connally was to be tested as Connally assumed the chairmanship of the Senate Foreign Relations Committee. He resented his predecessor's prestige and did whatever he could to outshine him. Vandenberg enjoyed telling his wife that "old Tawm" tried to talk him out of making a speech as the treaty debate opened in the Senate. When Vandenberg responded that he intended to give "the speech of his life," Connally was reported to say that he too was prepared to write "the speech of his life." The Michigan Republican "got a great kick out of that."[39] Not least of the difficulties in restoring consensus between the White House and the new Republican minority in the Senate were the natural hard feelings produced by the recent campaign.

That Vandenberg would continue the bipartisan policies toward Europe that had characterized his leadership in the Eightieth Congress was never in question. The Atlantic alliance was a direct consequence of his Vandenberg Amendment. To turn his back on this development would have meant repudiating his beliefs in the direction the nation had to move to achieve both containment of Soviet expansion, then centered on its failing blockade of West Berlin, and the security of both Western Europe and the United States.

His bipartisanship took a number of forms. He resisted Republican opposition to Acheson's appointment, even though his voice lacked enthusiasm. He had to repeat to such friends as Sumner Welles and Senator Raymond Baldwin (R-CT) that amending the UN Charter by removing the veto was not only unwise but also unnecessary; Article 51 allowed collective as well as individual defense.[40]

More difficult to resolve was Acheson's lack of appreciation for the limitations that the Vandenberg Resolution had placed on the obligations of the United States to provide military aid to the Europeans. Acheson was in general accord with the senator's position on Article 5 of the North Atlantic Treaty, but his "arrogance of expression," as Escott Reid observed, needlessly antagonized his European counterparts. Still, it seemed that Acheson was watering down the article's significance when he impatiently objected to inserting "military" as an "unnecessary embellishment." Vandenberg essentially agreed with the secretary's sentiments, uncomfortable as he always was with the military component of the alliance. But he understood that Article 5 needed a more nuanced response to appease the Allies.[41]

He was less appreciative of the way Chairman Connally expressed his suspicion that the Europeans were using the treaty to exploit America's military power for their own special interests. In an image worthy of Vandenberg's hyperboles on the Senate floor, Connally exclaimed, "We cannot . . . be Sir Galahads every time we hear a gun fired, plunge into war and take sides without knowing what we are doing and without knowing the issues involved." Although Vandenberg preferred to omit a specific reference to military action in Article 5, he felt that Connally's replacement of the assurance that "an attack against one . . . [would] be considered an attack against them all" with "an attack against one would be regarded as a threat to peace of all" too vague to satisfy the allies.[42] And it was unnecessary. The UN Charter's Article 51 provided the framework for defense of the West without the necessity of listing military details. The administration and its chief senatorial ally, Vandenberg, were now paying for the secrecy that had attended negotiations over the past year.

To circulate this message without being too precise was a priority for the senator. He responded to queries from a Grand Rapids friend, admitting that "there is no doubt that it is a 'calculated risk' for us [to] even partially arm the countries of Western Europe. It is also very much of a 'calculated risk' if we do *not*." There could be no economic security, the goal of the ECA, without physical security. How it should be managed was still an open question, and so he was withholding "his own final judgment until I see the precise terms of the treaty under which this new cooperation will be proposed."[43]

In conjunction with and usually in harmony with Connally, he used the executive sessions in the winter of 1949 to refine the language of the projected treaty. It had to be worded in a way that avoided automatic war in the event of an attack on members. This was the essence of Article IV of the Brussels Pact and was anathema to the Senate. It also had to be worded in such a way that if the adjective "military" was included it would not arouse the hostility of the European allies.

Vandenberg embarked on a whirlwind of negotiations in meetings with European colleagues in February 1949, seeking to lock in the triad of obligations that had to accompany the commitment to European security: (1) adherence to the authority of the United Nations Charter; (2) avoidance of automatic commitment to war; and (3) confirmation of the constitutional role of Congress in the forthcoming treaty. All of these prerequisites were set in the context of a Soviet threat to Western democracies that demanded an American response without resorting to war. He reminded a Michigan chemical executive that "Soviet Russia's Communist conspiracy is aimed chiefly at the United States. Therefore, our national security is involved" and the United States had to consider the whole situation from the standpoint of intelligent self-interest.[44]

Deference to the United Nations was the easiest requirement to fulfill, both in the Senate and in security talks with the Brussels Pact members. The Vandenberg Resolution had underscored the provenance of the UN Charter. Five of the six sentences that followed explicitly identified the role of the charter. The senator's imprint was particularly visible in the subsequent North Atlantic Treaty where the preamble reaffirmed the signatories' "faith in the purposes and principles of the Charter of the United Nations." They legitimated it with references to the charter in Articles 1, 5, and 12. Article 5 identified Article 51 of the charter as the authority for the alliance, and Article 7 was emphatic about the "primary responsibility of the Security Council" in underscoring the actions of the NATO allies.

The effort to define an appropriate response to an attack, however, created tensions in the Senate, as exemplified by Connally's Sir Galahad outburst. What gave senators pause at this moment was the detail of the draft's text: "What was an armed attack? Who would determine what should be done?" Meeting with Acheson on February 8, prior to the international gathering, Vandenberg pressed for elimination of "forthwith," "military," and "as may be necessary" from Article 5. He and Connally were concerned about who would determine what was necessary. They insisted on safeguards that would preserve the power of Congress to declare war.[45]

Six days later, on February 14, 1948, the senators met with Acheson and Charles E. Bohlen, counselor of the State Department, to argue even more forcibly than before that there must be no obligation in the treaty, "moral or otherwise," to go to war. A rancorous debate in the Senate made this denial all the more imperative. As noted, Vandenberg differed with Connally on how vague the language should be. He wanted the Rio model—"an attack on one as an attack on all"—to be retained, while making it plain "that the type of action should be a matter for individual determination." He insisted that the word "military" be omitted from the text. Vandenberg underscored the role of the Rio Pact when he wrote to a Grand Rapids friend that he was "heartily in favor of the North Atlantic pact provided it is modeled on the pattern of the Rio Pact. This means it must *not* involve any automatic commitments to war." He was convinced that the announcement in itself would deter war "if we notify all aggressors" that "an armed aggression upon any member of this Community [would be treated] as a potential armed aggression against us . . . which we shall deal with as the ultimate circumstances require."[46]

In executive session of the Senate Foreign Relation Committee on February 18 he fended off criticisms and applauded testimony from witnesses that supported the treaty before and after the twelve members signed it on April 4, 1949. He took the opportunity when it arose to elaborate on the utility of Article 51 of the UN Charter. As one of the authors of the charter he could confidently say that "it was written in recognition of the fact that in the event of an armed attack there would be an inevitable lag even under the most favorable circumstances before the Security Council could act." And if the council could not act because of a Soviet veto, the charter preserved the inherent right of individual or collective defense.[47]

By the end of the month Vandenberg had taken personal possession of the North Atlantic Treaty. His doubts had dissolved. He pointed out to a correspondent in South Carolina that he was "one of its authors. I heartily believe in it. I want to give it a maximum chance to help prevent World War III before it starts." To another in Michigan who wondered if he had misgivings about the forthcoming treaty, he said,

> You will be glad to know that your doubts about this attitude are *totally* without foundation. The best proof is the fact that the North Atlantic Pact is based originally on the so-called "Vandenberg Resolution" of which I was the principal author, and the development of this regional idea (*inside* the United Nations Charter but *outside* the Soviet veto) is the direct result of Article 51 of the Charter—and I was the chief author of Article 51. I

might further add that the North Atlantic Pact is modeled on the Rio Pact for which I was the chief sponsor. You may be very sure I have not changed my mind in any of these aspects.[48]

The senator's ego was on full display in these letters.

These were not private musings. After the State Department issued its white paper on the treaty he trumpeted to the world, or at least to the Conference of Mayors in Washington, on March 22, 1949, that the North Atlantic Treaty was "the most important step in American foreign policy since the promulgation of the Monroe Doctrine." He went on to claim "that this is the greatest war deterrent ever devised. No itching conqueror will lightly view such odds. Yet no other nation on the face of this earth needs spend one sleepless night over any sort of menace from this pact unless it is plotting armed aggression against neighbors."[49]

Vandenberg encountered a mild dissent, or at least an uneasy query, from his close friend and mentor, John Foster Dulles. Always pressing for the unification of Europe, Dulles wanted the senator to assure the nation that the pact would not retard unification by cementing the division between East and West. Testifying for the treaty on March 4, 1949, Dulles speculated that "it is possible that the historian may judge the Economic Recovery Act and the Atlantic Pact were the two things which prevented unity in Europe which in the long run may be more valuable than either of them." Vandenberg obliged with a resolution on March 29, stating that "the implementation of the treaty will be such as to advance the unification of Europe in accordance with the policy of the United States heretofore declared in relation to the European Recovery Program."[50]

There should have been no problems with the steps following the signing of the treaty on April 4. The Senate Foreign Relations Committee conducted sixteen days of hearings at the end of April and beginning of May. Chairman Connally listened to ninety-six witnesses, often shutting off those he disagreed with but nonetheless giving them all a platform. Vandenberg was a cooperative partner in these hearings. For the most part his comments were intended to confirm positions he had taken in February. The most urgent, in his judgment, was to minimize the military element in the treaty. He did so, often by putting words in the mouths of witnesses. He coached Secretary of Defense Louis Johnson to agree: "Is it not a fact that all of your answers are contingent entirely upon the success of the peace movement in the United Nations and under the North Atlantic Pact and that we may very well hope for the day when we will not need any such armament program at all, and are not all of our answers contingent upon the attitudes of Soviet Russia?"[51]

When issues arose that he felt had been settled before the signing of the treaty, he was quick to intervene. He extracted from Acheson assurance that if any additional countries were admitted to the alliance under Article 10, it would be through the advice and consent of the Senate. About the notion of any automatic reaction to an act of aggression against a member, he observed in executive session on June 6, 1949, "We accept the general obligation that the survival of France and the survival of Great Britain are essential to us, but we do not accept the basic thesis that an attack on Paris has got to be met precisely as if it were an attack on New York."[52]

Arguably, the most irritating issue raised in the hearings concerned the monies the allies were seeking immediately after the treaty was signed. He was annoyed that within forty-eight hours of the signing of this pact, and before, the Brussels Pact members released demands for arms. The senator wanted a conclusive statement that "the United States is under no obligation to assist the other parties to building up military establishments in their overseas territories. And I want to add this language, nor to engage in resisting attack outside the areas defined in article 6."[53]

That the North Atlantic Treaty could be identified as a traditional "military alliance" always disturbed Vandenberg. As he told a Baker University professor when his class voted against the alliance for that reason, he "too would disapprove a 'military alliance' in the historic pattern. But in my humble opinion the North Atlantic Pact is *fundamentally* of an entirely different character." Although bothered by this characterization of the alliance and by the cognate petition from the allies for military assistance, he joined his colleagues in reporting the treaty to the Senate on June 6 by a vote of thirteen to zero.[54] He continued to stand by his thesis that the treaty was a deterrent to Soviet aggression without reference to its military implications.

He coupled the Atlantic Pact with ECA as the key components in winning the Cold War: "In my opinion if it were not for these policies,

Soviet Communism would today be in substantial control of Europe and this would pose the greatest threat to our own national security in the lifetime of the republic." Accordingly, he strongly opposed Senator James P. Kem's (R-MO) amendment to an appropriation bill that would withdraw all ECA aid to any country that socialized any basic industry. He told a Flint dairy executive that while he agreed "that we should not promote 'socialism' at home or abroad, Britain and other allies share our values, and combat Communism at far closer range and therefore with far greater courage than we are called upon to exercise."[55]

The Kem amendment was defeated and the treaty survived debate in the Senate on July 21 by a convincing vote of eighty-two to thirteen. In the course of the two-week debate the senator found an occasion to deliver one of his trademark addresses to his colleagues that so often transfixed his audience. He opened with the declaration that "this treaty is the most sensible, powerful, practicable, and economical step the United States [could take] in the realistic interest of its own security." He then went on to justify his judgment. The results of the Senate debate pleased him, especially the size of the majority in its favor. True, he expressed some annoyance at the "little band of GOP isolationists" led by Senator Taft. But he had a right to feel "a great relief to have the battle over." More than that, he had "a feeling," he wrote to his wife, "that this day will go down in history as one of the big dates, and it all stems from the Vandenberg Resolution which you saw a-borning in [apartment] 500G with dear old Bob [Lovett] as the midwife."[56] He had no second thoughts about his own place in NATO's history.

THE MILITARY ASSISTANCE PROGRAM

The senator's note to his wife included a prediction that after the passage of the treaty, "we are going to have a God-awful time with the implementing arms bill a little later." He was not exaggerating. Although he implied that the trouble would come from Republican isolationists, he unintentionally placed himself in their camp when he referred in his July 6 speech to those who believed that the treaty called for arms aid: "I do not agree. Frankly, I should have much less interest in this Treaty if I though its repressive influence for peace is measured by or dependent on such an implementation."[57]

Vandenberg was familiar with the substance of military aid contemplated by the administration and with its links to the North Atlantic Treaty. Military aid had long been on the administration's agenda, reaching back to an annex to the ECA bill in 1948. It failed then because of possible encroachment upon the economic program. But it was reasonable to assume that if military aid accompanied economic aid to Korea, then the same arrangement could be made for Western Europe. Given Vandenberg's access to the administration's thinking in the winter of 1949, he knew of plans to implement the prospective treaty with a military assistance program. The machinery for implementing such a program was in place by the winter of 1949. The Joint Chiefs of Staff had recommended to the secretary of defense in March that more than half of the total estimated assistance of almost a billion dollars would go to Western Union nations in military aid for Western Union countries.[58]

Military aid posed a dilemma for the administration. Acheson and Connally knew the connections between a military assistance program and the treaty, and they knew that the Europeans had shown their eagerness to place Article 3, with its emphasis on mutual aid, above Article 5 after the treaty was signed on April 4. The Democratic leaders wanted quick action before the treaty was ratified, on the credible assumption that dissidents in their own party as well as Taft-led Republican critics would raise objections. Taft himself asked on July 8 whether it was possible for a senator to vote for the treaty and then take the positon that "we are not obligated to provide arms."[59] He equated support of the treaty with support of arms aid to Europe.

Vandenberg was ambivalent about military aid in general and angry in particular over the Western Union's unseemly request for a package of excessive military and financial aid from the United States so soon after the treaty was signed. But he unwittingly provided cover for the administration. He agreed with the State Department formula that military assistance "would be necessary even if there were no treaty just as the treaty would be necessary if the military assistance program had not been formulated. . . . The military assistance program is separate from the treaty except that the treaty and NATO both serve the national interest of the United States."[60]

The senator was not contradicting himself in repeating the words of the State Department announcement. The two in his mind were separate; the treaty was more important and yet military aid was also serving the nation and the alliance. But he believed his words were misconstrued. He was uncomfortable with the timing. In conversation with Secretary Acheson, Vandenberg felt "that the introduction of the Military Assistance Bill prior to ratification would present the Treaty to the country in the wrong light." By this he meant that the treaty would appear to be a mere prelude to the creation of forces in Europe that could resist Soviet aggression, whereas in his opinion the treaty would be enthusiastically accepted by Americans if it were presented simply as dealing with "potentialities to resist aggression if that should start."[61] Still, he would not make it a public issue even though he, unlike Connally, thought that introduction of a military assistance program prior to ratification was a mistake.

The senator's mild dissent from the administration's plans dissolved in July as he was confronted by a host of reasons to raise his voice. Fifty-six senators—Democrats and Republicans—had already sought to slash 5–10 percent from the billions in foreign aid appropriated to the executive branch for fiscal year 1950.[62] On the eve of ratification he complained to a sympathetic Lippmann about Senator Wayne Morse's (R-OR) claim that the United States had a moral as well as legal basis to furnish arms to the new allies. He was increasingly frustrated by the apparent inability of his Senate colleagues to understand that a military aid program had "*preceded* the negotiations of the Pact (even though its publication was more or less simultaneous)" and that "there are no obligations under Article Three of the Pact until *after* the Defense Committee of the Advisory [North Atlantic] Council has made a recommendation under Article Nine of the Pact." Article 9 instructed the council to "establish immediately a defence committee which shall recommend measures for the implementation of articles 3 and 5." Lippmann added to Vandenberg's concerns when he recalled from conversations with the French ambassador that the treaty would be valueless unless there was a military aid program. No wonder Acheson anticipated trouble "in view of the Vandenberg-Dulles attitude, which is that we should not take definitive action until the machinery under the Atlantic Pact has been set up and has had a chance to function."[63]

The secretary of state had reason to be worried. When the military assistance bill (H.R. 5748) was introduced on July 25 it provided for direct transfer of essential military items from U.S. stocks and for assistance in the use of military equipment, to be determined by the president. Truman tried to soften potential opposition by naming the initiative the Mutual Defense Assistance Program (MDAP). Although Vandenberg conceded that the president's emphasis on collective security was sound, he told the press, "My first impression is that his program must be rewritten and curtailed to get action this session. It is too wide in scope and too general in grant of power. . . . Its statement of policy puts too much emphasis upon arms."[64]

In Dulles's conversation with Acheson the day after the bill was submitted, the newly appointed New York senator spoke for Vandenberg in deploring the excessive power the president would have at his disposal. But he did suggest to Acheson that they could find common ground by delaying action until March or April 1950, when the Atlantic Pact machinery would have made recommendations. In the meantime, a modest interim aid program would be acceptable. Vandenberg admitted a few days later to a close friend that it would be "a supreme tragedy if this session of Congress should adjourn without passing some kind of a 'preliminary' arms bill."[65]

Acheson came away from this meeting comforted by Dulles's asking "only for an open mind on our part as the bill progressed through the Congress. I assured him that we would maintain an open mind and urged that he and Senator Vandenberg should not make their position more rigid, but should leave the matter with what they had already said until the testimony developed further. I understood from him that they were inclined to do this."[66]

Throughout the negotiations that followed in August and September 1949 under the joint auspices of Connally's Foreign Relations Committee and Millard Tydings's (D-MD) Armed Services Committee, Vandenberg worked closely with Dulles, now a fellow senator, and with Walter Lippmann, from his summer home in Maine, to cut down both the president's authority and the size of the military aid package. But the atmosphere dramatically changed even as Dulles seemed to give their blessing to the administration's program. Acheson "appreciated that he [Dulles] and Senator Vandenberg were not opposed to the program, but were advising me on their sincere conviction about the soundest way to proceed."[67]

But in place of the familiar bipartisan moderator, the Michigan sena-tor became the leader of angry protests, first against the original bill and then, after it was revised to accommodate him, against the subsequent bill. Writing to his wife on August 25, the day before Dulles's agreeable conversation with Acheson, Vandenberg reported, "I served blunt notice today that I simply would not support the President's bill. It is almost unbelievable in its grant of unlimited power to the chief Executive. It would permit the President to sell, lease or give away anything we've got at any time to any country in any way he wishes. It would virtually make him number one warlord of the world. . . . The old bipartisan business is certainly 'out the window' on this one." He even found a conspiracy in the making: "The President's pending proposal uses the existing situation as an *excuse* to seek more peace-time power than was ever concentrated in the White House in the history of the United States." He concluded a week-long tirade when he asked rhetorically, "Can you imagine that the American people would for an instant surrender such supreme and ex-clusive authority to the Chief Executive?"[68]

The administration backed off and withdrew H.R. 5748. Vandenberg professed to being "amused by all the dope stories today to the effect that Acheson is really getting ready to capitulate. They say he is working on an arms compromise. He better had—if he wants any legislation at all this session." The senator boasted about his victory to his wife on July 31.[69]

A new bill, H.R. 5895, introduced on August 5, cut the budget by $600 million. Vandenberg had extracted significant concessions from the administration, including reducing the president's authority in the pro-cess. Truman had no trouble with this change. Acheson recommended to the president that "we be authorized to rewrite the bill to meet the objections other than objections as to the amount."[70] Surprisingly, in light of Vandenberg's accommodating personality, there was nothing gra-cious in his recognition of victory. He displayed no appreciation for the president's voluntary reduction of the executive authority implied in the original bill. He crowed to his wife that the administration had no choice but to acknowledge its defeat: "We had our telltale show-down on the arms program in the joint meeting this morning of the Foreign Relations and Armed Services committees. I bluntly laid the 'facts of life' before Secretary of State Acheson and Secretary of Defense Johnson. I gave 'em an ultimatum—write a new and reasonable bill or you will get no bill and it will be your fault." As a postscript to this confrontation, he told Lippmann, "We have killed the 'war lord' bill which would have made the President the top military dictator of all time."[71]

The senator was never fully satisfied with the results of his intervention, although he believed that the changes he effected vastly improved the bill: "The new bill is in fairly satisfactory shape—except from my point of view, the new arms program is being developed on a two-year basis outside and independent of the implementation machinery set up by the North Atlantic Pact itself." Two weeks later he raised once again a principle that he believed had united the treaty and arms aid from the outset: namely that NATO's defense of the West was not dependent on extensive arms aid or on a massive buildup of European forces. "I would have infinitely preferred," he wrote, "to rely upon the *potentials* in the Atlantic Pact as a discouragement to Soviet aggression." By contrast, he feared that "*complete* rearmament would turn Western Europe (and America) into an armed camp."[72]

From the administration's perspective, Vandenberg should have been satisfied with the bill. As Acheson conceded on August 24, "Senator Tydings said he would talk this morning with Senator Connally, and if in their opinion, they were going to be licked on the full amount, they would consider the question of agreeing with Senator Vandenberg on his figure, provided there were no further cuts. Secretary Acheson said that if we were licked, we were licked and that was all there was to it."[73]

In fact, the senator was appeased. He told a Detroit correspondent that the revised bill, with all its flaws, was "adequately attempting to stop any new war before it starts." Whatever reservations he still had about the administration's bill crumbled in the face of the House Republicans' attempt to wreck the whole program. The House would cut in half military assistance funds, already reduced to the $1 billion level that satisfied Vandenberg and Dulles.[74] Vandenberg's voice helped to quash the effort, and the Mutual Defense Assistance Act passed on September 22, 1949. The bipartisan spirit was restored, if not quite to the status of 1947 and 1948, but sufficiently for the Michigan senator to endorse the administration's development of the Atlantic alliance.

Vandenberg's positions on the powers of the president, the authority of the UN, and the limited use of military assistance had never substantially changed. He was as annoyed with the Republican dissidents as he was with the Democratic leadership. The final vote was fifty-five to twenty-four, and as he noted to his wife, "the Republicans ran out on me right and left—only nine of 'em standing by to help beat the chief amendments with which we had to contend."[75]

What then accounted for the insulting language he used to force the administration into submission to his wishes? His loss of temper as well as his choice of words was out of character. More characteristic was his recognition that Truman was the only president the country had and his acknowledgment that "I want to help lick him when the time comes—but not at the expense of the national security, meanwhile."[76] His tantrums and tirades were an unnecessary aberration; the administration was prepared to compromise from the outset.

The answers may be found in the particular circumstances of the day. Without assigning priorities, his long-standing, visceral defense of Senate prerogatives in the face of presidential authority deserves pride of place. Connally's return to the chairmanship of the Senate Foreign Relations Committee after the Democratic electoral triumphs in 1948 undoubtedly added fuel to this flame. His most hyperbolic outbursts seemed to flare when he thought of the president's unilateral initiatives on foreign aid.

Second, the strong support of trusted friends and allies, particularly Dulles and Lippmann, buttressed his arguments. The pundit expressed shock at the president's "utter disrespect for our constitutional traditions" and recommended a "measured but stern lecture from you." Dulles was rightly bracketed with the senator in all stages of his protests. When Dulles spoke with Acheson about the Military Assistance Program (MAP) the day after the initial bill was introduced, he accurately said that "he was reflecting Senator Vandenberg's views as well as his own."[77] Parenthetically, Vandenberg was emboldened as well by the cheers he received from such Democrats as Senator Walter F. George (D-GA) and from traditional opponents in his own party. Taft played on his sensitivity about excessive powers in the hands of the president and enjoyed egging on his attacks. Arguably, Vandenberg's voice may have been all the more persuasive after Republicans finally understood that his "'so-called bi-partisan foreign policy' is not on a 'me-too' basis."[78]

A third source of his eruptions may have been his ongoing dislike of allies' eagerness to exploit the military aid program for national advantage, ignoring the collective and integrative objectives the alliance was intended to advance. This was apparent in the indecent haste that the Western Union members exhibited when they submitted their requests immediately after the North Atlantic Treaty was signed. Vandenberg repeatedly criticized the MAP for offering too much money for inappropriate purposes, most notably funds for tool production and raw materials for military production in Europe. The vote against Vandenberg over this issue was the rare exception in his long record of success on the Foreign Relations Committee. But in an address to a group of visiting European journalists a week before the passage of the Mutual Defense Assistance Act, he warned that Europe must face "definite limits to the American resources which we can safely invest in foreign aid." Europeans had to do more to help themselves.[79]

Last but perhaps not the least important factor in his loss of temper was his declining health. Vandenberg in September 1949 was a sick man, and he knew it. He stayed in Washington through the arduous negotiations in August and September out of a sense of duty. His headaches had been constant and were growing worse. His letters to his wife in the closing days of the debate reveal the extent of his exhaustion and the limits of his patience. With the arms bill battle in the Senate over, he was "going to let 'em 'worry along' the House-Senate conference (on the bill) without me. This means—and you may tell our doctor—that I am ready to report at Ann Arbor next Tuesday or Wednesday to suit his convenience."[80]

His flare-ups, most vividly demonstrated in conversations and private letters in the summer of 1949, reflected frustration with the limits of his own aspirations for the nation and his party. Did his conflict with the administration over the Military Assistance Program signify retreat from his conversion to an internationalist foreign policy? The MAP by its nature disturbed his vision of how America should deal with the world. There was the existential danger of NATO, through the military aid program, evolving into a traditional military alliance, itself threatening world peace and the integrity of the United Nations. Yet given the genuine menace of Soviet-led Communism he felt he had no choice but to accept the risk of perverting the meaning of the Atlantic alliance. News of the Soviet success in exploding a nuclear device underscored the reasons for the concessions he made.[81] The consequence of the existential threat to the nation's security ultimately trumped reliance on the supremacy of the UN Charter—repeatedly mentioned in the North Atlantic Treaty—as the institution primarily responsible for international peace and security.

10

In Retrospect, 1950–1951

Senator Vandenberg died of cancer on April 18, 1951, after more than a year and a half of painful operations and incomplete convalescences. A lung lesion was removed in a six-hour operation on October 3, 1949, leaving "50 well intentioned stitches which are more annoying than a Senate filibuster." Despite a "stubborn convalescence"—a description he used frequently, almost to his deathbed, in writing to correspondents—he returned to Washington in December in the hope of resuming his seat when the Eighty-First Congress convened in January. He admitted that "I find major surgery something like war. You win the war but you are a long way from peace." Humor aside, he was right; a photograph of him during his brief return to Washington showed him thin, wan, and tired.[1]

A relapse accompanied his premature return to Washington. On April 11, 1950, he had a tumor near his spine removed at the Georgetown University Hospital. Aside from a difficult trip to the Senate for a vote on behalf of the Fair Employment Practices Commission, he was confined to his apartment at the Wardman Park Hotel, with no improvement in his health. The death of his wife in June after a long illness further depressed his spirits. He returned to Grand Rapids in September 1950, realizing, without explicitly admitting it, that he would never occupy his Senate seat again. He died at his home in the presence of his son and two daughters.

The senator knew what he was risking when he refused to be hospitalized until Congress had approved the MAP. In responding to Acheson's congratulations over victory in the Senate on September 22, 1949, he expressed satisfaction about his contribution to its passage. While he would be out of contact "for a few weeks," he was pleased to continue the search "for the American *unity* which is so essential to the authority with which we speak abroad." Robert Lovett was effusive in claiming that Vandenberg saved "the day on M.A.P. with darn little help from the quarters which should have eagerly accepted the sage counsel given them."[2]

What the senator did not say at the time was that he had postponed a needed operation for a year and a half, until the North Atlantic Treaty and MAP were secured. He had been taking digitalis for ten years for a heart ailment. A check after the Republican convention in July 1948 revealed a tiny spot on one lung. He brushed it aside when tests for tuberculosis proved negative, but there was no doubt in his own mind that he was testing his endurance to a dangerous degree. Lurking in the background were constant headaches, which he dismissed as no worse than ever. The cigar-smoking senator was overworked, a prime candidate for physical collapse. He knew the risks he was taking. His frequent allusions to President Wilson's collapse in 1919, his age, his refusal to run for president in 1948, and his intention to retire at the end of his term all portended a sense that his time in life was limited. But pride in his accomplishments as well as a sense of duty to his country justified whatever sacrifices he had made.[3]

COMMENTARIES ON FOREIGN RELATIONS
AFTER SEPTEMBER 1949

The senator's enforced absence from the Senate floor and from his role as Republican leader of the Foreign Relations Committee in the Eighty-First Congress did not mean he had resigned his post or withdrawn from concern about the direction of the nation's foreign policies. The closest he came to giving up his office was his resignation from the Joint Congressional Atomic Energy Committee in light of his inability to take an active role in its work. He did not give up his membership on the Senate Foreign Relations Committee. And his decision to keep his seat was heartily endorsed by Democrats and Republicans alike. The president's letters grew more urgent as he reported how much he missed Vandenberg's leadership in effecting a unified foreign policy. As the end drew near his Democratic colleague Tom Connally expressed his outrage over the demand by the Detroit and Wayne County Federation of Labor that he resign from the

Senate, given his infrequent presence since his lung operation eighteen months earlier. Connally felt that his old sparring partner "should be continued in office indefinitely." The call for his resignation "is shameful in view of his distinguished service to the State of Michigan and the United States and to the peace of the world."[4]

Vandenberg felt some discomfort from time to time over his absence from the fray. But his voice was not altogether silent. Nor was it always used in endorsement of the Truman policies. In the only press conference he gave during his brief return to the Senate in December 1950, he asked for sharply reduced foreign aid in the 1950 budget. "Never let us forget," he warned, "that so-called foreign aid is dictated by our own intelligent self-interest." His criticism of the administration's excessive largesse did not lessen his support for continuing the foreign military aid program in opposition to the position of Senator Arthur V. Taft (R-UT).[5]

Vandenberg clarified his views in a letter to Senator Watkins, a major antagonist in the NATO hearings, when he dismissed the Idaho senator's assertion that he had taken "*anything* the Administration hands us." On the contrary, the military assistance bill that the administration handed the Foreign Relations Committee "was largely rewritten in line with the Dulles-Vandenberg amendments. It stemmed from [a] Senate Resolution sponsored by a Republican and unanimously approved by Republican Senate Committee votes." In brief, both NATO and the restructured military aid program were essentially Republican accomplishments.[6]

Similarly, he cited his long-standing opposition to the administration's China policy as evidence of his Republican credentials He consistently had excluded the administration's approach to Nationalist China from his bipartisan backing of its European policies. President Truman's response to North Korea's invasion of South Korea offered another opportunity for Vandenberg to distance himself from the administration's behavior. He did not take full advantage of it. While he felt that the administration had mishandled the Korean situation, particularly in its lack of clarity over the defense of South Korea, he strongly backed the president's response once North Korea had attacked: "It is only fair to add that our Government did meet the crisis bravely when it arose." Despite his respect for President Syngman Rhee "as a great Patriot," he opposed his intention of taking control "north of the 38th parallel unless a northern referendum establishes this design." The ultimate decision over the unification of Korea should, he argued, be decided by the United Nations.[7]

The senator's reactions to the Korean War did not mesh with his party's charges of executive overreach. Vandenberg would agree that the president ideally should have consulted with Congress before dispatching troops abroad. He repeatedly asserted his preference for presidential restraint. But he undercut his objections in observing to a Detroit publisher, "We confront a condition and not a theory. He is Commander-in-Chief. His constitutional function must not be impaired lest it tie our hand behind our backs." Although he was writing in February 1951 in reference to the Wherry resolution on troops to Europe, his words applied to Korea as well. He told Senator Kenneth S. Wherry (R-NE) in gentle terms that he could approve of a Senate resolution expressing its desire to have the president "seek the advance approval of Congress" before dispatching troops to Europe. Congressional partnership was an important consideration, but it should not infringe on presidential authority or damage national unity.[8]

The senator was not unaware of the perils of his middle way, the danger of being pilloried by partisans on both sides of the aisle. He did his best to maintain a civil relationship with critics, at least in his communications with such right-wing stalwarts as Senators Watkins and Wherry. He rarely allowed his feelings to be on public display. The one major exception occurred when he consciously tried to exercise his influence in Congress during his long absences from the Washington arena. In a letter to Paul Hoffman, the ECA administrator, on the second anniversary of the European Recovery Program, he appealed to both parties to continue supporting the ERP. "The least I can do," he wrote, "is to take advantage of this occasion to say that, in my humble opinion, you and your ECA associates, at home and abroad, have rendered incalculably vital service to our country and its indispensable leadership for liberty."[9]

This was vintage Vandenberg—the touch of false humility, along with a heartfelt conviction of the importance of the goals he had sought in securing the future of both the United States and Europe. He won tributes from the president that were replicated frequently in his final year. Both Truman and Acheson frequently expressed their regrets in missing his voice in Washington, as they thanked him for his public endorsement of the president's call for unity.[10]

No one was more conscious of his missing voice than Vandenberg himself. No matter how many times he might criticize the Democrats' Asian policies or presidential infringement on the Senate's prerogatives, he directed his anger primarily at his own party—at the right-wing extremists who, he believed, would endanger the nation by turning their backs on the policies he championed. The bedridden senator felt they were a threat to both the party and the country. He had only contempt for the unfounded charges of Communism that made Senator Joseph R. McCarthy (R-WI) a notorious figure in 1950. He would distinguish McCarthy's demagoguery from the strongly held, if wrongheaded, convictions of Watkins and Wherry. At least there was civility in their exchanges, and even some accommodation in his last communications with his colleagues. Taft, writing to Vandenberg a month before his death, noted, "As I went over my speeches on foreign policy the other day, I did not think I had departed in any substantial respect from your own views in spite of the violence of the Administration partisans."[11]

He closely followed events in Washington almost to the day of his death. If he rarely made his views public, his friends and adversaries knew where he stood. Despite all the current challenges, he was sure that the nation would surmount the frictions plaguing Congress. He expected that General Dwight D. Eisenhower, then NATO's supreme commander, Allied Powers, Europe (SACEUR), not only would resolve the most urgent problems but deservedly would be a Republican candidate for president in 1952. When a reporter called him from Philadelphia to ask his opinion about the general's address to the nation upon his return from a European inspection tour in January 1951, he replied, "I feel as though a great load had just been lifted from my back. Things will be all right with Ike at the helm."[12] Eisenhower assumed the roles Theodore Roosevelt and Douglas MacArthur had played in Vandenberg's life.

THE VANDENBERG LEGACY

Vandenberg fostered the impression that his conversion from isolationism to internationalism was less a long odyssey from Troy to Ithaca than a sudden Pauline experience on the road to Damascus. Pearl Harbor was the instrument of his conversion. He wrote later that "in my own mind my convictions regarding international cooperation and collective security took firm form on that afternoon of the Pearl Harbor attack. That day ended isolation for any realist."[13]

In reality Vandenberg's conversion to internationalism was gradual and hesitant. He first had to overcome his suspicions of the president's use of the war to advance executive power at the expense of the Senate's prerogatives. But without admitting that his isolationism before Pearl Harbor was a mistake, he recognized that new circumstances required a new approach to achieving a peaceful world for America in the future. He felt that this would be unlikely until fruitful collaborations between the executive and legislative branches of government had been established, and this required the administration to share with congressional Republicans its secret agreements with the World War II Allies. Mutual distrust between the administration and the Senate Foreign Relations Committee stood in the way of developing bipartisan policies for a postwar world.

It was the prospect of a new international organization more than any other issue during the war that dislodged Vandenberg from his ideological moorings. His conversion involved pride in the unusual attention the administration paid in appointing him to an influential committee that pondered the future of America in a postwar world. Seeking to chart a middle position of influence between his isolationist admirers and the energized internationalist wing of his party, he welcomed Roosevelt's belated steps toward bipartisanship.

The election of 1944 inevitably postponed new links between the parties in the campaign for the presidency. While his doubts about the Roosevelt administration's sincerity in offering a role in postwar planning to Republicans were never fully allayed, Vandenberg, now clearly the leader of the party's moderates, revealed a new view of foreign relations in his seminal speech to the Senate on January 10, 1945. He not only categorically renounced isolationism in light of the technology of modern warfare but also championed a four-power treaty between the allies that could be solemnized in the proposed United Nations organization. It was a decisive moment in his career, followed quickly by the administration's appointment of him as a delegate to the conference in San Francisco that produced the charter of the United Nations.

He perceived himself to be a founder of the United Nations and immediately became its chief American defender. His fervor in denouncing Soviet Communists increased as he saw them abusing the UN Charter, thereby threatening the security of the democratic West. The Vandenberg Resolution that made NATO possible was intended not simply to defend the West against Soviet aggression but to maintain the supremacy of the UN Charter as the primary keeper of world peace. Once he left his isolationist past behind he reveled in his status as the voice of harmony, bridging the gaps between the executive and legislative branches. As chairman of the Senate Foreign Relations committee in the Eightieth Congress he envisioned himself, even as he deprecated the notion, as coequal to the secretary of state in responding to challenges to the United States and the United Nations Charter.

An uneasy alliance with Senator Taft, the leader of the isolationist faction in his party and majority leader in postwar America, allowed Vandenberg freedom to speak informally for his party in the years that produced the Truman Doctrine, the Marshall Plan, and the North Atlantic Treaty. His towering ego accounted for his presence in every stage of legislation in post–World War II America. When Connally replaced him as chairman of the Senate Foreign Relations Committee in the Eighty-First Congress, the two self-important men, each with his own florid style, intensified an old rivalry. Vandenberg's loss of the chairmanship made his demands for recognition even more annoying to the administration. Acheson, as secretary of state, was less tolerant than Lovett in catering to the Michigan senator to win his approbation for legislation both men wanted. Yet Vandenberg was also able to force the administration to rewrite such bills as the Mutual Defense Assistance Act in August 1949, when the initial bill appeared to grant too much power to the president.

Vandenberg was not posturing in his railing against aspects of the administration's foreign policies. While he accepted and supported steps to contain Soviet expansionism, he demanded that they be conducted within the jurisdiction of the UN Charter. This was the message of the Vandenberg Resolution, which opened the way for the United States to depart from its tradition of nonentanglement with Europe. The purpose of the Atlantic alliance was to reinforce the UN, which had been prevented by the Soviet veto from fulfilling its mission.

The militarization of NATO was constantly on his mind as an obstacle in its relationship to the UN, which helps to explain the concerns he repeatedly expressed deprecating the military elements in the implementation of the North Atlantic Treaty. His vision of NATO serving the UN was evident in the preamble to the treaty and in Articles 1, 2, 5, 7, and 12. His identification of the United Nations with a new world order might have ruled NATO as a military alliance that violated the terms of the UN Charter as well as deviated from America's historical abhorrence of militarism. It did not. His ultimate acceptance of a major military component of NATO rested on his perception that the nation's security required a vigorous defense program. The menace of Soviet-led Communism trumped his reservations about NATO's functions. It also suppressed his doubts about the NATO allies' commitment to the common cause. The changes he personally imposed on the administration safeguarded the principles he had espoused since World War II.

No matter how severe the tensions between the Senate and the presidency, Vandenberg's legacy as an internationalist was never in question. He fought to the end of his life for the bipartisanship that appeared to be dissolving in partisan divisions exacerbated by the Korean War. Had he lived longer, it is likely that his faith in Eisenhower would have restored his optimism about America and the world. Vandenberg's contributions to America's foreign policy after World War II mark him as an equal of Marshall and Acheson. He deserves to be remembered as a partner in their company.

Excerpts from "The Need for Honest Candor: Clarification of Our Foreign Policy"

By Arthur H. Vandenberg, U.S. Senator from Michigan
Delivered in the Senate, Washington, D.C., January 10, 1945

There are critical moments in the life of every nation which call for the straightest, the plainest and the most courageous thinking of which we are capable. We confront such a moment now. It is not only desperately important to America. It is important to the world. It is important not only to this generation which lives in blood. It is important to future generations if they shall live in peace.

No man in his right senses will be dogmatic in his viewpoint at such an hour. A global conflict which uproots the earth is not calculated to submit itself to the domination of any finite mind. The clash of rival foreign interests, which have motivated wars for countless centuries, are not likely suddenly to surrender to some simple man-made formula, no matter how nobly meditated.

Each of us can only speak according to his little lights—and pray for a composite wisdom that shall lead us to high, safe ground. It is only in this spirit of anxious humility that I speak today. Politics, in any such connection, would be as obnoxious at home as they are in international manipulations abroad.

Mr. President, we still have two major wars to win. I said "We."

That does not mean America alone. It means the continued and total battle fraternity of the United Nations. It must mean one for all and all for one; and it will mean this—unless somewhere in this grand alliance the stupid and sinister folly of ulterior ambitions shall invite the enemy to postpone our victory through our own rivalries and our own confusion.

The United Nations, in even greater unity of military action than heretofore, must never, for any cause, permit this military unity to fall apart. If it does, we shall count the cost in mortal anguish—even though we stumble on to a belated, though inevitable, victory. . . .

Then, in honest candor, Mr. President, I think we have the duty and the right to demand that whatever immediate unilateral decisions have to be made in consequence of military need, and there will be such even in civil affairs, they shall all be temporary, and subject to final revision in the objective light of the post-war world and the post-war peace league as they shall ultimately develop.

As President Roosevelt put it in his annual message:

"During the interim period, until conditions permit a genuine expression of the people's will, we and our Allies have a duty, which we cannot ignore, to use our influence to the end that no temporary or provisional authorities in the liberated countries block the eventual exercise of the peoples' right freely to choose the Government and the institutions under which as free men they are to live."

I agreed to that. Indeed, I would go further. I would write it in the bond. If Dumbarton Oaks should specifically authorize the ultimate international organization to review protested injustices in the peace itself, it would at least partially nullify the argument that we are to be asked to put a blank-check warrant behind a future status quo which is unknown to us, and which we might be unwilling to defend.

We are standing by our guns with epic heroism. I know of no reason why we should not stand by our ideals. If they vanish under ultimate pressures, we shall at least have kept the record straight; we shall have kept faith with our soldier sons; and we than shall clearly be free agents, unhampered by tragic misunderstandings, in determining our own course when Berlin and Tokyo are in Allied hands.

Let me put it this way for myself: I am prepared, by effective international cooperation, to do our full part in charting happier and safer tomorrows. But I am not prepared to permanently guarantee the spoils of an unjust peace. It will not work.

Mr. President, we need honest candor even with our foes. Without any remote suggestion of appeasement, I wish we might give these Axis peoples some incentive to desert their own tottering tyrannies by at least indicating to them that the quicker they "unconditionally surrender" the cheaper will be "unconditional surrender's" price. Here again we need plain speaking, which has been too conspicuous by its absence, and, upon at least one calamitous occasion, by its error.

Source: Vital Speeches of the Day 11, no. 8 (February 1, 1945): 226, 229. © Copyright 2003, Ebsco Publishing.

Appendix 2

The Vandenberg Resolution

Whereas peace with justice and the defense of human rights and fundamental freedoms require international cooperation through more effective use of the United Nations:

Therefore be it

Resolved, That the Senate reaffirm the policy of the United States to achieve international peace and security through the United Nations, so that armed force shall not be used except in the common interest, and that the President be advised of the sense of the Senate that this Government, by constitutional process, should particularly pursue the following objectives within the United Nations Charter:

(1) Voluntary agreement to remove the veto from all questions involving pacific settlements of international disputes and situations, and from the admission of new members.

(2) Progressive development of regional and other collective arrangements for individual and collective self-defense in accordance with the purposes, principles, and provisions of the Charter.

(3) Association of the United States, by constitutional process, with such regional and other collective arrangements as are based on continuous and effective self-help and mutual aid, and as affect its national security.

(4) Contributing to the maintenance of peace by making clear its determination to exercise the right of individual or collective self-defense under article 51 should any armed attack occur affecting its national security.

(5) Maximum efforts to obtain agreements to provide the United Nations with armed forces as provided by the Charter, and to obtain agreement among member nations upon universal regulation and re-

duction of armaments under adequate and dependable guaranty against violation.

(6) If necessary, after adequate effort toward strengthening the United Nations, review of the Charter at an appropriate time by a general conference called under article 109 or by the General Assembly.

Source: S. Res. 239, 80th Cong., 2d sess., *Congressional Record* 94 (June 11, 1948): 7791.

Notes

1. Hamilton's Impact, 1906–1928

1. Tompkins, *Senator Arthur H. Vandenberg*, 1–2. Much of the information in this chapter is drawn from Tompkins's valuable study of Vandenberg's early years.

2. James Reston, March 24, 1948, article in *Life,* quoted in ibid., 2.

3. Ibid., 6.

4. Rychard Fink, ed., *Horatio Alger's Struggle Upward; or, Luke Larkin's Luck* (North Plainfield, NJ: Nautilus Books, 1971). As the 1940 election approached, journalist Robert Albright observed that the "background of probably none of the other Presidential candidates follows the Horatio Alger tradition more faithfully [than Vandenberg's]. . . . No Alger youth's rise was ever more rapid." *Washington Post,* March 3, 1940.

5. Tompkins, *Senator Arthur H. Vandenberg*, 3.

6. Vandenberg to Randolph G. Adams, director of the William L. Clements Library, May 10, 1949, Vandenberg Papers, Bentley Library, roll 11. The senator's dispatch of copies of documents compiled by the Senate Foreign Relations Committee relating to the pending North Atlantic Treaty typified his interest in the Clements Library's collections. His autograph was included on one of them, at Randolph's suggestion.

7. Tompkins, *Senator Arthur H. Vandenberg*, 28.

8. Ibid., 28.

9. Ibid., 29.

10. Address at annual award dinner of Theodore Roosevelt Memorial Association, New York City, April 25, 1949, accepting 1948 Theodore Roosevelt Medal for public service, Vandenberg Papers, Bentley Library, roll 8.

11. Vandenberg to Gen. Robert E. Wood, co-chairman for MacArthur candidacy September 15, 1943; Vandenberg to A. I. Miller, May 5, 1944, ibid., roll 3.

12. *Grand Rapids (MI) Herald,* March 15, 1907, 4.

13. *Grand Rapids Herald,* August 5, 1906, 4.

14. Ibid.

15. Tompkins, *Senator Arthur H. Vandenberg*, 15–16.

16. 71st Cong., 2d sess., *Congressional Record* 72, pt. 3 (January 31, 1931): S 2734–36; hereafter cited as *CR.*

17. Vandenberg to Col. Theodore Roosevelt Jr., Governor-General, P.I., July 11, 1932; Vandenberg to W. N. Wallace, General Manager, Michigan Sugar Co., Saginaw, November 23, 1932, Vandenberg Papers, Bentley Library, roll 1; *New York Times*, May 8, 1931, 44.

18. Tompkins, *Senator Arthur H. Vandenberg*, 12–13.

19. Ibid., 13.

20. Ibid.

21. *Grand Rapids Herald*, July 7, 1914, 4.

22. *Grand Rapids Herald*, August 10, 1914, 4.

23. *Grand Rapids Herald*, August 24, 1914, 4.

24. *Grand Rapids Herald*, February 5, 1917, 4.

25. Tompkins, *Senator Arthur H. Vandenberg*, 19–20.

26. Ibid., 20.

27. *Grand Rapids Herald*, July 11, 1919, 6.

28. Ibid.

29. Margulies, *Mild Reservationists*, 2; Bailey, *Woodrow Wilson and the Great Betrayal*, 157.

30. Borah to Vandenberg, December 19, 1921, Vandenberg Papers, Bentley Library, roll 1.

31. Vandenberg to Col. Frank Knox, August 18, 1919, ibid., roll 1.

32. Ibid.; *Grand Rapids Herald*, July 24, 1919, 1.

33. Vandenberg to Earl Kettle, October 1, 1919, Vandenberg Papers, Bentley Library, roll 1.

34. *Grand Rapids Herald*, March 20, 1920, 6.

35. Vandenberg, *Trail of a Tradition*, 376.

36. Tompkins, *Senator Arthur H. Vandenberg*, 25.

37. Ibid., 27.

38. Ibid., 34–35.

39. Vandenberg, *If Hamilton Were Here Today*, 109.

40. Vandenberg to editor, *Hackensack (NJ) Record*, December 19, 1939, Vandenberg Papers, Bentley Library, roll 2.

41. Vandenberg, *If Hamilton Were Here Today*, v.

42. Ibid., 349–50.

43. Ibid., 336–37.

44. Coolidge to Vandenberg, March 8, 1924, Vandenberg Papers, Bentley Library, roll 1; Knox to Vandenberg, October 1, 1928, General Correspondence, Knox Papers, Library of Congress; Lodge to Vandenberg, November 17, 1924, Vandenberg Papers, Bentley Library, roll 1.

45. Lodge to Vandenberg, May 2, 1924, Vandenberg Papers, Bentley Library, roll 1.

46. Vandenberg, *Trail of a Tradition*, v.

47. Tompkins, *Senator Arthur H. Vandenberg*, 34.

2. The Republican Moderate, 1928–1936

1. Tompkins, *Senator Arthur H. Vandenberg*, 35.

2. Ibid., 36.

3. Tompkins, "Arthur Vandenberg Goes to the Senate," 29.

4. Address to S.A.N.E. (Society of American Newspaper Editors), April 28, 1928, Vandenberg Papers, Bentley Library, roll 6.

5. Tompkins, "Arthur Vandenberg Goes to the Senate," 25–27, 34. The journalist Bill Davidson speculated that Governor Green wanted the Senate seat for himself and "expected that the long-winded editor would talk himself out of the job before he came up for re-election." Davidson, "Two Mr. Vandenbergs," 91.

6. *Grand Rapids Herald*, April 6, 1928, 1, 4.

7. Tompkins, *Senator Arthur H. Vandenberg*, 46.

8. Remarks of Senator Vandenberg, May 29, 1928, on reapportionment of House of Representatives, Vandenberg Papers, Bentley Library, roll 6; see also 70th Cong., 1st sess., *CR* 69, pt. 10 (May 29, 1928): S 10598.

9. Ibid.

10. Ibid.

11. Myers and Newton, *Hoover Administration*, 394.

12. Dawes, *Notes as Vice President*, 280.

13. Tompkins, *Senator Arthur H. Vandenberg*, 52–55.

14. Ibid., 46–47.

15. Hoover, *Memoirs*, 209.

16. *New York Times*, June 5, 1930, 5.

17. Vandenberg to Albert J. Beveridge, June 11, 1923, Beveridge Papers, Library of Congress, box 241.

18. *New York Times*, January 5, 1930, 2; December 18, 1930, 2.

19. Speech on World Court, U.S. Senate, January 18, 1935, Vandenberg Papers, Bentley Library, roll 6. See 74th Cong., 1st sess., *CR* 79, pt. 1 (June 14, 1935): S 407.

20. *New York Times*, February 22, 1931, 11; February 28, 1931, 1.

21. *New York Times*, February 19, 1932, 4.

22. Tompkins, *Senator Arthur H. Vandenberg*, 146–47.

23. Vandenberg to Roosevelt, August 19, 1937; Roosevelt to Vandenberg, September 24, 1937; Vandenberg to Roosevelt, September 29, 1937, Vandenberg Papers, Bentley Library, roll 2.

24. Roosevelt to Vandenberg, December 21, 1937, ibid.

25. Speech in Philadelphia, October 1936, ibid., roll 6.

26. Speech in Battle Creek, Michigan, September 5, 1940, ibid.

27. Vandenberg to Roosevelt, November 7, 1940, ibid., roll 3.

28. Barnard, *Independent Man*, 196–97.

29. *New York Times*, June 10, 1933, 2.

30. Tompkins, *Senator Arthur H. Vandenberg,* 98–100.

31. Fine, *Sit Down,* 334.

32. Timmons, *Jesse H. Jones,* 184.

33. Ibid., 194–95.

34. Vandenberg to A. D. Hunt, The Farmers Bank, Lincoln, MO, December 20, 1943, Vandenberg Papers, Bentley Library, roll 3.

35. Vandenberg to Leo T. Crowley, October 12, 1945, ibid., roll 4; Vandenberg to Rep. Roy G. Woodruff (R-MI), July 25, 1944, ibid., roll 3.

36. Vandenberg to Frederick Nelson, December 11, 1949, ibid., roll 5.

37. Tompkins, *Senator Arthur H. Vandenberg,* 99.

38. Ibid., 132; Krock, *Memoirs,* 179.

39. Independence Day speech in Grand Rapids, July 4, 1936; Speech in Philadelphia, October 1, 1936, Vandenberg Papers, Bentley Library, roll 6.

40. *New York Times,* June 23, 1936, 12.

41. Cole, "And Then There Were None!," 240.

42. Leuchtenburg, *Franklin D. Roosevelt and the New Deal,* 231–35.

43. Rosenman, *Public Papers and Addresses of Roosevelt,* 6:51–59.

44. "The Latest Constitutional Challenge," broadcast over NBC, June 20, 1935; "Layman's View of the Supreme Court," NBC, March 2, 1936; Vandenberg radio address, NBC, February 21, 1937, Vandenberg Papers, Bentley Library, roll 6.

45. Vandenberg to President, telegram, July 13, 1938, Roosevelt Papers.

46. Vandenberg to Beveridge, November 19, 1923, Beveridge Papers, box 241.

3. Toward Insulation, 1934–1937

Vandenberg preferred to identify his views as "insulationism" rather than "isolationism." Vandenberg, *Private Papers,* 1.

1. 73rd Cong., 2nd sess., *CR* 78, pt. 6 (April 12, 1934): S 6475.

2. Connally, *My Name Is Tom Connally,* 219.

3. Vandenberg, "Can America Stay Out of the Next War?," address at Michigan Press Club, Ann Arbor, November 14, 1935, Vandenberg Papers, Bentley Library, roll 6.

4. Cole, "And Then There Were None!," 233; Wilz, *In Search of Peace,* 26.

5. Wilz, *In Search of Peace,* 27.

6. Coulter, *Senate Munitions Inquiry,* 14–15.

7. Cole, *Senator Gerald P. Nye,* 48.

8. 73rd Cong., 2nd sess., *CR* 78, pt. 6 (April 12, 1934): S6477.

9. Cole, *Senator Gerald P. Nye,* 61.

10. Ibid., 67–69; Detzer, *Appointment on the Hill,* 157–58.

11. 73rd Cong., 1st sess., *CR* 77, pt. 2 (April 15, 1933): S1789.

12. Cole, "Senator Key Pittman," 662–64; Detzer, *Appointment on the Hill,* 157–59.

13. Coulter, *Senate Munitions Inquiry*, 24.

14. Ibid.

15. Detzer, *Appointment on the Hill*, 159; "Arms and Men," *Fortune*, March 9, 1934, 53–57, 113–26; Leuchtenburg, *Franklin D. Roosevelt and the New Deal*, 217.

16. Detzer, *Appointment on the Hill*, 160–61; Wilz, *In Search of Peace*, 35–37.

17. Cole, *Senator Gerald P. Nye*, 71–72; Hull, *Memoirs*, 1:398.

18. Wilz, *In Search of Peace*, 45; Senate Special Committee Investigating the Munitions Industry, *Hearings on S.R. 206*, 74th Cong., 1st sess., pt. 21, February 27, 1935, 5819–58. Wilz believed that most writers have exaggerated the Nye committee's responsibility for the neutrality legislation: "It is possible that by talking so much about peace the committee unwittingly helped create a climate favorable to isolationist neutrality legislation." Doenecke and Wilz, *From Isolation to War*, 51.

19. Tompkins, *Senator Arthur H. Vandenberg*, 125.

20. 73rd Cong., 2nd sess., *CR* 78, pt. 6 (June 18, 1934): S6477.

21. *Washington Daily News*, January 21, 1936, 2.

22. Address by Senator Vandenberg, "Can America Stay Out of the Next War?" Michigan Press Club, Ann Arbor, November 14, 1935, Vandenberg Papers, Bentley Library, roll 6.

23. *New York Times*, December 19, 1934, 2; December 6, 1934, 1.

24. *New York Times*, December 28, 1936, 4.

25. Ibid.

26. Bolt, *Bullets before Ballots*, 152.

27. Ludlow, *From Cornfield to Press Gallery*, 400–401.

28. Bolt, *Bullets before Ballots*, 155.

29. Ibid., 430; 74th Cong., 1st sess., *CR* 79, pt. 1 (January 14, 1936): H430.

30. Bolt, *Bullets before Ballots*, 157, 158, 161.

31. Jonas, *Isolationism in America*, 161–62.

32. Cole, *Senator Gerald P. Nye*, 100–101; Tompkins, *Senator Arthur H. Vandenberg*, 126–28.

33. Cole, *Senator Gerald P. Nye*, 101–2; S.J. Res. 173, August 31, 1935, ch. 173, *U.S. Statutes at Large* 49 (1935): 1081.

34. Wilz, *In Search of Peace*, 217; H.J. Res. 491, Neutrality Act amendments, February 29, 1936, ch. 106, *U.S. Statutes at Large* 49 (1936): 1152.

35. Jonas, *Isolationism in America*, 144; Hull, *Memoirs*, 1:399.

36. Adler, *Isolationist Impulse*, 218–19; Connally, *My Name Is Tom Connally*, 219.

37. S.J. Res. 51, May 1, 1937, ch. 146, *U.S. Statutes at Large* 50 (1937): 121; Connally, *My Name Is Tom Connally*, 223; Jonas, *Isolationism in America*, 241.

38. McKenna, *Borah*, 353.

39. Divine, *Illusion of Neutrality*, 166–67.

40. *New York Times,* December 28, 1936, 4.

41. Senate Committee on Foreign Relations, *Hearings on S. 3474,* 74th Cong., 2nd sess., February 10, 1936, 290.

42. 75th Cong., 1st sess., *CR* 81, pt. 1 (January 22, 1937): S337; Divine, *Illusion of Neutrality,* 171, 173.

43. Senate Committee on Foreign Relations, *Hearings Relative to Proposed Legislation on Neutrality,* 75th Cong., 1st sess., February 15, 1937, 4–5.

44. Divine, *Illusion of Neutrality,* 174.

45. Ibid., 192; 75th Cong., 1st sess., *CR* 81, pt. 4 (April 29, 1937): S3943.

46. Cole, "And There Were None!," 239.

47. *New York Times,* October 27, 1936, 34.

48. *New York Times,* December 28, 1936, 4.

49. *New York Times,* August 31, 1937, 1.

4. Isolationism Challenged, 1938–1941

1. *Newsweek,* December 10, 1937, 10.

2. Jonas, *Isolationism in America,* 202.

3. Senate Committee on Foreign Relations, *Hearings on Neutrality, Peace Legislation, and Our Foreign Policy,* May 4, 1939, 76th Cong., 1st sess., 601.

4. Vandenberg to Alton Roberts, September 19, 1939, Vandenberg Papers, Bentley Library, roll 2; Divine, *Illusion of Neutrality,* 313. Unless otherwise noted, any emphasis is in the original.

5. Israel, *Nevada's Key Pittman,* 6; Cole, *Senator Gerald P. Nye,* 113–14.

6. *New York Times,* April 29, 1939, 7.

7. Langer and Gleason, *Challenge to Isolation,* 157–58.

8. Berle quoted in ibid., 158; Hull, *Memoirs,* 1:636–37.

9. Vandenberg to Secretary of State, August 7, 1939, in U.S. Department of State, *Foreign Relations of the United States, 1939* (Washington, D.C.: GPO), 3:568–69 (hereafter *FRUS*); Welles to Vandenberg, August 22, 1939; Vandenberg to Welles, August 24, 1939; and Vandenberg to Welles, August 11, 1939, Vandenberg Papers, Bentley Library, roll 2.

10. Vandenberg to Lippmann, January 30, 1940, Vandenberg Papers, Bentley Library, roll 3.

11. Vandenberg to C. M. Saunders, editor, *Jackson (MI) Patriot,* February 16, 1940, ibid.

12. Ibid.

13. Vandenberg to John H. Ferry, September 6, 1941; and Vandenberg to Claire Merrill, managing editor, *Midland (MI) Daily News,* January 29, 1940, ibid.

14. Vandenberg to Hiram H. Walker, May 22, 1940, ibid.

15. Cole, "And There Were None!," 239.

16. Vandenberg to Hiram H. Walker, May 22, 1940; and Vandenberg to John

T. Flynn, May 15, 1940, Vandenberg Papers, Bentley Library, roll 3; Vandenberg to S. L. A. Marshall, September 13, 1940, ibid., roll 8.

17. *Washington Post,* April 3, 1938, 5; *Baltimore Sun,* May 30, 1939, 1, 2; Howard G. Lawrence, chairman, the Vandenberg Movement, "War Times Demand Experienced Leadership," Vandenberg Papers, Bentley Library, roll 8; *Baltimore Sun,* April 28, 1939, 1.

18. McCoy, *Landon of Kansas,* 423, 428; Vandenberg, "New Deal Must Be Salvaged," 2, 9.

19. Espil diary, July 1, 1940, 1189–91, Espil Papers.

20. Vandenberg to John W. Blodgett, September 18, 1940, Vandenberg Papers, Bentley Library, roll 3.

21. Tompkins, *Senator Arthur H. Vandenberg,* 171–72; Jonas, *Isolationism in America,* 226, 228.

22. Adler, *Isolationist Impulse,* 273–74. For an authoritative study of the America First movement, see Cole, *America First.*

23. 80th Cong., 2nd sess., *CR* 85, pt. 1 (October 4, 1939): S95–104; Meijer, "Arthur Vandenberg and the Fight for Neutrality," 14–16; Divine, *Illusion of Neutrality,* 318.

24. Vandenberg diary, September 15, 1939, in Vandenberg, *Private Papers,* 2–3.

25. Vandenberg diary, October 27, 1939, ibid., 4.

26. Jonas, *Isolationism in America,* 216; responses to interventionist sentiment from constituents: F. W. Newton, secretary-treasurer, Saginaw Chapter, Committee to Defend America by Aiding the Allies, to Vandenberg, August 22, 1940; to Mayor George W. Welsh, Grand Rapids, August 19, 1940; and to Rev. Milton M. McGerrill, October 4, 1940, Vandenberg Papers, Bentley Library, roll 3.

27. Newbold Noyes to Vandenberg, October 9, 1949, ibid.

28. Vandenberg to Noyes, October 10, 1939, ibid.

29. Adler, *Isolationist Impulse,* 262–63. The committee was more Republican than Democrat.

30. Doenecke, *Storm on the Horizon,* 114.

31. Ibid., 173; Kimball, *Most Unsordid Act,* 68.

32. Vandenberg to Walter Meiden, May 1, 1941, Vandenberg Papers, Bentley Library, roll 3.

33. 76th Cong., 3rd sess., *CR* 86, pt. 9 (August 12, 1940): S10128; J. Clifford, *First Peacetime Draft,* 186.

34. Tompkins, *Senator Arthur H. Vandenberg,* 186; Vandenberg to Stuart H. Perry, August 20, 1940, Vandenberg Papers, Bentley Library, roll 3.

35. Vandenberg to S. L. A. Marshall, September 13, 1940; Voting Record of Vandenberg Compared with That of Taft, 1939, ibid., roll 8.

36. Kimball, *Most Unsordid Act,* 151–53; Churchill quoted in Martel, *Lend-Lease,* 3.

37. Kimball, *Most Unsordid Act,* 244.

38. Vandenberg diary, March 8, 1941, in Vandenberg, *Private Papers,* 10; Martel, *Lend-Lease,* 5.

39. Vandenberg diary, January 7, 1941, in Vandenberg, *Private Papers,* 8; *New York Times,* January 7, 1941, 2.

40. 77th Cong., 1st sess., *CR* 87, pt. 2 (March 7, 1941): S1991.

41. Vandenberg diary, March 8, 1941, in Vandenberg, *Private Papers,* 9–10.

42. 77th Cong., 1st sess., *CR* 87, pt. 3 (March 24, 1941): S2506-7.

43. Vandenberg to Walter Meiden, May 1, 1941, Vandenberg Papers, Bentley Library. roll 3.

44. Vandenberg to Joseph Alsop, January 15, 1941, ibid.

45. *New York Times,* January 2, 1941, 2; January 3, 1941, 4.

46. Mahl, *Desperate Deception,* 142–46; Lord Halifax to Lord Beaverbrook, December 3, 1941, FO 954/29, U.K. National Archives, Kew.

47. Vandenberg to Carl M. Saunders, March 19, 1941, Vandenberg Papers, Bentley Library, roll 3; Vandenberg, *Private Papers,* 11–12.

48. Ibid.

49. Vandenberg to John W. Blodgett, March 13, 1941; Vandenberg to E. Wallace Heck, November 4, 1941, Vandenberg Papers, Bentley Library, roll 3.

50. Langer and Gleason, *Undeclared War,* 264.

51. Vandenberg to E. Wallace Heck, November 4, 1941, Vandenberg Papers, Bentley Library, roll 3.

52. Ibid.

53. Vandenberg to Ralph Ennis, October 6, 1941, and Vandenberg to John W. Stalker, October 18, 1941, ibid.; "The Case against Repealing the Neutrality Act," Speech in the Senate, October 27, 1941, 77th Cong., 1st sess., *CR* 87, pt. 8 (October 27, 1941): S8252.

54. Vandenberg to Stalker, October 18, 1941, Vandenberg Papers, Bentley Library, roll 3; *New York Times,* October 28, 1941.

55. Vandenberg diary, December 8, 11, 1941, in Vandenberg, *Private Papers,* 16, 18–20.

56. Vandenberg diary, December 8, 1941, ibid., 16.

57. Ibid., 1, 12.

58. Vandenberg maintained close personal relations with Frank Januszewski, editor of Detroit's *Polish Daily News,* and with Philip Slomovitz, editor of Detroit's *Jewish News;* his awareness of political advantage with Michigan's Polish community is reflected in his request to the Clements Library for any original material relating to General Pulaski in the American Revolution when the country was commemorating the 150th anniversary of Pulaski's death. Vandenberg to Clements Librarian, September 18, 1929, Vandenberg Papers, Bentley Library, roll 1.

59. See Vandenberg to editor, *Hackensack (NJ) Record,* December 19, 1939,

ibid., roll 2, emphasizing his opposition to recognition of the Soviet Union in 1933. He urged breaking relations after Soviet actions in Poland and Finland in 1939, in *Liberty*, June 8, 1940, 15–19.

60. Vandenberg diary, June 8, 1939, in Vandenberg, *Private Papers*, 5.

61. Vandenberg to President, December 15, 1941, ibid., 24.

5. The Impact of World War, 1941–1945

1. Vandenberg, *Private Papers*, 1.

2. Vandenberg to President, December 15, 1941, ibid., 24; President to Vandenberg, December 27, 1941, folder 2529, Roosevelt Papers.

3. Vandenberg diary, January 7, 1942, in Vandenberg, *Private Papers*, 25–26.

4. Vandenberg diary, January 12, 1942, ibid., 27.

5. Vandenberg to Henry Hazlitt, *New York Times*, February 20, 1942, Vandenberg Papers, Bentley Library, roll 3; Vandenberg diary, April 21, 1942, in Vandenberg, *Private Papers*, 30; President to Vandenberg, December 27, 1941, Roosevelt Papers.

6. Vandenberg diary, June 4, 1942, in Vandenberg, *Private Papers*, 31–32.

7. Vandenberg to Editor, *Hackensack (NJ) Record*, December 19, 1939, Vandenberg Papers, Bentley Library, roll 2; Arthur H. Vandenberg, "Shall We Break with Russia," *Liberty*, December 5, 1939, ibid., roll 8; *New York Times*, December 5, 1939, urging recall of the U.S. ambassador to the USSR.

8. Vandenberg to John Williams, Pontiac, MI, January 8, 1942; and Vandenberg to Paul Wengel, Adrian, MI, March 2, 1943, Vandenberg Papers, Bentley Library, roll 3.

9. Vandenberg to Howard Ellis, Chicago, February 12, 1942, ibid.

10. Vandenberg to Henry Wallace, March 12, 1942; October 1, 1942; October 16, 1942, Wallace Papers.

11. Divine, *Second Chance*, 65; Vandenberg diary, March 26, 1943, in Vandenberg, *Private Papers*, 35.

12. Vandenberg to Major George Fielding Eliot, February 10, 1943, ibid., 35; Memorandum for Mr. Early, March 11, 1943, folder 3524, Roosevelt Papers. Vandenberg and Connally justified the extension of the bill as vital to the nation's war effort. See *New York Times*, May 9, 1944, 1, 5.

13. Vandenberg Resolution, 78th Cong., 1st sess., *CR* 89, pt. 5 (July 6, 1943): S7237.

14. Vandenberg to Senator Charles McNary (R-OR), July 7, 15, 1943, in Vandenberg, *Private Papers*, 67–68; Connally, *My Name Is Tom Connally*, 252–53.

15. Vandenberg to unnamed newsman, August 24, 1943, in Vandenberg, *Private Papers*, 72.

16. Ibid., 73–74.

17. Acheson, *Present at the Creation*, 71.

18. Vandenberg diary, July 8, 1943, in Vandenberg, *Private Papers,* 69.

19. 78th Cong., 1st sess., *CR* 89, pt. 2 (March 16, 1943): S2030.

20. Vandenberg diary, March 16, 1943, in Vandenberg, *Private Papers,* 40–41.

21. Vandenberg diary, March 24, 1943, ibid., 41–42; Vandenberg to Alex Smolenski, March 17, 1943, Vandenberg Papers, Bentley Library, roll 3.

22. Vandenberg to Walter George, March 27, 1943; and Vandenberg to Major George Fielding Eliot, March 26, 1943, Vandenberg Papers, Bentley Library, roll 3; letter to Eliot excerpted in Vandenberg, *Private Papers,* 35.

23. Ibid.; Vandenberg diary, August 24, 1943, in Vandenberg, *Private Papers,* 56.

24. Vandenberg to Major George Fielding Eliot, February 10, 1943, Vandenberg Papers, Bentley Library, roll 3.

25. Connally resolution, 78th Cong., 1st sess., *CR* 89, pt. 7 (November 5, 1943): S9222; Divine, *Second Chance,* 153.

26. *New York Times,* September 6, 1943, 1, 30.

27. *New York Times,* December 15, 1942, 1.

28. Vandenberg to Thomas W. Lamont, August 4, 1943, in Vandenberg, *Private Papers,* 55–56.

29. "The Mackinac Charter," address on the National Radio forum, conducted by the *Washington Evening Star,* September 23, 1943, quoted in Divine, *Second Chance,* 131–32.

30. Vandenberg, September 17, 1943, in Vandenberg, *Private Papers,* 60.

31. Taft to Vandenberg, March 29, 1944, in Taft, *Papers of Robert A. Taft,* 2:536.

32. Vandenberg to Frank Shakespeare, Kalamazoo, March 18, 1944, Vandenberg Papers, Bentley Library, roll 3; excerpted in Vandenberg, *Private Papers,* 92.

33. Vandenberg to Gen. Robert E. Wood, September 15, 1943, Vandenberg Papers, Bentley Library, roll 3; Vandenberg diary, April 30, 1944, in Vandenberg, *Private Papers,* 86.

34. Vandenberg to Dewey, May 22, 1944, Correspondence, 1943–1944, Dulles Papers, Princeton University, copy in Dulles Papers, Library of Congress, roll 3; undated statement by Vandenberg to Resolutions Committee, Vandenberg Papers, Bentley Library, roll 7.

35. Hull, *Memoirs,* 2:1658–59.

36. Vandenberg diary, May 2, 1944, in Vandenberg, *Private Papers,* 96; the text mistakenly gives the date as May 14.

37. Hull, *Memoirs,* 2:1659.

38. Vandenberg diary, May 2, 1944, in Vandenberg, *Private Papers,* 95–96.

39. Vandenberg to Hull, May 3, 1944, Vandenberg Papers, Bentley Library, roll 3, excerpted in Vandenberg, *Private Papers,* 97–98.

40. Vandenberg diary, May 19, 23, 26, 29, 1944, in Vandenberg, *Private Papers,* 99–101, 101–2, 103, 104–6; Israel, *War Diary of Breckinridge Long,* 346.

41. *New York Times,* August 17, 1944, 11.

42. Hull, *Memoirs,* 2:1691.

43. Vandenberg to Hull, August 29, 1944, in Vandenberg, *Private Papers,* 117.

44. Ibid., 118.

45. Vandenberg to Lippmann, September 14, 1944, ibid., 118–19.

46. Dulles, Suggested Statement on Dumbarton Oaks Plan, September 28, 1944, Correspondence, 1942–1944, Dulles Papers, Library of Congress, roll 5; Vandenberg to John K. Ormond, Birmingham, MI, September 30, 1944, Vandenberg Papers, Bentley Library, roll 3, excerpted in Vandenberg, *Private Papers,* 120.

47. "Proposal for the Establishment of a General International Organization," U.S. Department of State, *Bulletin* 11 (October 8, 1944): 368–74; Vandenberg speech on Dumbarton Oaks Conference, August 22, 1944, 78th Cong., 2nd sess., *CR* 90, pt. 5 (August 22, 1944): S7177; Vandenberg diary, November 24, 1944, in Vandenberg, *Private Papers,* 121–22.

48. Dulles recollections, February 28, 1944, Correspondence, 1942–1944, Dulles Papers, Princeton, box 23, and Dulles Papers, Library of Congress, roll 5.

49. Vandenberg to Dulles, November 11, 1944, in Vandenberg, *Private Papers,* 124; speech by Dulles to Massachusetts Committee of 1000, Boston, January 10, 1945, Correspondence, 1945, Dulles Papers, Library of Congress, roll 5.

50. Vandenberg to John T. Flynn, August 18, 1944, Vandenberg Papers, Bentley Library, roll 3.

51. Vandenberg to W. E. Fisher, Royal Oak, MI, November 22, 1944, ibid.

52. Ibid.

53. The address may be found in 69th Cong., 1st sess., *CR* 91, pt. 1 (January 10, 1945): S164–67. The quotations in this chapter are drawn from Arthur H. Vandenberg, "The Need for Honest Candor: Clarification of Our Foreign Policy," February 1, 1945, *Vital Speeches of the Day* 11: 226–30.

54. Vandenberg to Fred S. Noble, Ann Arbor, MI, July 8, 1948, in Vandenberg, *Private Papers,* 130–31.

55. Connally, *My Name Is Tom Connally,* 269; Vandenberg to Noble, July 8, 1948, in Vandenberg, *Private Papers,* 140.

56. *Washington Star,* January 20, 1945, 7; quotations drawn from "For Michigan—For America—Re-Elect Senator Vandenberg—A Tale of Two Speeches," 1946 election campaign literature, Vandenberg Papers, Bentley Library, roll 9.

57. Vandenberg, *Private Papers,* xx xxi.

58. Ibid., 35, 131.

59. *Vital Speeches of the Day,* 11:226–27.

60. Ibid., 11:229.

61. Ibid., 11:228.

62. Ibid., 11:229.

63. Gregg, "Rhetorical Re-examination," 167. In a more critical view, Thomas

Michael Hill emphasized the anti-Russian elements in the January 19, 1945, speech. Hill, "Senator Arthur H. Vandenberg," 231.

64. Vandenberg, "Try to Prevent World War III," *Saturday Evening Post,* March 17, 1945, 16.

65. Ibid.; Dulles to Hamilton Owens, *Baltimore Sun,* January 11, 1945, Dulles Papers, Library of Congress, roll 6.

66. *Washington Post,* January 14, 1945, B14.

6. The Conversion Experience, 1945

1. *FRUS, 1945,* February 13, 1945, 1:70.

2. Israel, *War Diary of Breckinridge Long,* 346.

3. Vandenberg diary, April 12, 1945, in Vandenberg, *Private Papers,* 165.

4. Vandenberg to Roosevelt, February 15, 1945, ibid., 149.

5. Vandenberg to Lippmann, March 15, 1945, ibid., 157–58.

6. Vandenberg to Roosevelt, March 1, 1945, ibid., 153; Roosevelt to Vandenberg, March 3, 1945, ibid., 153–54; Vandenberg to Dulles, February 17, 1945, ibid., 151–52.

7. Vandenberg to Dulles, February 17, 1945, Dulles Papers, Library of Congress, roll 6, copy in Vandenberg, *Private Papers,* 151; Vandenberg to Dulles, March 6, 1945, and Vandenberg diary, March 13, 1945, in Vandenberg, *Private Papers,* 151, 157.

8. Dulles to Vandenberg, March 20, 1945, Dulles Papers, Library of Congress, roll 6.

9. Dulles to Secretary of State, April 4, 1945; Dulles to Vandenberg, April 6, 1945, ibid.

10. Dulles to Vandenberg, February 21 and March 5, 1945, ibid.

11. Dulles to Vandenberg, February 22 and March 6, 1945, ibid.

12. Vandenberg to Dulles, March 22, 1945, ibid.

13. Vandenberg diary, May 13, 1945, in Vandenberg, *Private Papers,* 191.

14. Minutes of the Thirty-Sixth Meeting of the U.S. Delegates, May 11, 1945, *FRUS, 1945,* 1:667.

15. Pearson, *Mike,* 1:275.

16. Minutes of the First Four-Power Consultative Meeting on Charter Proposals, May 2, 1945, *FRUS, 1945,* 1:555.

17. Ibid., 1:561.

18. Minutes of the Thirty-Third Meeting of the U.S. Delegation, May 8, 1945, *FRUS, 1945,* 1:648.

19. Dulles to Pvt. W. P. Welling, September 14, 1944; Dulles to Marquis Childs, May 4, 1944, Correspondence, 1943–1944, Dulles Papers, Princeton, boxes 24, 25, and Dulles Papers, Library of Congress, roll 5.

20. Dulles Papers, Library of Congress, roll 5.

21. Memo for files, Acheson conversation with Lehman, April 5, 1950; Acheson to Vandenberg, April 10, 1950, Acheson Papers.

22. Vandenberg, *Private Papers*, xx–xxi.

23. Vandenberg to Lippmann, May 9, 1935; Vandenberg to Leon B. Gridley, Director, Servicemen's Bureau, Detroit, May 13, 1935, box 107, folder 2145, series III, Select Correspondence, 1931–1974, reel 96, Lippmann Papers.

24. Vandenberg to Lippmann, January 30, 1940, Lippmann Papers; Vandenberg to Saunders, February 16, 1940, Vandenberg Papers, Bentley Library, roll 3.

25. Lippmann to Vandenberg, October 2, 1939, quoted in Steel, *Walter Lippmann*, 379–80.

26. Vandenberg to Lippmann, September 14, 1944, in Vandenberg, *Private Papers*, 118–19.

27. Steel, *Walter Lippmann*, 419.

28. Vandenberg to Lippmann, March 15, 1945, Lippmann Papers.

29. Steel, *Walter Lippmann*, 419, 455.

30. Lippmann to Vandenberg, April 28, 1948, Lippmann Papers.

31. Vandenberg to Januszewski, March 7, 1945, in Vandenberg, *Private Papers*, 155–56.

32. Januszewski to Vandenberg. March 10, 1945, Vandenberg Papers, Bentley Library, roll 3.

33. Vandenberg diary, March 23, 1945, in Vandenberg, *Private Papers*, 159.

34. Vandenberg diary, March 27, 1945; Vandenberg press statement, March 29, 1945; and Vandenberg diary, April 2, 1945, ibid., 159–60.

35. Vandenberg to Harry G. Hogan, March 20, 1945, Vandenberg Papers, Bentley Library, roll 3.

36. Amendments to Dumbarton Oaks proposals, in Vandenberg, *Private Papers*, 162–63; Divine, *Second Chance*, 281.

37. Vandenberg diary, April 16, 1945, in Vandenberg, *Private Papers*, 168.

38. Vandenberg diary, March 20, 1945, ibid., 158.

39. Vandenberg to Rev. Paul Wengel, Adrian MI, Vandenberg Papers, Bentley Library, roll 3.

40. Vandenberg diary, March 20, April 2, 3, 1945, in Vandenberg, *Private Papers*, 160, 161–62.

41. Arthur Vandenberg Jr. provides the setting in ibid., 175; see also Divine, *Second Chance*.

42. Divine, *Second Chance*, 276.

43. Vandenberg diary, April 27, 1945, in Vandenberg, *Private Papers*, 181–82.

44. Vandenberg diary, April 24, 1945, ibid., 175–76.

45. Ibid., 176.

46. Arthur Vandenberg Jr. describes the emotional reaction in the Senate on April 20, 1945, ibid., 171.

47. See ibid., 175; Divine, *Second Chance*.

48. Vandenberg diary, April 27, 1945, in Vandenberg, *Private Papers*, 180.

49. Ibid.

50. Vandenberg diary, April 25, 1945, ibid., 176–77.

51. Vandenberg diary, April 30, 1945, ibid., 182; Reid, May 4, 1945, *On Duty*, 33.

52. Vandenberg diary, April 30, 1945, in Vandenberg, *Private Papers*, 182; Vandenberg diary, May 1, 1945, Vandenberg Papers, Bentley Library, roll 10.

53. Reid, May 18, August 24, 1945, *On Duty*, 43, 78.

54. Vandenberg diary, May 20, 1945, in Vandenberg, *Private Papers*, 196–97.

55. Vandenberg diary, May 13, 1945, ibid., 191.

56. Vandenberg diary, May 13, 1945, Vandenberg Papers, Bentley Library, roll 10, excerpted in Vandenberg, *Private Papers*, 192.

57. Briggs, "Senator Vandenberg, Bipartisanship," 168; Vandenberg to Henry M. Robbins, Secretary of the Detroit Committee on Foreign Relations, December 9, 1948, in Vandenberg, *Private Papers*, 419.

58. Vandenberg diary, June 3, 1945, ibid., 202.

59. Vandenberg diary, June 5, 7, 1945, ibid., 203–4, 208.

60. Vandenberg diary, June 17, 20, 1945, ibid., 212–13, 213–14.

61. Russell, *History of the United Nations Charter*, 758–60.

62. Ibid., 759.

63. Vandenberg diary, June 23, 1945, Vandenberg Papers, Bentley Library, roll 10 (not included in the Vandenberg, *Private Papers*, excerpts).

64. Vandenberg, "Device to Put Men's Minds in Gear," 9.

65. Vandenberg diary, June 23, 1945; Vandenberg to Mrs. Vandenberg, in Vandenberg, *Private Papers*, 215, 225.

66. Vandenberg diary, June 23, 1945, ibid., 215.

67. Divine, *Second Chance*, 300.

68. 79th Cong., 1st sess., *CR* 91, pt. 7 (June 28, 1945): S6874–78; (June 29, 1945), S6981.

69. Ibid., S6981; Gazell, "Arthur H. Vandenberg, Internationalism, and the United Nations," 392.

70. 79th Cong., 1st sess., *CR* 91, pt. 7 (June 29, 1945), S6981.

71. Vandenberg to Floyd McGriff, August 29, 1945, Vandenberg Papers, Bentley Library, roll 3; Vandenberg to Detroit Economic Club, July 13, 1945, ibid., roll 7.

72. Vandenberg to Dulles, July 3, 1945, ibid., roll 3.

73. Ibid.

74. Senate Committee on Foreign Relations, *Hearings*, 79th Cong., 1st sess., July 6, 1945, 237; July 10, 1945, 451.

75. *New York Times*, July 12, 1945, 1; Vandenberg to Mrs. Vandenberg, undated, in Vandenberg, *Private Papers*, 218.

76. Vandenberg to Mrs. Vandenberg, undated, in Vandenberg, *Private Papers*, 218–19.

77. Acheson, *Present at the Creation*, 223.

7. The Senator as Diplomat, 1945–1946

1. Vandenberg, *Private Papers,* 238.

2. 79th Cong., 1st sess., *CR* 8 (November 18, 1945): S10696–97. Churchill used the metaphor in a message to Truman a year before he unveiled it in Fulton, Missouri, but there is no evidence that Vandenberg was aware of it.

3. Smith, "Russia's Favorite Whipping Boy," 19; Vandenberg to Frank Januszewski, July 2, 1946, in Vandenberg, *Private Papers,* 314.

4. Vandenberg diary, April 2, 1946, in Vandenberg, *Private Papers,* 245.

5. Ibid.

6. Vandenberg to wife, undated, ibid., 225. He seemingly places Byrnes at Yalta.

7. Ibid., 226.

8. Vandenberg diary, December 10, 1945, ibid., 228.

9. Vandenberg diary, December 11, 1945, ibid., 211; Hill, "Senator Arthur H. Vandenberg," 234–35.

10. Vandenberg to Dulles, December 19, 1945, Vandenberg Papers, Bentley Library, roll 4; excerpted in Vandenberg, *Private Papers,* 230–31.

11. Vandenberg to President, December 21, 1945, expressing his appreciation for the appointment as a U.S. representative to the first session of the UN General Assembly, General File, Truman Papers.

12. Vandenberg diary, December 29, 1945, in Vandenberg, *Private Papers,* 235–36.

13. Ibid., 242–44. Britain's and France's withdrawal of their forces from Syria and Lebanon was praised by Secretary Byrnes in his speech on February 28 to the Overseas Press Club in New York. U.S. Department of State, *Bulletin* 14, no. 349 (March 10, 1946): 356.

14. U.S. Delegation Position Paper, [January 1946], *FRUS, 1946,* 1:725–26.

15. Byrnes, *All in One Lifetime,* 347–48.

16. 79th Cong., 2nd sess., *CR* 92, pt. 2 (February 27, 1946): S1692–95.

17. Ibid., S1694.

18. Campbell and Herring, *Diaries of Edward R. Stettinius Jr.,* 4.

19. Byrnes speech, February 28, 1946, quoted in Vandenberg, *Private Papers,* 250; Vandenberg address, Grand Rapids, March 23, 1946, ibid., 251.

20. Quoted in ibid., 220.

21. Vandenberg to Rev. Leonard Saunders, March 6, 1946, Vandenberg Papers, Bentley Library, roll 4.

22. Hewlett and Anderson, *History,* 424.

23. Truman, *Memoirs,* 2:15.

24. Ibid., 19; Vandenberg, *Private Papers,* 259–60.

25. Walter Brooks to Vandenberg, March 2, 1946; and Vandenberg to Brooks, March 28, 1946, Vandenberg Papers, Bentley Library, roll 4; Vandenberg diary, March 14, 1946, in Vandenberg, *Private Papers,* 257.

26. Vandenberg, *Private Papers,* 254; Wallace quotation on 255.

27. Vandenberg to L. F. Beckwith, November 13, 1945, Vandenberg Papers, Bentley Library, roll 5.

28. Vandenberg to Editor, *Baltimore Sun,* March 14, 1946, ibid.; excerpted in Vandenberg, *Private Papers,* 257–58.

29. Vandenberg to L. G. Carmick Jr., Detroit, April 18, 1946; and Vandenberg to L. T. Girdler, Muskegon, July 28, 1946, Vandenberg Papers, Bentley Library, roll 4. Vandenberg expressed these sentiments about totalitarian control of atomic energy on July 20, 1946; see Vandenberg, *Private Papers,* 253.

30. Vandenberg to Walter Brooks, March 24, 1946, Vandenberg Papers, Bentley Library, roll 4.

31. Hewlett and Duncan, *History,* 279.

32. Ibid., 279–84.

33. Lilienthal, *Journals,* 2:133–34.

34. B. E. Hutchinson to Vandenberg, February 13, 1946, Vandenberg Papers, Bentley Library, roll 4; Vandenberg to Hutchinson, February 17, 1946, ibid.; relevant quotation in Vandenberg, *Private Papers,* 354.

35. Vandenberg, *Private Papers,* 354–55.

36. 80th Cong., 1st sess., *CR* 93, pt. 9 (April 3, 1947): S3108; excerpted in Vandenberg, *Private Papers,* 355.

37. Vandenberg to Mrs. Vandenberg, May 24, 1949, in Vandenberg, *Private Papers,* 357–58.

38. President Truman to Vandenberg, July 18, 1946, Vandenberg Papers, Bentley Library, roll 4.

39. Quoted in memcon, Associate Chief of the Division of International Security Affairs, April 1, 1946, notes on conference between State Department officials and certain Senators, April 1, 1946, Senate Foreign Relations Committee room in the Capitol, *FRUS, 1946,* 1:772

40. Ibid., 1:773.

41. Vandenberg diary, April 28, 1946, in Vandenberg, *Private Papers,* 266.

42. Ibid., 267.

43. Vandenberg diary, May 28, 1946, ibid., 285.

44. Vandenberg diary, July 10, 1946, AHV Diary, 1946, re: Paris Peace Conference, 2nd session, June–July, and Council of Foreign Ministers, Vandenberg Papers, Bentley Library, roll 10.

45. 79th Cong., 2nd sess., *CR* 92, pt. 7 (July 16, 1946): S9061.

46. Ibid., S9062.

47. Ibid., S9064–65.

48. Ibid., S9065.

49. Close of the Third Session of the Council of Foreign Ministers in New York, December 12, 1946, *FRUS, 1946,* 2:1556; Byrnes, *Speaking Frankly,* 149; Vandenberg, *Private Papers,* 302–3.

50. Byrnes, *Speaking Frankly,* 242; also in Vandenberg, *Private Papers,* 302.

51. Vandenberg, *Private Papers,* 301.

52. John Foster Dulles to Irving Fisher, September 18, 1946, Dulles Papers, Princeton, box 29, and Dulles Papers, Library of Congress, roll 7.

53. Vandenberg to Dulles, December 19, 1945, Vandenberg Papers, Bentley Library, roll 4; excerpted in Vandenberg, *Private Papers,* 230–31.

54. Taft to Vandenberg, September 29, 1946; and Vandenberg to Taft, October 19, 1946, Vandenberg Papers, Bentley Library, roll 4; Patterson, *Mr. Republican,* 340; speech to Economic Club of Detroit, February 23, 1946, in Taft, *Papers of Robert A. Taft,* 3:406.

55. Vandenberg to Howard C. Lawrence, Grand Rapids, May 28, 1946, Vandenberg Papers, Bentley Library, roll 4.

56. Forty-Sixth Plenary Meeting, U.S. Delegation Journal, October 14, 1946, *FRUS, 1946,* 3:841.

57. Minutes of the Thirteenth Meeting of the U.S. Delegation, New York, November 1, 1946, *FRUS, 1946,* 1:469.

58. Vandenberg to Kim Sigler, Lansing, July 16, 1946, Vandenberg Papers, Bentley Library, roll 4.

59. Vandenberg to campaign headquarters, September 21, 1946, in Vandenberg, *Private Papers,* 311.

60. Ibid., 312.

61. Ibid., 309.

62. Vandenberg to Robert E. Hannegan, Postmaster General, October 28, 1946, Vandenberg Papers, Bentley Library, roll 4.

63. Ibid.

64. Vandenberg, *Private Papers,* 315–17.

8. The Senator as Statesman, 1947–1948

1. *New York Herald-Tribune,* January 11, 1947, 2.

2. Vandenberg to President, [February 1947], in Vandenberg, *Private Papers,* 319.

3. Vandenberg to Capper, November 8, 1946, Vandenberg Papers, Bentley Library, roll 4.

4. Vandenberg to Roberts, December 20, 1946, in Vandenberg, *Private Papers,* 320–21.

5. Vandenberg to Roberts, January 23, 1947, ibid., 321.

6. *New York Times,* January 20, 1947, 7.

7. Vandenberg to Januszewski, May 27, 1946; and Vandenberg to Slomovitz, February 28, 1948, Vandenberg Papers, Bentley Library, roll 4.

8. NBC symposium, *New York Times,* January 20, 1947, 1; address before the Cleveland Council on World Affairs, January 11, 1947, in Vandenberg, *Private Papers,* 334–35.

9. Hoover, *Memoirs,* 209; *New York Times,* June 5, 1930, 5.

10. Vandenberg, *Private Papers,* 335.

11. *New York Times,* August 2, 1947, 6.

12. Vandenberg to Eleanor Roosevelt, January 9, 1947, Vandenberg Papers, Bentley Library, roll 4; excerpted in Vandenberg, *Private Papers,* 331 (without italics).

13. Ibid.

14. Vandenberg to Stettinius, May 5, 1945, diary of the San Francisco Charter Conference on the United Nations, March 13–June 25, 1945, Vandenberg Papers, Bentley Library, roll 10; see also Vandenberg, *Private Papers,* 187.

15. Vandenberg diary, June 13, 1945, Vandenberg Papers, Bentley Library, roll 10.

16. Vandenberg speech to the Senate on Rio Pact, December 8, 1947, 80th Cong., 1st sess., *CR* 93, pt. 9 (December 8, 1947): S11122; Vandenberg, *Private Papers,* 369.

17. Vandenberg to Marshall, August 8, 1947, Vandenberg Papers, Bentley Library, roll 4.

18. Vandenberg to Alberto Lleras Carmago, Director General, Pan American Union, March 16, 1948, complaining about the slow progress in ratifications; and Vandenberg to Taft, December 2, 1947, ibid., roll 4.

19. Acheson to Vandenberg, July 7, 1950, ibid., roll 5.

20. Vandenberg to Lovett, September 14, 1948, ibid., roll 5; quoted in Woyke, "Foundation and History of NATO," 253.

21. Vandenberg summation of results of Rio conference in speech to Senate, December 8, 1947, in Vandenberg, *Private Papers,* 371.

22. For Mrs. Vandenberg's comments on Marshall, see ibid., 372.

23. On Vandenberg's interest in Philippine independence, see *New York Times,* June 5, 1930, 5.

24. Vandenberg to Ickes, July 22, 1947; and Vandenberg to Leon Henderson, Chairman, Executive Committee, Americans for Democratic Action, July 21, 1947, Vandenberg Papers, Bentley Library, roll 4.

25. Vandenberg to A. Scott Peterson, June 4, 1947; and Vandenberg to Styles Bridges, March 25, 1947, ibid.

26. Vandenberg to Knowland, August 18, 1948, ibid.

27. Vandenberg to Frederick B. Newton, November 22, 1948, ibid., roll 5; Vandenberg to C. Reid Webber, October 14, 1947, ibid., roll 4.

28. Vandenberg to J. B. Montgomery, January 27, 1947, ibid., roll 4.

29. Vandenberg, *Private Papers,* 327–28; Fetzer, "Senator Vandenberg and the American Commitment to China," 300; Westerfield, *Foreign Policy and Party Politics,* 260.

30. Vandenberg diary, February 10, 1947, in Vandenberg, *Private Papers,* 523.

31. Vandenberg to Frederick B. Newton, November 22, 1948, Vandenberg Papers, Bentley Library, roll 5.

32. Vandenberg to C. Reid Webber, October 14, 1947, ibid., roll 4; Vandenberg to F. Smith, January 28, 1949, ibid., roll 5.

33. Vandenberg presented the China Aid Bill to the Senate, March 29, 1948. See Vandenberg, *Private Papers*, 524; Vandenberg to Knowland, October 28, 1948, ibid., 525.

34. Vandenberg to Eugene Zeimet, January 18, 1949, Vandenberg Papers, Bentley Library, roll 5.

35. Memcon, Connally, Acheson, Wilcox, Gross, June 19, 1947, Acheson Papers; 81st Cong., 1st sess., *CR* 95, pt. 5 (June 24, 1949): S8294; Vandenberg to Donald F. Zorn, August 25, 1949, Vandenberg Papers, Bentley Library, roll 5, excerpted in Vandenberg, *Private Papers*, 536 (without italics).

36. Vandenberg to Bernard C. Yunck, January 17, 1950; and Vandenberg to D. M. Fraser Jr., January 23, 1950, Vandenberg Papers, Bentley Library, roll 5.

37. Vandenberg to Acheson, June 5, 1950; and Acheson to Vandenberg, June 23, 1950, ibid.

38. 81st Cong., 1st sess., *CR* 95, pt. 5 (June 24, 1949): S8294; Vandenberg, *Private Papers*, 532–33.

39. Vandenberg to Mrs. Vandenberg, [June 1949], in Vandenberg, *Private Papers*, 534; Taft quoted in Acheson, *Present at the Creation*, 355.

40. Vandenberg to President, July 3, 1950, Vandenberg Papers, Bentley Library, roll 5; excerpted in Vandenberg, *Private Papers*, 543; Vandenberg to President, October 20, 1950, in Vandenberg, *Private Papers*, 544.

41. Vandenberg to unnamed recipient, November 15, 1950, ibid., 545.

42. Jones, *Fifteen Weeks*, 11. Jones, special assistant to the assistant secretary of state for public affairs, was the leading draftsman of the president's message to Congress on aid to Greece and Turkey. His book, a history and memoir on the background of the Truman Doctrine and the Marshall Plan, celebrates his own role in those crucial days.

43. Quoted in Jones, *Fifteen Weeks*, 91.

44. Special Message to the Congress on Greece and Turkey: Truman Doctrine, March 12, 1947, in *Public Papers of the Presidents of the United States: Harry S. Truman, 1947* (Washington, D.C.: GPO, 1963), 178–79.

45. Acheson's version of Marshall's presentation in Jones, *Fifteen Weeks*, 139.

46. Ibid.; Acheson, *Present at the Creation*, 219, quoting Vandenberg.

47. Vandenberg to newsmen [about March 13, 1947], in Vandenberg, *Private Papers*, 343.

48. Vandenberg to R. F. Moffett, May 12, 1947, ibid., 341–42.

49. Vandenberg to Bruce Barton, March 24, 1947, ibid., 342; Taft to Vandenberg, March 14, 1947, Taft Papers, box 887.

50. Jones, *Fifteen Weeks*, 193.

51. Vandenberg to Acheson, March 20, 1947, Vandenberg Papers, Bentley Library, roll 4.

52. Vandenberg to newsmen [about March 13, 1947], in Vandenberg, *Private Papers,* 343.

53. Quoted in Jones, *Fifteen Weeks,* 182.

54. Ibid., 177.

55. 80th Cong., 1st sess., *CR* 93, pt. 2 (March 21, 1947): S2378.

56. 80th Cong., 1st sess., *CR* 93, pt. 3 (March 31, 1947): S2848; "colossal blunder" was in penciled notes in Vandenberg, *Private Papers,* 345.

57. Acheson, *Present at the Creation,* 223. Acheson earlier had made these points without the sarcasm and with appreciation for Vandenberg's contributions, in *Sketches from Life,* 108–9.

58. Acheson, *Present at the Creation,* 224; Connally, *My Name Is Tom Connally,* 319; Jones, *Fifteen Weeks,* 184.

59. Jones, *Fifteen Weeks,* 197–98.

60. Vandenberg to Rep. John S. Bennett (R-MI), March 5, 1947, Vandenberg Papers, Bentley Library, roll 4.

61. Dulles to Vandenberg, August 28, 1947, ibid.

62. Special Message to Congress, Requesting Appropriations for Aid to Liberated Countries, February 21, 1947, in *Public Papers of the Presidents: Truman, 1947,* 150; Westerfield, *Foreign Policy and Party Politics,* 273.

63. 80th Cong., 1st sess., *CR* 93 (May 14, 1947): S5242–44.

64. Bohlen, *Witness to History,* 264; Ruddy, *Cautious Diplomat,* 74–75. Bohlen's role is diminished in Marshall's records. See Stoler, "And Perhaps a Little More," 57.

65. Acheson speech before Delta Council, Cleveland, MS, May 8, 1947, *Vital Speeches of the Day,* 13:486–87; Truman, *Memoirs,* 2:137; Truman quoted in Jones, *Fifteen Weeks,* 233.

66. Lippmann, *Cold War,* 54–55; Kennan, *Memoirs,* 379.

67. *New York Times,* May 23, 1947, 1; Jones, *Fifteen Weeks,* 236–37.

68. Marshall quoted in Vandenberg, *Private Papers,* 375.

69. Vandenberg comment to White House, June 13, 1947, ibid., 376.

70. Ibid., 377.

71. Vandenberg to R. J. Winter, June 20, 1947, Vandenberg Papers, Bentley Library, roll 4.

72. Lovett to Vandenberg, January 2, 1948, ibid.

73. *New York Times,* January 23, 1948, 1, 3.

74. Vandenberg to Mrs. Vandenberg, [November 13, 1947], in Vandenberg, *Private Papers,* 379.

75. Vandenberg to Eichelberger, June 25, 1947, Vandenberg Papers, Bentley Library, roll 4; excerpted in Vandenberg, *Private Papers,* 381.

76. Vandenberg to Lovett, October 30, 1947, Vandenberg Papers, Bentley Library, roll 4.

77. *New York Times,* November 25, 1947, 15; Vandenberg to Mrs. Vandenberg, undated, in Vandenberg, *Private Papers,* 378.

78. Vandenberg quoted in Hartmann, *Truman and the 80th Congress*, 119.

79. Vandenberg to Prof. Kenneth Colegrove, June 6, 1947; and Vandenberg to C. Reid Webber, October 14, 1947, Vandenberg Papers, Bentley Library, roll 4.

80. Vandenberg to Lovett, December 10, 1947; and Lovett to Vandenberg, December 11, 1947, ibid.

81. Vandenberg to Marshall, March 24, 1948, ibid.; Vandenberg, *Private Papers*, 394; Senate Committee on Foreign Relations, European Recovery Program, *Hearings*, 80th Cong., 2nd sess., January 8, 1948, 21–22.

82. Vandenberg to Snyder, January 28, 1948; and Snyder to Vandenberg, February 2, 1948, Vandenberg Papers, Bentley Library, roll 4.

83. Hartmann, *Truman and the 80th Congress*, 160–61.

84. Vandenberg, speech to Senate, March 1, 1948, in Vandenberg, *Private Papers*, 391–92.

85. Vandenberg to Dulles, June 4, 1948, Vandenberg Papers, Bentley Library, roll 4; Vandenberg, speech to Senate, June 9, 1948, in Vandenberg, *Private Papers*, 397.

86. Vandenberg, speech to Senate, June 9, 1948, in Vandenberg, *Private Papers*, 398; Vandenberg to B. E. Hutchinson, September 28, 1948, Vandenberg Papers, Bentley Library, roll 5.

9. Charter and Treaty, 1948–1949

1. Achilles, *Fingerprints on History*, 11.

2. Vandenberg to Lovett, November 5, 1947, Vandenberg Papers, Bentley Library, roll 4.

3. Achilles, *Fingerprints on History*, 12–13.

4. Vandenberg to Dr. John W. Dunning, September 19, 1947, Vandenberg Papers, Bentley Library, roll 4, excerpted in Vandenberg, *Private Papers*, 400–401; *New York Times*, October 6, 1947.

5. Resolution 10, 80th Cong., 1st sess., *CR* 93, pt. 2 (March 21, 1947): S2437.

6. 80th Cong., 2nd sess., *CR* 94, pt. 2 (March 3, 1948): S2034, 2037.

7. Vandenberg to Arthur B. Langlie, February 19, 1948, Vandenberg Papers, Bentley Library, roll 4.

8. Vandenberg diary, April 21, 1948, in Vandenberg, *Private Papers*, 404.

9. Kaplan, *Community of Interests*, 207–9.

10. Renaud quoted in Millard [U.S. chargé d'affaires, Belgium] to Secretary of State, telegram, March 15, 1948, no. 1349, 840.00/3–1548, U.S. National Archives and Records Administration, College Park, MD.

11. Vandenberg to James W. Sheppard, January 27, 1948, Vandenberg Papers, Bentley Library, roll 4.

12. Memcon, Gladwyn Jebb with Sir Orme Sargent, Sir Ivone Kirkpatrick, and Ernest Bevin, March 3, 1948, FO 371, 73050, U.K. National Archives, Kew;

Special Message to the Congress on the Threat to the Freedom of Europe, March 17, 1948, in *Public Papers of the Presidents of the United States: Harry S. Truman, 1948* (Washington, D.C.: GPO, 1964), 404.

13. Achilles, *Fingerprints on History*, 14; Minutes of the Sixth Meeting of the United States–United Kingdom–Canada Security Conversations, Washington, D.C., April 1, 1948, *FRUS, 1948*, 3:72.

14. NSC 9: The Position of the United States with Respect to Support for Western Union and Other Related Free Countries, April 13, 1948, *FRUS, 1948*, 3:86.

15. Achilles, *Fingerprints on History*, 16.

16. Cook, *Forging the Alliance*, 162; Vandenberg, *Private Papers*, 404.

17. Vandenberg, *Private Papers*, 404.

18. Memcon with Vandenberg, acting secretary of state, April 11, 1948, *FRUS, 1948*, 3:82–84.

19. Meeting at Blair House, April 27, 1948—Marshall, Lovett, Vandenberg, Dulles, Dulles Papers, Princeton, box 37, and Dulles Papers, Library of Congress, roll 11.

20. 80th Cong., 2nd sess., *CR* 94, pt. 6 (June 11, 1948): S7791.

21. Cook, *Forging the Alliance*, 162–63; Achilles, *Fingerprints on History*, 17.

22. Hudson, "Vandenberg Reconsidered," 47–48.

23. Lovett quoted in ibid., 49.

24. Ibid., 63.

25. Vandenberg to Arthur B. Langlie, February 19, 1948, Vandenberg Papers, Bentley Library, roll 4; Vandenberg to Lodge, December 11, 1948, in Vandenberg, *Private Papers*, 415.

26. Vandenberg to Henry M. Robbins, December 1948, in Vandenberg, *Private Papers*, 419; Senate Committee on Foreign Relations, *Hearings in Executive Session on the Vandenberg Resolution and the North Atlantic Treaty, S. Res. 239*, 80th Cong., 2nd sess., Historical Series, May 11, 1948, 3, 8.

27. Senate Committee on Foreign Relations, *Hearings in Executive Session S. Res. 239*, 80th Cong., 2nd sess., May 19, 1948, 65; 80th Cong., 2nd sess., *CR* 94, pt. 8 (June 11, 1948): S7809, 7848.

28. C. Clifford, *Counsel to the President*, 234.

29. Vandenberg to Milton Carmichael, September 1, 1947, Vandenberg Papers, Bentley Library, roll 4.

30. Quoted in Vandenberg, *Private Papers*, 427.

31. Vandenberg to Sumner Welles, July 3, 1948; and Vandenberg to Harold Ickes, July 29, 1948, Vandenberg Papers, Bentley Library, roll 5.

32. Vandenberg diary, Philadelphia, 1948, in Vandenberg, *Private Papers*, 434–36.

33. Vandenberg to J. K. Kane, July 1, 1948, Vandenberg Papers, Bentley Library, roll 5.

34. Vandenberg to Dulles, June 4, 1948, ibid., roll 4; joint statement, September 11, 1948, Dulles Papers, Princeton, box 38, and Dulles Papers, Library of Congress, roll 11; Vandenberg to Dulles, July 2, 1948, Vandenberg Papers, Bentley Library, roll 5.

35. Dulles memo of Washington Conference, July 19, 1948, Dulles Papers, Princeton, box 37, and Dulles Papers, Library of Congress, roll 11; Vandenberg diary, October 5, 1948, in Vandenberg, *Private Papers,* 458.

36. Vandenberg to Dulles, August 9, 1948, Vandenberg Papers, Bentley Library, roll 5; excerpted in Vandenberg, *Private Papers,* 448. A similar message was sent to Herbert Brownell Jr., Dewey's campaign manager, on September 22, 1948; see Vandenberg, *Private Papers,* 448.

37. Vandenberg to Curtis P. Nettels, November 17, 1948, Vandenberg Papers, Bentley Library, roll 5.

38. Vandenberg statement, September 11, 1948, Dulles Papers, Princeton, box 38, and Dulles Papers, Library of Congress, roll 11; Vandenberg to President, telegram, November 3, 1948, Vandenberg Papers, Bentley Library, roll 5.

39. Vandenberg to Mrs. Vandenberg, [June 1949], in Vandenberg, *Private Papers,* 489.

40. 81st Cong., 1st sess., *CR* 95, pt. 1 (January 18, 1949): S460; Vandenberg to Sumner Welles, December 7, 1948; and Vandenberg to Sen. Raymond Baldwin (R-CT), Vandenberg Papers, Bentley Library, roll 5.

41. Reid, *Time of Fear and Hope,* 150; Memcon by Secretary of State—Bohlen, Connally, Vandenberg, February 14, 1949, *FRUS, 1949,* 4:109–10; 81st Cong., 1st sess., *CR* 95, pt. 1 (February 14, 1949): S1164; Henderson, *Birth of NATO,* 90–91.

42. Memcon by Secretary of State—Bohlen, Connally, Vandenberg, February 14, 1949, *FRUS, 1949,* 4:109.

43. Vandenberg to James H. Sheppard, January 27, 1949, Vandenberg Papers, Bentley Library, roll 5.

44. Vandenberg to Neil M. Morgan, April 15, 1949, ibid.

45. Minutes, Twelfth Meeting of the Washington Exploratory Talks on Security, February 8, 1949, *FRUS, 1949,* 4:73–74; memcon by Secretary of State—Bohlen, Connally, Vandenberg, February 8, 1949, Vandenberg Papers, Bentley Library, roll 5.

46. Memcon by Secretary of State—Bohlen, Connally, Vandenberg, February 14, 1949, *FRUS, 1949,* 4:109; Vandenberg to Glenwood C. Fuller, February 21, 1949, Vandenberg Papers, Bentley Library, roll 5.

47. Senate Committee on Foreign Relations, *The Vandenberg Resolution and North Atlantic Treaty: Hearings in Executive Session,* 81st Cong., 1st sess., Historical Series, February 18, 1949, 96.

48. Vandenberg to R. B. Wilson, February 22, 1949; and Vandenberg to Barbara Lossman, February 24, 1949, Vandenberg Papers, Bentley Library, roll 5.

49. *New York Times,* March 23, 1949, 1, 15.

50. Senate Committee on Foreign Relations, *Vandenberg Resolution and North Atlantic Treaty: Hearings*, 81st Cong., 1st sess., March 4, 1949, 2:368–69.

51. Ibid., April 21, 1949, 2:239.

52. Vandenberg, *Private Papers*, 482–83; Senate Committee on Foreign Relations, *Vandenberg Resolution and North Atlantic Treaty: Hearings*, June 6, 1949, 302.

53. Senate Committee on Foreign Relations, *Vandenberg Resolution and North Atlantic Treaty: Hearings*, June 2, 1949, 255.

54. Vandenberg to W. A. Young, April 15, 1949, Vandenberg Papers, Bentley Library, roll 5.

55. Vandenberg, *Private Papers*, June 29, 1949, 489; Vandenberg to W. A. McDonald, June 2, 1949, Vandenberg Papers, Bentley Library, roll 5.

56. Vandenberg, speech in the Senate, July 6, 1949; Vandenberg to Mrs. Vandenberg, [July 1949]; and Vandenberg to Mrs. Vandenberg, [July 21, 1949], in Vandenberg, *Private Papers*, 493, 501, 501–2.

57. Vandenberg to Mrs. Vandenberg, [July 21, 1949]; and Vandenberg, speech in the Senate, July 6, 1949, ibid., 495, 501.

58. Rearden, *Formative Years*, 501.

59. 81st Cong., 1st sess., *CR* 95, pt. 7 (July 8, 1949): S9100.

60. 81st Cong., 1st sess., *CR* 95, pt. 8 (July 21, 1949): S9885.

61. Memcon by Acheson—telephone conversations with Connally and Vandenberg, June 24, 1949, Acheson Papers, box 65.

62. *New York Times*, June 24, 1949, 1.

63. Vandenberg to Lippmann, July 18, 1949; and Lippmann to Vandenberg, July 22, 1949, Vandenberg Papers, Bentley Library, roll 5; Acheson to Ambassador David K. E. Bruce, July 22, 1949, Acheson Papers, box 65.

64. Vandenberg statement for the press, July 25, 1949, in Vandenberg, *Private Papers*, 503.

65. Memcon, Acheson with Senator Dulles, July 26, 1949, p. 2, Acheson Papers, box 65; Vandenberg to Carl M. Saunders, August 1, 1949, in Vandenberg, *Private Papers*, 506.

66. Memcon, Acheson with Dulles, July 26, 1949, p. 4, Acheson Papers, box 65.

67. Ibid., 3.

68. Vandenberg to Mrs. Vandenberg, July 25, 1949; and Vandenberg to Carl M. Saunders, August 1, 1949, in Vandenberg, *Private Papers*, 503–4, 506–7.

69. Vandenberg to Mrs. Vandenberg, July 31, 1949, ibid., 506.

70. Memcon, Acheson with the President—MAP Amendments, August 2, 1949, Acheson Papers, box 65.

71. Vandenberg to Mrs. Vandenberg, [August 2, 1949]; and Vandenberg to Lippmann, August 9, 1949, in Vandenberg, *Private Papers*, 508.

72. Vandenberg to Lippmann, August 9, 1949, ibid., 509; Vandenberg to

James P. Warburg, August 23, 1959, Vandenberg Papers, Bentley Library, roll 5, excerpted in Vandenberg, *Private Papers*, 512.

73. Memtel, L. D. B. [Lucius D. Battle], aide to Acheson, August 24, 1949, Acheson Papers, box 65.

74. Vandenberg to Clyde Beck, September 14, 1949, Vandenberg Papers, Bentley Library, roll 5.

75. Vandenberg to Mrs. Vandenberg, [September 22, 1949], in Vandenberg, *Private Papers*, 516–17.

76. Vandenberg to Mrs. Vandenberg, September 24, 1949, ibid., 518.

77. Lippmann to Vandenberg, August 8, 1949; quoted in memcon, Acheson with Dulles, July 26, 1949, p. 1, both in Vandenberg Papers, Bentley Library, roll 5.

78. *New York Times*, July 16, 1949, 2; Vandenberg to Lippmann, August 9, 1949, in Vandenberg, *Private Papers*, 509.

79. *New York Times*, August 30, 1949, 16; September 16, 1949, 4.

80. Vandenberg to Mrs. Vandenberg, [September 22, 1949], in Vandenberg, *Private Papers*, 517.

81. Vandenberg to Mrs. Vandenberg, [September 23, 1949], ibid., 518.

10. In Retrospect, 1950–1951

1. Vandenberg to George W. Calver, November 15, 1949, Vandenberg Papers, Bentley Library, roll 5; Vandenberg, *Private Papers*, 551–52; Reston quoted in *New York Times*, December 22, 1949, 1; photograph in *New York Herald-Tribune*, December 22, 1949, 1.

2. Vandenberg to Acheson, September 22, 1949, Vandenberg Papers, Bentley Library, roll 5; Lovett to Vandenberg, October 5, 1949, Lovett Papers, box 28, folder 404.

3. Vandenberg diary, July 3, 1948, in Vandenberg, *Private Papers*, 446; Vandenberg to Lippmann, July 6, 1950, box 107, folder 2145, Lippmann Papers.

4. Vandenberg, *Private Papers*, 553; *Washington Star*, March 11, 1951, 41.

5. *New York Times*, December 22, 1949, 1, 48.

6. Vandenberg to Watkins, December 28, 1949, Vandenberg Papers, Bentley Library, roll 5.

7. Letters to constituents, August 5, 20, 1950, in Vandenberg, *Private Papers*, 543–44 (quote in August 20 letter); Vandenberg to George Haines, October 24, 1950, Vandenberg Papers, Bentley Library, roll 5; Vandenberg, *Private Papers*, 544–45.

8. Vandenberg to W. S. Gilmore, February 12, 1951, in Vandenberg, *Private Papers*, 568; Vandenberg to Wherry, February 2, 1951, Vandenberg Papers, Bentley Library, roll 5.

9. Vandenberg to Hoffman, March 24, 1950, in Vandenberg, *Private Papers*,

557; a letter in Vandenberg Papers, Bentley Library, roll 5, asks for "release for all editions Sunday March 26, 1950."

10. Truman to Vandenberg, March 27, 31, 1950; and Truman to Vandenberg, telegram, March 6, 1951, in Vandenberg, *Private Papers,* 558–60, 577; Acheson to Vandenberg, January 9, 1951, Vandenberg Papers, Bentley Library, roll 5.

11. Taft to Vandenberg, March 21, 1951, Vandenberg Papers, Bentley Library, roll 5.

12. Vandenberg, *Private Papers,* 575.

13. Ibid., 1. Acheson questioned the relevance of the Pauline comparison in *Sketches from Life,* 123.

Bibliography

Archives

Acheson, Dean. Papers. Harry S. Truman Library, Independence, MO.

Beveridge, Albert J. Papers. Library of Congress.

Dulles, John Foster. Papers. Seeley Mudd Library, Princeton University. Microform copies at Library of Congress.

Espil, Courtney Letts de. Papers. Library of Congress.

Fulbright, J. William. Papers. University of Arkansas.

Knox, Franklin. Papers. Library of Congress.

Lippmann, Walter. Papers. Yale University.

Lovett, Robert A. Papers. Yale University.

NATO Archives, Brussels.

Roosevelt, Franklin D. Papers. Franklin D. Roosevelt Library, Hyde Park, NY.

Taft, Robert A. Papers. Library of Congress.

Truman, Harry S. Papers. Harry S. Truman Library, Independence, MO.

U.K. National Archives, Kew.

U.S. National Archives and Records Administration, College Park, MD.

Vandenberg, Arthur H. Papers. Bentley Historical Library, University of Michigan.

Wallace, Henry A. Papers. Franklin D. Roosevelt Library, Hyde Park, NY.

Western European Union Archives, Brussels.

Government Serials

Congressional Record

Foreign Relations of the United States

Public Papers of the Presidents of the United States

U.S. Department of State. *Bulletin.*

U.S. Senate, Committees on Foreign Relations and Armed Services. Hearings.

Newspapers and Journals

American Mercury

Collier's

Detroit Free Press
Foreign Correspondent (UK)
Grand Rapids (MI) Herald
Jackson (MI) Patriot
Liberty
Life
Michigan Historical Review
Mississippi Valley Historical Review
Newsweek
New York Herald-Tribune
New York Times
Saturday Evening Post
Vital Speeches of the Day
Washington Daily News
Washington Evening Star
Washington Post

Articles and Books

Acheson, Dean. *Present at the Creation: My Years in the State Department.* New York: W. W. Norton, 1969.

———. *Sketches from Life of Men I Have Known.* New York: Harper & Bros., 1961.

Achilles, Theodore C. *Fingerprints on History: The NATO Memoirs of Theodore C. Achilles.* Edited by Lawrence S. Kaplan and Sidney R. Snyder. Occasional Paper 1. Kent, OH: Lyman L. Lemnitzer Center for NATO and European Community Studies, Kent State University, 1992.

Adler, Selig. *The Isolationist Impulse: Its Twentieth-Century Reaction.* New York: Free Press, 1957.

Bailey, Thomas A. *Woodrow Wilson and the Great Betrayal.* New York: Macmillan, 1945.

Barnard, Harry. *Independent Man: The Life of James Couzens.* New York: Scribner's, 1958.

Bohlen, Charles E. *Witness to History.* New York: W. W. Norton, 1973.

Bolt, Ernest C. *Bullets before Ballots: The War Referendum Approach to Peace in America, 1914–1941.* Charlottesville: University of Virginia Press, 1966.

Briggs, Philip J. "Senator Vandenberg, Bipartisanship and the Origins of the United Nation's Article 51." *Mid-America* 60, no. 1 (October 1978): 163–69.

Byrnes, James F. *All in One Lifetime.* New York: Harper & Brothers, 1958.

———. *Speaking Frankly.* New York: Harper & Brothers, 1947.

Campbell, Thomas M., and George C. Herring, eds. *The Diaries of Edward R. Stettinius Jr., 1943–1945.* New York: New Viewpoints, 1975.

Carlyle, Margaret, ed. *Documents in International Affairs, 1947–1948*. London: Oxford University Press, 1951.

Clifford, Clark M. *Counsel to the President: A Memoir*. With Richard Holbrooke. New York: Random House, 1991.

Clifford, J. Garry. *The First Peacetime Draft*. With Samuel R. Spencer Jr. Lawrence: University Press of Kansas, 1986.

Cole, Wayne S. *America First: The Battle against Intervention, 1940–1941*. Madison: University of Wisconsin Press, 1953.

———. "And There Were None! How Arthur H. Vandenberg and Gerald P. Nye Separately Departed Isolationist Leadership Roles." In *Behind the Throne: Servants of Power to Imperial Presidents, 1898–1968*, edited by Thomas J. McCormick and Walter LaFeber, 232–56. Madison: University of Wisconsin Press, 1993.

———. *Roosevelt & the Isolationists, 1932–1942*. Lincoln: University of Nebraska Press, 1983.

———. *Senator Gerald P. Nye and American Foreign Relations*. Minneapolis: University of Minnesota Press, 1962.

———. "Senator Key Pittman and American Neutrality Politics, 1933–1940." *Mississippi Valley Historical Review* 46 (March 1960): 644–62.

Connally, Tom. *My Name Is Tom Connally*. As told to Alfred Steinberg. New York: Thomas Crowell, 1954.

Cook, Don. *Forging the Alliance: NATO, 1945–1950*. London: Secker & Warburg, 1989.

Coulter, Matthew Ware. *The Senate Munitions Inquiry of the 1930s: Beyond the Merchants of Death*. Westport, CT: Greenwood Press, 1997.

Davidson, Bill. "The Two Mr. Vandenbergs." *Collier's*, June 19, 1948.

Dawes, Charles. *Notes as Vice President, 1928–1929*. Boston: Little Brown, 1935.

Detzer, Dorothy. *Appointment on the Hill*. New York: Henry Holt, 1948.

Divine, Robert A. *The Illusion of Neutrality*. Chicago: University of Chicago Press, 1962.

———. *Second Chance: The Triumph of Internationalism in America during World War II*. New York: Atheneum, 1967.

Doenecke, Justus. *Storm on the Horizon: The Challenge of American Intervention, 1935–1941*. Lanham, MD: Rowman & Littlefield, 2000.

Doenecke, Justus, and John Wilz. *From Isolation to War, 1931–1941*. Arlington Heights, IL: Harlan Davidson, 1991.

Fetzer, James. "Senator Vandenberg and the American Commitment to China, 1945–1950." *Historian* 36 (February 1974): 283–303.

Fine, Sidney. *Sit Down: The General Motors Strike of 1936–1937*. Ann Arbor: University of Michigan Press, 1969.

Forrestal, James V. *The Forrestal Diaries*. Edited by Walter Millis. New York: Viking Press, 1951.

Gazell, James A. "Arthur H. Vandenberg, Internationalism, and the United Nations." *Political Science Quarterly* 88 (September 1973): 375–94.

Gregg, Richard R. "A Rhetorical Re-examination of Arthur Vandenberg's Dramatic Conversion, January 10, 1945." *Quarterly Journal of Speech* 61 (April 1975): 154–68.

Hartman, Susan. *Truman and the 80th Congress.* Columbia: University of Missouri Press, 1971.

Henderson, Nicholas. *The Birth of NATO.* Boulder, CO: Westview Press, 1983.

Hewlett, Richard G., and Oscar E. Anderson Jr. *A History of the United States Atomic Energy Commission.* Vol. 1, *The New World, 1939/1946.* University Park: Pennsylvania State University Press, 1962.

Hewlett, Richard G., and Francis Duncan. *A History of the United States Atomic Energy Commission.* Vol. 2, *Atomic Shield, 1947/1952.* University Park: Pennsylvania State University Press, 1969.

Hill, Thomas Michael. "Senator Arthur H. Vandenberg, the Politics of Bipartisanship, and the Origins of Anti-Soviet Consensus, 1941–1946." *World Affairs* 138, no. 3 (Winter 1975–1976): 219–41.

Hoover, Herbert. *The Memoirs of Herbert Hoover: The Cabinet and Presidency.* New York: Macmillan, 1952.

Hudson, Daryl J. "Vandenberg Reconsidered: Senate Resolution 239 and American Foreign Policy." *Diplomatic History* 1 (Winter 1977): 46–63.

Hull, Cordell. *The Memoirs of Cordell Hull.* 2 vols. New York: Macmillan, 1948.

Israel, Fred I. *Nevada's Key Pittman.* Lincoln: University of Nebraska Press, 1963.

———, ed. *The War Diary of Breckinridge Long: Selections from the Years 1939–1944.* Lincoln: University of Nebraska Press, 1966.

Jebb, Gladwyn. *The Memoirs of Lord Gladwyn.* New York: Weybridge and Talley, 1972.

Jonas, Manfred. *Isolationism in America, 1935–1941.* Ithaca, NY: Cornell University Press, 1966.

Jones, Joseph M. *The Fifteen Weeks (February 21–June 5, 1947).* New York: Viking Press, 1955.

Kaplan, Lawrence S. *A Community of Interests: NATO and the Military Assistance Program, 1948–1951.* Washington, D.C.: Office of the Secretary of Defense Historical Office, 1980.

Kennan, George F. *Memoirs, 1925–1950.* New York: Bantam Books, 1969.

Kimball, Warren F. *The Most Unsordid Act: Lend-Lease, 1939–1941.* Baltimore: Johns Hopkins University Press, 1969.

Krock, Arthur. *Memoirs: Sixty Years on the Firing Line.* New York: Funk and Wagnalls, 1968.

Langer, William L., and S. Everett Gleason. *The Challenge to Isolation, 1937–1940.* New York: Harper & Row, 1951.

———. *The Undeclared War, 1940–1941.* New York: Harper & Row, 1953.

Leuchtenburg, William E. *Franklin D. Roosevelt and the New Deal.* New York: Harper & Row, 1963.

Lie, Trygve. *In the Cause of Peace: Seven Years with the United Nations.* New York: Macmillan, 1954.

Lilienthal, David E. *The Journals of David E. Lilienthal.* Vol. 2, *The Atomic Energy Years, 1945–1950.* New York: Harper & Row, 1964.

Lippmann, Walter. *The Cold War: A Study in U.S. Foreign Policy.* New York: Harper & Bros., 1947.

Ludlow, Louis. *From Cornfield to Press Gallery: Adventures of a Veteran Washington Correspondent.* Washington, DC: W. F. Robert, 1924.

Mahl, Thomas H. *Desperate Deception: British Covert Operations in the United States, 1939–1944.* Washington, D.C.: Brassey's, 1998.

Margulies, Herbert F. *The Mild Reservationists and the League of Nations Controversy in the Senate.* Columbia: University of Missouri Press, 1989.

Martel, Leon. *Lend-Lease, Loans, and the Coming of the Cold War: A Study of the Implementation of Foreign Policy.* Boulder, CO: Westview Press, 1979.

Mazuzan, George T. *Warren R. Austin at the U.N., 1949–1953.* Kent, OH: Kent State University Press, 1977.

McCoy, Donald B. *Landon of Kansas.* Lincoln: University of Nebraska Press, 1966.

McKenna, Marion C. *Borah.* Ann Arbor: University of Michigan Press, 1961.

Meijer, Hank. "Arthur Vandenberg and the Fight for Neutrality." *Michigan Historical Review* 16 (Fall 1990): 1–21.

Myers, William Starr, and Walter H. Newton. *The Hoover Administration: A Documented Narrative.* New York: Scribner's, 1936.

Patterson, James T. *Mr. Republican: A Biography of Robert A. Taft.* Boston: Houghton Mifflin, 1972.

Pearson, Lester B. *Mike: The Memoirs of Lester B. Pearson.* 3 vols. Toronto: University of Toronto Press, 1972.

Rearden, Steven L. *The Formative Years, 1947–1950.* Washington, D.C.: Historical Office, Office of the Secretary of Defense, 1984.

Reid, Escott. *On Duty: A Canadian at the Making of the United Nations, 1945–1946.* Kent, OH: Kent State University Press, 1983.

———. *Time of Fear and Hope: The Making of the North Atlantic Treaty, 1947–1949.* Toronto: McClelland and Stewart, 1977.

Rosenman, Samuel I., ed. *Public Papers and Addresses of Franklin Delano Roosevelt, 1938–1950.* 13 vols. New York: Random House/Macmillan/Harper, 1938–1950.

Ruddy, T. Michael. *The Cautious Diplomat: Charles E. Bohlen and the Soviet Union, 1929–1960.* Kent, OH: Kent State University Press, 1986.

Russell, Ruth. *A History of the United Nations Charter: The Role of the United States.* Washington, D.C.: Brookings Institution, 1958.

Smith, Beverly. "Russia's Pet Whipping Boy." *Saturday Evening Post*, April 5, 1947.

Smith, E. Timothy. *Opposition Beyond the Water's Edge: Liberal Internationalists, Pacifists, and Containment, 1945-1953*. Westport, CT: Greenwood Press, 1999.

Steel, Ronald. *Walter Lippmann and the American Century*. Boston: Little, Brown, 1980.

Stoler, Mark A. "'And Perhaps a Little More': The George C. Marshall Secretary of State Papers." *Passport* 43 (January 2013): 56-58.

Strauss, Lewis L. *Men and Decisions*. New York: Macmillan, 1963.

Taft, Robert A. *The Papers of Robert A. Taft*. Edited by Clarence E. Wunderlin. 4 vols. Kent, OH: Kent State University Press, 1997.

Timmons, Bascom M. *Jesse H. Jones: The Man and Statesman*. New York: Henry Holt, 1956.

Tompkins, C. David. "Arthur Vandenberg Goes to the Senate." *Michigan History* 51 (Spring 1967): 19-35.

———. *Senator Arthur H. Vandenberg: The Evolution of a Modern Republican, 1884-1945*. East Lansing: Michigan State University Press, 1970.

Truman, Harry S. *Memoirs*. Vol. 2, *Years of Trial and Hope, 1946-1952*. New York: New American Library, 1965.

Vandenberg, Arthur H. "A Device to Put Men's Minds in Gear." *New York Times*, September 16, 1945.

———. *The Greatest American, Alexander Hamilton*. New York: G.P. Putnam's Sons, 1921.

———. *If Hamilton Were Here Today: American Fundamentals Applied to Modern Problems*. New York: G.P. Putnam's Sons, 1923.

———. "The New Deal Must Be Salvaged." *American Mercury* 49 (January 1940): 1-10

———. *The Private Papers of Senator Vandenberg*. Edited by Arthur H. Vandenberg Jr. with the collaboration of Joe Alex Morris. Boston: Houghton Mifflin, 1952.

———. *The Trail of a Tradition*. New York: G.P. Putnam's Sons, 1926.

———. "Try to Prevent World War III." *Saturday Evening Post*, March 17, 1945.

Westerfield, H. Bradford. *Foreign Policy and Party Politics: Pearl Harbor to Korea*. New Haven, CT: Yale University Press, 1955.

Wilz, John E. *In Search of Peace: The Senate Munitions Inquiry, 1934-1936*. Baton Rouge: Louisiana State University Press, 1963.

Woyke, Wichard. "Foundation and History of NATO, 1948-1950." In *The Western Security Community, 1948-1950*, edited by Norbert Wiggershaus and Richard Foerster, 251-72. Oxford: Berg, 1993.

Index

Plan and, ix, 180–81, 189, 191,
192–201, 204–5, 214, 218, 241;
neutrality and, 49–60, 61–66,
67–68, 71–73, 74–75; New Deal
and, 28–32, 34–35, 36, 37; as
newspaper editor, 2, 3–4, 7–9, 10,
11, 12–15, 16, 17, 21, 25, 26, 42;
North Atlantic Treaty, military
aid and, x, 125, 226–34, 235–36,
241–42; North Atlantic Treaty and,
x, 135, 177, 201, 220–26, 249n6;
Nye munitions inquiry and, 42–49,
52–53, 55, 59; Philippines and,
6–7, 177; political ambitions and,
14, 15–16, 19–20, 21–23, 35–36,
70, 215; Progressive movement
and, 4, 5–6, 7, 8, 9, 15, 17, 18,
27–28, 31, 43; Republican Party
after 1945 and, 161, 162–64, 167,
169, 172–73, 177–78, 200, 203,
215, 220; Republican Party before
1945 and, 7–9, 10, 17, 28, 29–30,
32, 35, 38, 61, 66–67, 68–70, 83,
93, 97; Franklin D. Roosevelt
and, 4, 28–30, 34, 36, 84–85, 87,
91, 95–96, 99, 103, 109, 115, 116,
126–27, 128, 129; San Francisco
United Nations Charter formation
and, 115–42, 143, 173; sickness
and, 184, 233, 235, 236–37; speech,
1945 and, 107, 108–14, 115, 124,
141, 150, 240, 243–45; United
Nations beginnings and, 143–68,
170–77, 184, 187–89, 190–91,
197, 203–7, 212, 213–14, 263n11;
United Nations Charter and, 144,
146, 159, 163, 174, 175, 184, 186,
203, 240–41; UNRRA and, 90–93,
107, 189, 191–92; Western Europe
and, 208–9, 210–13, 218, 221–22,
225–26, 263n2; Woodrow Wilson
and, 4, 8–10, 11, 12, 14, 15, 25;

world peace and, 3, 11, 26–27;
World War II and, 82–85, 87–90,
257n12; World War II in Europe
and, 73–82; as writer, 4, 17–19,
108–9, 124; as "young Turk,"
23–28. *See also* Acheson, Dean;
communism; Grand Rapids, MI;
internationalism; isolationism;
Lippmann, Walter; Lovett, Robert
A.; Taft, Robert A.; U.S. Senate,
Foreign Relations Committee
Vandenberg, Arthur, Jr., 83, 110,
122–23, 261n46
Vandenberg Papers, x, xi
Vandenberg Resolution (S. Res. 239),
x, 211, 212–13, 214–15, 218, 219,
220, 222, 226, 241, 247–48
Versailles treaty, 11, 13, 14, 50, 115,
117
Villard, Oswald Garrison, 52
Vincent, John Carter, 178
Vinson, Fred, 218
Vishinski, Andrei, 149–50
Vital Speeches of the Day, 110

Wagner, Robert, 35, 38, 53
Wallace, Henry A., 89, 95, 153, 159,
162, 163, 165, 166, 188, 215
Wall Street, 25, 31, 32, 33, 42, 44, 47,
49, 54, 59
Wall Street Journal, 50
Walsh, Thomas J., 44
War Industries Board, 56
War Policies Commission, 46, 47, 50
Washington Evening Star, 73
Washington Exploratory Talks on
Security, 219
Washington Merry-Go-Round
column, 35
Washington Naval Conference, 63
Washington Post, 122, 199
Washington Star, 37

The Gulf: The Bush Presidencies and the Middle East
Michael F. Cairo

Diplomatic Games: Sport, Statecraft, and International Relations since 1945
Edited by Heather L. Dichter and Andrew L. Johns

Nothing Less Than War: A New History of America's Entry into World War I
Justus D. Doenecke

Grounded: The Case for Abolishing the United States Air Force
Robert M. Farley

The American South and the Vietnam War: Belligerence, Protest, and Agony in Dixie
Joseph A. Fry

Obama at War: Congress and the Imperial Presidency
Ryan C. Hendrickson

The Conversion of Senator Arthur H. Vandenberg: From Isolation to International Engagement
Lawrence S. Kaplan

The Currents of War: A New History of American-Japanese Relations, 1899–1941
Sidney Pash

So Much to Lose: John F. Kennedy and American Policy in Laos
William J. Rust

Lincoln Gordon: Architect of Cold War Foreign Policy
Bruce L. R. Smith